AMERICAN WOMEN FICTION WRITERS 1900-1960

VOLUME TWO

AMERICAN WOMEN FICTION WRITERS 1900–1950 VOLUME TWO

Edited and with an Introduction by

Harold Bloom

CHELSEA HOUSE PUBLISHERS

Philadelphia

ON THE COVER: Beatrice Whitney Van Ness (American, 1888–1981), *Summer Sunlight*, ca. 1936. Oil on canvas, 39" x 49". The National Museum of Women in the Arts, gift of Wallace and Wilhelmina Holladay.

CHELSEA HOUSE PUBLISHERS

PRODUCTION MANAGER   Pamela Loos
PICTURE EDITOR   Judy Hasday
ART DIRECTOR   Sara Davis
SENIOR PRODUCTION EDITOR   Lisa Chippendale

WOMEN WRITERS OF ENGLISH AND THEIR WORKS:
   American Women Fiction Writers, 1900–1960: Volume Two

SERIES EDITOR   Jane Shumate
CONTRIBUTING EDITOR   Tenley Williams
SENIOR EDITOR   Therese De Angelis
INTERIOR AND COVER DESIGNER   Alison Burnside
EDITORIAL ASSISTANT   Anne Hill

Introduction © 1997 by Harold Bloom

First Printing
1 3 5 7 9 8 6 4 2

Library of Congress Cataloging-in-Publication Data

American women fiction writers / edited and with an introduction by
   Harold Bloom.
      p.   cm. — (Women writers of English and their works)
   Includes bibliographical references.
   ISBN 0-7910-4480-7 (v. 1). — ISBN 0-7910-4496-3 (pbk. : v. 1)
      1. American fiction—Women authors—History and criticism.
   2. American fiction—Women authors—Bio–bibliography. 3. Women and
   literature—United States.   I. Bloom, Harold. II. Series.
   PS374.W6A455 1997
   813.009' 9287—dc21
   [B]   97-6310
                                                                                    CIP

CONTENTS

THE ANALYSIS OF WOMEN WRITERS

HAROLD BLOOM

I APPROACH THIS SERIES with a certain wariness, since so much of classical feminist literary criticism has founded itself upon arguments with that phase of my own work that began with *The Anxiety of Influence* (first published in January 1973). Someone who has been raised to that bad eminence—*The Patriarchal Critic*—is well advised that he trespasses upon sacred ground when he ventures to inquire whether indeed there are indisputable differences, imaginative and cognitive, between the literary works of women and those of men. If these differences are so substantial as pragmatically to make an authentic difference, does that in turn make necessary different aesthetic standards for judging the achievements of men and of women writers? Is Emily Dickinson to be read as though she has more in common with Elizabeth Barrett Browning than with Ralph Waldo Emerson?

Is Elizabeth Bishop a great poet because she triumphantly meets the same aesthetic criteria satisfied by Wallace Stevens, or should we evaluate her by criteria she shares with Marianne Moore, but not with Stevens? Are there crucial gender-based differences in the representations of Esther Summerson by Charles Dickens in *Bleak House*, and of Dorothea Brooke by George Eliot in *Middlemarch*? Does Samuel Richardson's Clarissa Harlowe convince us that her author was a male when we contrast her with Jane Austen's Elizabeth Bennet? Do women poets have a less agonistic relationship to female precursors than male poets have to their forerunners? Two eminent pioneers of feminist criticism, Sandra Gilbert and Susan Gubar, have suggested that women writers suffer more from an anxiety of authorship than they do from influence anxieties, while another important feminist critic, Elaine Showalter, has suggested that women writers, early and late, work together in a kind of quiltmaking, each doing her share while avoiding any contamination of creative envy in regard to other writers, provided that they be women. Can it be true that, in the aesthetic sphere, women do not beware women and do not suffer from the competitiveness and jealousy that alas do exist in the professional and sexual domains? Is there something in the area of literature, when practiced by women, that changes and purifies mere human nature?

I cannot answer any of these questions, yet I do think it is vital and clarifying to raise them. There is a current fashion, in many of our institutions of higher education, to insist that English Romantic poetry cannot be studied in the old way, with an exclusive emphasis upon the works of William Blake, William Wordsworth, Samuel Taylor Coleridge, Lord Byron, Percy Bysshe Shelley, John Keats, and John Clare. Instead, the Romantic poets are taken to include Felicia Hemans, Laetitia Landon, Charlotte Smith, and Mary Tighe, among others. It would be heartening if we could believe that these are unjustly neglected poets, but their current revival will be brief. Similarly, anthologies of 17th-century English literature now tend to include the Duchess of Newcastle as well as Aphra Behn, Lady Mary Chudleigh, Anne Killigrew, Anne Finch, Countess of Winchilsea, and others. Some of these— Anne Finch in particular—wrote well, but a situation in which they are more read and studied than John Milton is not one that is likely to endure forever. The consequences of making gender a criterion for aesthetic choice must finally destroy all serious study of imaginative literature as such.

In their *Norton Anthology of Literature by Women*, Sandra Gilbert and Susan Gubar conclude their introduction to Elizabeth Barrett Browning by saying that "she constantly tested herself against the highest standards of male-defined poetic genres," a true if ambiguous observation. They then print her famous "The Cry of the Children," an admirably passionate ode that protests the cruel employment of little children in British Victorian mines and factories. Unfortunately, this well-meant prophetic affirmation ends with this, doubtless its finest stanza:

XIII

They look up with their pale and sunken faces,
  And their look is dread to see,
For they mind you of their angels in high places,
  With eyes turned on Deity.
"How long," they say, "how long, O cruel nation,
  Will you stand, to move the world, on a child's heart,—
Stifle down with a mailèd heel its palpitation,
  And tread onward to your throne amid the mart?
Our blood splashes upward, O goldheaper,
  And your purple shows your path!
But the child's sob in the silence curses deeper
  Than the strong man in his wrath."

If you read this aloud, then you may find yourself uncomfortable, on a strictly aesthetic basis, which would not vary if you were told that this had been composed by a male Victorian poet. In their selections from Elizabeth Bishop, Gilbert and Gubar courageously reprint Bishop's superb statement explaining her refusal to permit her poems to be included in anthologies of women's writing:

> Undoubtedly gender does play an important part in the making of any art, but art is art and to separate writings, paintings, musical compositions, etc., into sexes is to emphasize values in them that are *not* art.

That credo of Elizabeth Bishop's is to me the Alpha and Omega of critical wisdom in regard to all feminist literary criticism. Gender studies are precisely that: they study gender, and not aesthetic value. If your priorities are historical, social, political, and ideological, then gender studies clearly are more than justified. Perhaps they are a way to justice, or at least to more justice than women have received throughout thousands of years of male domination and aggression. Yet that is a very different matter from the now vexed issue of aesthetic value. Biographical criticism, like the different modes of historicist and psychological criticism, always has relied upon a kind of implicit gender studies and doubtless will benefit, as other modes will, by a making explicit of such considerations, particularly in regard to women writers.

Each volume in this series contains copious refutations of, and replies to, the traditionally aesthetic stance that I have advocated here. These introductory remarks aspire only to a questioning, and not a challenging, of feminist literary criticism. There are no longer any Patriarchal Critics; they are all dinosaurs, fabulous beasts fit for revival only in horror films. Sometimes I sadly think of myself as Bloom Brontosaurus, amiably left behind by the fire and the flood. But more often I go on reading the great women writers, searching for the aesthetic difference that yet may prove to be there, but which has not yet been found.

Introduction

THOUGH THERE ARE OTHER writers of authentic literary eminence studied in this volume—such as Zora Neale Hurston and Carson McCullers—it seems clear to me that Flannery O'Connor was the most remarkable. Her mode was Southern Gothic, following the Faulkner of *As I Lay Dying* and *Sanctuary* in particular, but in O'Connor this is the Southern Gothic of an aggressive Roman Catholic moralist. That blend is astonishing and spiritually very problematic, though the frequent aesthetic splendor that ensues is indisputable.

What mattered most to O'Connor were transcendental entities and verities, no matter how high the cost was to naturalistic experience, whether her own or that of her doom-eager characters. The terrible violence depicted in O'Connor's work was, for her, the inevitable effect of the sacred breaking in upon the fallen world of unbelief. Sacred violence was not only O'Connor's subject but also constituted her stance toward her readers, most of whom she accurately assumed would be skeptics or unbelievers. Myself a Gnostic heretic, a knower rather than an unbeliever, I tend to discover in O'Connor's work an uncanny tension between a Gnostic sensibility and a Catholic believer's morality. Though she fiercely denounced all heresy and affirmed the Church's primacy on all questions of faith and morals, O'Connor's imagination nevertheless manifested heretical tendencies, to the great advantage of her fiction.

John Burt, one of O'Connor's most acute critics, said that "she herself rejects the inward power which her characters take as their sole authority, and through irony and even ridicule she forcefully keeps her point of view separate from theirs." O'Connor's favorite characters are wild Protestants who each form sects of one, American Religionists rather than mainline believers. They tend therefore to be Gnostic seekers and prophets, like Hazel Motes in *Wise Blood* and the boy Francis Tarwater in *The Violent Bear It Away*. Burt shrewdly observes that these figures win the respect of both the author and the reader. From O'Connor's perspective, they are fearfully mistaken persons who should seek salvation in the one true authority: the Roman Catholic Church. Yet O'Connor's imagination thrills to them and to their grotesque quests.

Young Tarwater in particular moves O'Connor greatly, as he does any sensitive reader. I once described Tarwater as "the Huck Finn of visionaries" and cite that here because I cannot improve upon it. Perhaps Tarwater is clinically schizophrenic: he hears the voice of the Devil speaking to him from within as a nameless "friend," and he achieves liberation from the Devil only by setting a forked tree ablaze until it becomes "an arch of fire." And yet Tarwater is in most other respects as sane as Huck Finn, valuing freedom above all, as Huck does. Though Tarwater longs for freedom even from his prophetic vocation, he cannot evade his calling, and O'Connor ends *The Violent Bear It Away* with a vision of the boy accepting what is likely to become a religious martyrdom:

> By midnight he had left the road and the burning woods behind him and had come out on the highway once more. The moon, riding low above the field beside him, appeared and disappeared, diamond-bright, between patches of darkness. Intermittently the boy's shadow slanted across the road ahead of him as if it cleared a rough path toward his goal. His singed eyes, black in their deep sockets, seemed already to envision the fate that awaited him but he moved steadily on, his face set toward the dark city, where the children of God lay sleeping.

The sublime power of this is hardly qualified by its implicit irony; O'Connor may not be at one with Tarwater, but she confessed he was her favorite character in all her work. Perhaps his quest, eloquent and doom-eager, constitutes O'Connor's best metaphor for her own enterprise as a writer. Her chosen mode was romance, the way of Hawthorne and of Faulkner, and in Francis Tarwater's story she created a quest-romance worthy of her literary masters.

PAULINE ELIZABETH HOPKINS

1859-1930

PAULINE ELIZABETH HOPKINS was born in 1859 in Portland, Maine, the daughter of Northrup and Sarah Allen Hopkins. Shortly after her birth, her parents moved to Boston, where she attended public schools. At 15 she won a writing contest sponsored by William Wells Brown and the Congregational Publishing Society on the theme of temperance.

Hopkins's first literary work was a play, *Slaves' Escape: or, the Underground Railroad*, written in 1879 and produced the next year by a touring group organized by her family, the Hopkins' Colored Troubadours, in which her mother, her stepfather, and Hopkins herself acted. The play was later published as *Peculiar Sam: or, the Underground Railroad*, although the date of publication is not known. Hopkins earned considerable renown as an actress and singer, acquiring the nickname "Boston's Favorite Colored Soprano." She also wrote at least one further play, *One Scene from the Drama of Early Days*, but it was apparently never performed, and the manuscript is now lost.

Around 1892, Hopkins enrolled in a stenography course and began earning her livelihood in this profession, working for four years at the Bureau of Statistics. In 1900, the founding of *The Colored American Magazine* changed the course of her career and her writing. She began writing voluminously for the magazine and by the second issue had joined its staff. Her earliest work for it was a short story, "The Mystery Within Us," published in the magazine's first issue (May 1900).

Hopkins's one separately published novel, *Contending Forces: A Romance Illustrative of Negro Life North and South*, was issued in 1900 by the Colored Co-operative Publishing Company, the publisher of *The Colored American*. This historical romance about an octoroon, Sappho Clark, and a mulatto, Will Smith, is a powerful examination of the life of black women within white society and touches upon many fundamental issues of black social life. Although it employs many of the conventions of the popular sentimental romance of the period, it probes such concerns as the sexual exploitation of black women, the searing effects of slavery, and the need for strong family ties.

The Colored American also serialized three novels by Hopkins: *Hagar's Daughter: A Story of Southern Caste Prejudice* (1901–2); *Winona: A Tale of Negro Life in the South and Southwest* (1902); and *Of One Blood: or, the Hidden Self* (1902–3). All three treat themes of race and interracial love affairs.

1

In addition to fiction, Hopkins wrote a considerable amount of nonfiction and journalism for *The Colored American*. A series of articles entitled "Famous Men of the Negro Race" (1901–2) dealt with such figures as Frederick Douglass and William Wells Brown, while "Famous Women of the Negro Race" (1901–2) discussed Sojourner Truth, Harriet Tubman, Frances E. W. Harper, and others.

By 1904, Hopkins had become too ill to work on the magazine. She continued writing, however, and published a series, "The Dark Races of the Twentieth Century," in *Voice of the Negro* (1905). This was, however, the last of her major writings, aside from a novelette, *Topsy Templeton*, published in 1916 in *New Era*.

Hopkins resumed her stenographic work, being employed by the Massachusetts Institute of Technology. She died in a house fire on August 13, 1930. Her work suffered critical neglect until the 1970s, when *Contending Forces* was hailed as a pioneering work of black American fiction.

CRITICAL EXTRACTS

ANN ALLEN SHOCKLEY

By November, 1903, ⟨Hopkins⟩ had become Literary Editor of the *Colored American*. Much of her personal time and effort was now spent in promoting the magazine. For example, in January, 1904, she was one of the founders of the Colored American League in Boston (fictionalized in a chapter of her *Contending Forces* as "The American Colored League")—an organization comprised of "some twenty or more representative ladies and gentlemen of the colored citizens of Boston" ⟨*Colored American*, March 1904⟩ which helped sustain the *Colored American* during the summer months in a series of public meetings over the country to gain interest and support for the magazine.

Miss Hopkins's spirit and love for the magazine were demonstrated as well by her prolific contributions to it. Six of her short stories appeared in the publication, among these "Talma Gordon," "George Washington: A Christmas Story," and "Bro'r Abr'm Jimson's Wedding. A Christmas Story." Two short novels which dealt with interracial love were also serialized in the *Colored American*. The first one, *Winona: A Tale of Negro Life in the South and Southwest in the 1840's*, was serialized in twenty-four chapters. Winona was the daughter of a white man in Buffalo, New York, who joined an Indian tribe and became its chief. The chief married a fugitive slave girl who died while giving birth to Winona. The plot was sensational and complicated, filled with adventurous escapades, murder, and romance. In the conclusion, Winona and her white English lover go to England where the "American caste prejudice could not touch them beyond the sea." Her second short novel, *Of One Blood or The Hidden Self*, began serializing in the October, 1902 issue immediately following the conclusion of *Winona*. It was a similarly complicated tale of interracial romance, and filled with the mysticism of the mind and spirit.

The recurring theme of interracial love in Miss Hopkins's serials was noted by a white reader, Cornelia A. Condict, who wrote a letter to the editor saying: "Without exception, they have been of love between the colored and white. Does that mean that your novelists can imagine no love beautiful and sublime within the range of the colored race, for each other?" Miss Hopkins replied to this with candor while stating the basic philosophy of her fiction:

> . . . My stories are definitely planned to show the obstacles persis-
> tently placed in our paths by a dominant race to subjugate us spiritu-
> ally. Marriage is made illegal between the races and the mulattoes
> increase. Thus the shadow of corruption falls on the blacks and on
> the whites, without whose aid the mulattoes would not exist.

—Ann Allen Shockley, "Pauline Elizabeth Hopkins: A Biographical Excursion into Obscurity," *Phylon* 33, no. 1 (Spring 1972): 24–25

CLAUDIA TATE

The structure of ⟨*Winona*⟩ conforms to basic conventions. But *Winona* is even more sensational than *Contending Forces* in that there are more incredible coincidences, swashbuckling adventures, and exaggerated heroic descriptions, all held together with a very sentimental love story. Winona's appearance, as we might expect, conforms to the tragic mulatto mold: "Her wide brow, about which the hair clustered in dark rings, the beautifully chiselled features, the olive complexion with a hint of pink." And her hero, Maxwell, is equally as handsome, though fair: ". . . a slender, well-knit figure with a bright, handsome face, blue eyes and a mobile mouth slightly touched with down on his upper lip." The virtuous pair are rewarded with prosperity and happiness, while the villain suffers a painful death.

Hopkins placed this novel into the genre of the fugitive slave story and identified her protest as that against the arbitrary segregation and subjection of black Americans:

> Many strange tales of romantic happenings in this mixed community
> of Anglo-Saxons, Indians and Negroes might be told similar to the
> one I am about to relate, and the world stand aghast and may try to
> find the dividing line supposed to be a natural barrier between the
> whites and the dark-skinned race.

Thus, as is the case with *Contending Forces*, the central issue of *Winona* is its protest against racial injustice, but unlike *Contending Forces*, *Winona* outlines no program of social reform other than that offered by escape. Whereas escape offered a possible resolution to the slave's dilemma prior to 1864, Hopkins's contemporary scene of 1901 afforded virtually no ostensible reason for her to write an abolitionist novel. Perhaps she wrote the novel as an exercise in nostalgia, intended to arouse sympathy for oppressed black Americans. There was, however, more than sufficient reason to condemn the practices of employment and housing discrimination, separate public accommodations, mob violence, and lynching, as she had done in *Contending Forces*. Whereas her first novel was very sensitive to the racial issues of 1900 and consequently addressed each of them, *Winona* seems to be essentially an escapist, melodramatic romance in which Hopkins used sentimental love as a means for supporting an appeal for racial justice. Though, granted, Hopkins does dramatize the fact that being black in America means being subjected to racial abuse, she offers little hope to those who cannot escape like Winona and Jude.

Women's issues, which were central to the argument of *Contending Forces*, have been abandoned entirely in *Winona*. Although marriage is depicted as woman's ambition in both *Contending Forces* and *Winona*, in the latter novel a woman's role is seen exclusively as finding a suitable husband and tending to his needs. Love is translated singularly into duty, and duty finds expression only on the domestic front. We do not see women, like Mrs. Willis of *Contending Forces*, who are their husbands' helpmates in the struggle for racial advancement. On the contrary, marriage offers women its own blissful escape in *Winona*, and marital love is portrayed as the balm which soothes their worldly wounds. When we turn our attention to the subject of the advancement of black women, we find no discussion of this topic at all. Although Hopkins was, nevertheless, a product of the nineteenth century's rising consciousness of women's concerns, it is surprising to find that this issue appears so inconsistently in her work.

—Claudia Tate, "Pauline Hopkins: Our Literary Foremother," *Conjuring: Black Women, Fiction, and Literary Tradition*, ed. Marjorie Pryse and Hortense J. Spillers (Bloomington: Indiana University Press, 1985), 60–61

JANE CAMPBELL

Contending Forces fictionalizes women's collective efforts to create a countermythology. In the chapter entitled "The Sewing Circle," a large group of women gather to make garments for a church fair. Mrs. Willis, who plays a significant role in this chapter, serves as the embodiment of the black women's club movement. Although women's organizations existed before the Civil

War, during the 1890s these clubs, led by such esteemed members as Frances Harper, Mary Church Terrell, and Fannie Barrier Williams, achieved greater prominence than they had earlier, in part because of the formation of the National Association of Colored Women in 1896. Gerda Lerner notes that it is unclear whether this association spawned new clubs or whether existing clubs began to attain recognition; nevertheless, the club movement as a whole deserves credit for uniting black women in the crusades against lynching and Jim Crow and for integration. When characters in the sewing circle discuss woman's role in racial upbuilding, they turn to Mrs. Willis for direction. Mrs. Willis echoes Harper's injunction that mothers, as culture bearers, constitute black America's future, and she applauds African women's native virtue, suggesting that black American women, by extension, are innately virtuous. She goes on to caution her listeners that black women must not assume responsibility for the sexual exploitation of their ancestors and themselves. With this chapter, Harper charts black woman's role in changing history through her solidarity with other women, who help her to forge a new vision that runs counter to the one white culture promulgates. At the same time, the cult of domesticity, a motif pervading *Contending Forces*, enshrines the possibilities inherent in the home, where a sewing circle can become a political forum.

Hopkins's concept of history, exhibited in the aforementioned chapter and elsewhere, presupposes an educated, "cultured" class of leaders who will foster the rest of Afro-America so that it may evolve into ideal humanity. Patronizing as her mythmaking seems, it mirrors the attitudes of other post-Reconstruction black writers in its evolutionary concept of history. Unlike Harper, however, Hopkins conveys no notion that blacks are inherently more moral than whites or that black leaders will enhance white evolution. If anything, Hopkins hazards the idea that racial intermixture with Anglo-Saxons, however much it exploits women, has improved Afro-Americans, infusing blacks with characteristics of "the higher race." This blatant endorsement of racial supremacy has been responsible, in part, for the critical neglect of Hopkins's fiction; whether she was collapsing under the weight of the dominant cultural ideology or merely appealing to a white audience fails to excuse her. Yet paradoxically, Hopkins insists that, regardless of skin color, African descent people must identify with Afro-American. In addition, she avows in her epigraph from Emerson that whites have debased themselves by racial oppression. Finally, *Contending Forces* challenges "the best" of both races to consolidate in order to bring about historical change. Denouncing violence for agitation, Hopkins seeks to arouse moral urgency in black and white readers alike.

—Jane Campbell, *Mythic Black Fiction: The Transformation of History* (Knoxville: University of Tennessee Press, 1986), 39–40

HAZEL V. CARBY

What Hopkins concentrated on ⟨in *Contending Forces*⟩ was a representation of the black female body as colonized by white male power and practices; if oppositional control was exerted by a black male, as in the story of Mabelle's father, the black male was destroyed. The link between economic/political power and economic/sexual power was firmly established in the battle for the control over women's bodies. Hopkins repeatedly asserted the importance of the relation between histories: the contemporary rape of black women was linked to the oppression of the female slave. Children were destined to follow the condition of their mothers into a black, segregated realm of existence from where they were unable to challenge the white-controlled structure of property and power. Any economic, political, or social advance made by black men resulted in accusations of a threat to the white female body, the source of heirs to power and property, and subsequent death at the hands of a lynch mob. A desire for a pure black womanhood, an uncolonized black female body, was the false hope of Sappho's pretense. The only possible future for her black womanhood was through a confrontation with, not denial of, her history. The struggle to establish and assert her womanhood was a struggle of redemption: a retrieval and reclaiming of the previously colonized. The reunited Mabelle/Sappho was a representation of a womanhood in which motherhood was not contingent upon wifehood, and Will was a representation of a black manhood that did not demand that women be a medium of economic exchange between men. The figure of Mabelle/Sappho lost her father when he refused to accept that his daughter was a medium of cash exchange with his white stepbrother. Beaubean had his fatherhood denied at the moment when he attempted to assert such patriarchal control and was slaughtered by a white mob. Instead of representing a black manhood that was an equivalent to white patriarchy, Hopkins grasped for the utopian possibility that Will could be a husband/partner to Mabelle/Sappho, when he accepted her sexual history, without having to occupy the space of father to her child.

Contending Forces was the most detailed exploration of the parameters of black womanhood and of the patriarchal limitations of black manhood in Hopkins's fiction. In her following three novels, Hopkins would adopt the more popular conventions of womanhood and manhood that defined heroes and heroines as she produced a magazine fiction that sought a wide audience. Hopkins continued to write popular fiction at the same time as she adopted popular fictional formulas and was the first Afro-American author to produce a black popular fiction that drew on the archetypes of dime novels and story papers.

—Hazel V. Carby, *Reconstructing Womanhood: The Emergence of the Afro-American Woman Novelist* (New York: Oxford University Press, 1987), 143–44

DICKSON D. BRUCE, JR.

⟨Hagar's Daughter⟩ begins with a version of the tragic mulatto story, as Hagar, the beautiful young wife of a southern planter named Ellis Enson, is discovered to have black ancestry. In her grief and despair, she jumps with her child from a high bridge crossing the Potomac, apparently to her death. The scene is virtually identical to a similar episode at the conclusion of William Wells Brown's *Clotel*. But Hopkins departed from the usual treatment of the tragic mulatto. Commonly, in such stories, the heroine's tragedy is a result of the sexual hypocrisy of the white man. In Hopkins' story, the element of sexual hypocrisy does not appear. Hagar decides upon suicide because Ellis has apparently died while trying to arrange for their removal to Europe, where they can continue to live openly as husband and wife, away from the prejudices of white America. Like ⟨George Marion⟩ McClellan's "Old Greenbottom Inn," Hopkins' *Hagar's Daughter* held out the possibility of a real interracial love that triumphed over prejudice.

But Hopkins also went a step further than McClellan in her treatment of interracial love. As the word *apparently* in the synopsis indicates, neither Hagar nor Ellis actually dies in the early going of the novel. After spinning a complex tale of Washington intrigue, set twenty years beyond the apparent deaths of husband and wife, Hopkins reunited them through a series of coincidences. Again, Ellis, knowing full well Hagar's background, wants her to be his wife, creating a marriage that makes race irrelevant. The only tragic sidelight is that a young white man in love with Hagar's daughter spurns the girl because of her ancestry. In the end, he sees the error of his ways; but he cannot do anything about it. She has died, the victim of a fever. Here, of course, is the tragic mulatto, but presented in a way—balanced by her parents' unhappiness—that displays the alternative to, rather than the inevitability of, the young girl's tragic end, an alternative that even her misguided young man has come to see.

Hagar's Daughter was a frank espousal of the possibility and rightness of interracial romance. It was like "Talma Gordon" ⟨*The Colored American*, October 1900⟩ in this regard, portraying a perspective consistent with but still more fully assimilationist than that of *Contending Forces*. Hopkins recognized that if racial barriers were to be represented as truly possible to overcome, then even the barrier to intermarriage had to be seen as artificial. Critic Claudia Tate has pointed out that marriage as a source of identity and stability was important in all of Hopkins' novels. In *Hagar's Daughter*, Hopkins used interracial marriage to encapsulate a vision of the irrelevance of racial identity in a decent world.

—Dickson D. Bruce, Jr., *Black American Writing from the Nadir: The Evolution of a Literary Tradition 1877–1915* (Baton Rouge: Louisiana State University Press, 1989), 150–51

CLAUDIA TATE

Mrs. Willis (in *Contending Forces*) is the principal proponent for the law of the mother. In the chapter entitled "The Sewing Circle," she advises Sappho, on hearing her fictitious version of her personal history. Sappho recalls: "I once knew a woman who had sinned. . . . She married a man who would have despised her had he known her story; but as it is, she is looked upon as a pattern of virtue for all women. . . . Ought she not to have told her husband before marriage? Was it not her duty to have thrown herself upon his clemency?" Mrs. Willis replies: "I am a practical woman of the world and I think your young woman builded wiser than she knew. I am of the opinion that most men are like the lower animals in many things—they don't always know what is for their best good." Mrs. Willis's advice does not sanction the father's law; instead, she insists that man's view is finite, while God's judgment is infinite. She interprets God's infinity as "[Sappho's] duty . . . to be happy and bright for the good of those about [her]." The preeminence of the mother's law also directs the lives of Will Smith and his sister, Dora. For them their father is a sacred memory, connecting them to a history of racial strength as well as oppression. However, his absence also mitigates the strength of patriarchal values on their immediate lives and permits their mother to become the authority figure who not only nurtures them but manages the household affairs. Although the text makes no explicit mention of her managerial skills, it informs us that she runs a comfortable rooming house, and has a son enrolled at Harvard and a daughter who does not work outside the home. These details represent Mrs. Smith's proficiency in financial management and encourages the characters (and us) to regard women not as masculine complements but as individuals in their own right, deserving respect. Equally important to the evolving plot, the absence of the father and his law permits Will to follow his own desire in selecting his wife, rather than institutionalized patriarchal desire for premarital virginity. As a result he is free to marry the so-called ruined woman and to father her child as if it were his own.

The fact that Mrs. Willis is also a widow is important because she and Mrs. Smith are the principal means for inscribing the absence of the black patriarch. Mrs. Smith is the ideal maternal figure, which the text underscores by repeatedly referring to her as Ma Smith. Her widowhood is idealized, while Mrs. Willis's widowhood is problematic. The text describes Mrs. Willis's deceased husband as "a bright Negro politician" who had secured "a seat in the Legislature." In addition, she had "loved [him] with a love ambitious for his advancement." Despite "the always expected addition to [their] family," she was the woman behind the man. However, at his death there was no trust fund to meet her financial needs, and she has to work. For her the question becomes what line of work can fulfill both her financial needs and ambition. No longer able to represent her ambition as desire for her husband's advancement, Mrs. Willis has to find a cause. "The best opening, she decided after looking carefully about her, was in the great cause of the evolution of true womanhood in the work of the 'Woman Question' as embodied in marriage and suffrage." Thus, Mrs. Willis comes to the Woman Question not out of a burning passion for women's rights but out of a desire to advance herself as well as black women and the race. In short, she is a professional, or, in her own words, "a practical woman of the world" who has "succeeded well in her plans," which the text continues to describe as "conceived in selfishness, they yet bore glorious fruit in the formation of clubs of colored women banded together . . . [to] better the condition of mankind." To her audience she is a "brilliant widow" who "could talk dashingly on many themes." However, Mrs. Willis incites "a wave of repulsion" in Sappho; yet "Sappho [is] impressed in spite of herself, by the woman's words." Mrs. Willis is a model for the successful professional woman of that epoch who has stepped far into the public realm of political ambition. Sappho detects Mrs. Willis's conscious desire for power as well as the will to grasp it, and this detection excites her contradictory feelings about women's ambitions for power and conventional gender prescriptives designating it as inappropriate, which Hopkins's contemporaries no doubt also experienced.

   —Claudia Tate, "Allegories of Black Female Desire; or, Rereading Nineteenth-Century Sentimental Narratives of Black Female Authority," in *Changing Our Own Words: Essays on Criticism, Theory, and Writing by Black Women*, ed. Cheryl A. Wall (New Brunswick, NJ: Rutgers University Press, 1989), 122–23

Elizabeth Ammons

Very far removed from the social-documentary style of *Contending Forces*, *Of One Blood* mixes in unstable and therefore highly productive and unsettling combinations the ingredients of narrative realism, travelog, allegory, and dream prophecy. Unlike ⟨Frances E. W.⟩ Harper's work, in which much the same mixing of forms suggests generic searching, Hopkins's fusion, confusion, and irresolution of genre—the strange complexity of *Of One Blood*'s "fantastical plot," to recall Watson's characterization—suggests brilliant, even if not totally realized, purpose. Hopkins is not entering herself in the American romance tradition. She does not, like Hawthorne, use the supernatural as symbol. Rather, like Toni Morrison after her, she asserts the supernatural as reality. She breaks boundaries—enters the secret, long lost kingdom of black power in Africa—not in a mind trip but in a *real* trip, as *Of One Blood*'s literal volatility of form expresses. She moves with complete logic and ease between material and supernatural reality, past and present. In Charlotte Perkins Gilman's work about a woman artist, spirits and the supernatural are products of mind—and of a deranged mind at that (the wobbling heads in the wallpaper, the creeping female forms). In Hopkins's narrative, experience from the other side (of life/of the world) is not the product of mind, much less of insanity. It is part of what is here. To "say" this in fiction—to say the opposite of what a Poe or Gilman might imply in their contextualizing of the supernatural in madness, or what Hawthorne might suggest in using the supernatural as moral or psychological symbol—Hopkins *does* create, by "realistic" high-culture western standards, a most strange and fantastical narrative: elaborate, dense, utterly decentered in its instability as realism. Clearly her last published long fiction, *Of One Blood*, suggests her desire to break out of the inherited high western narrative tradition, her desire to craft new form by drawing on antidominant realities of multiconsciousness and pan-African wholeness.

As an allegory about art, Hopkins's elaborate, bitter story shows the black woman artist, whose roots go deep into African history, half-dead and then completely dead in the United States. Dianthe, Candace's spiritual double and daughter, should be strong like her African forbear: regal, powerful, constantly renewed by the society in which she lives, and ready to unite with the black man to redeem the past and create the future. In Hopkins's myth, however, this tremendous possibility for creativity, including union with her black brother, meets total destruction at the hands of the white man, whose policy it is to deceive, silence, exploit sexually, and finally kill the black woman if she attempts to free herself from him. Whatever guarded optimism Hopkins might have felt about the future of the African American woman artist at the time she wrote *Contending Forces* was gone by the time she wrote *Of One Blood*. Grounding the black woman artist's story in unrequited heterosexual desire, violent sexual violation by white America, and erasure of her empowering African heritage, Hopkins tells in her "fairy tale," her wildly unbelievable fiction (if looked at in conventional western realistic terms), the awful truth about the African American woman artist's reality at the beginning of the twentieth century. In *Of One Blood* the black American woman artist *has* a past. It is ancient, potent, brilliant—full of voice. What she does not have is ownership of that past, or a future. ⟨. . .⟩

With *Of One Blood* Pauline Hopkins changed history. She pushed narrative form fully over into the mode of allegorical vision, prophecy, and dream projection that African American fiction, and particularly fiction by women—Toni Morrison, Rosa Guy, Gloria Naylor—would brilliantly mine later in the twentieth century. Without the *Colored American Magazine*, however, Pauline Hopkins, whose last major fiction in that magazine dramatized the violent silencing and death of the black American woman artist, disappeared as a productive artist.

—Elizabeth Ammons, *Conflicting Stories: American Women Writers at the Turn into the Twentieth Century* (New York: Oxford University Press, 1991), 83–85

B I B L I O G R A P H Y

Slaves' Escape: or, the Underground Railroad. 1879.

Contending Forces: A Romance Illustrative of Negro Life North and South. 1900.

Hagar's Daughter: A Story of Southern Caste Prejudice. Serialized 1901–2.

Winona: A Tale of Negro Life in the South and Southwest. Serialized 1902.

Of One Blood: or, the Hidden Self. Serialized 1902–3.

*A Primer of Facts Pertaining to the Greatness of the African Race and the Possibility of
 Restoration by Its Descendants.* 1905.

Topsy Templeton. 1916.

ZORA NEALE HURSTON

1891-1960

ZORA NEALE HURSTON, although she gave her birthdate as 1901 or 1903, was probably born on January 7, 1891, in America's first all-black incorporated town, Eatonville, Florida. Her father, John Hurston, was a sharecropper who became a carpenter, preacher, and three-term mayor of Eatonville. Her mother, Lucy Hurston, died in 1904. As a child, she recounts in her autobiography, she listened to the "lying sessions" of the men on a storefront porch "straining against each other in telling folks tales. God, Devil, Brer Rabbit, Brer Fox, Sis Cat, Brer Bear, Lion, Tiger, Buzzard and all the wood folk walked and talked like natural men." The richness and singularity of black folklore would permeate all her work.

In her teens, five years after her mother's death, Hurston left Eatonville to work as a maid and wardrobe girl for a traveling Gilbert and Sullivan troupe. Some biographers have conjectured that she was married during this period, but no evidence supports or disproves it. In 1917, her travels brought her to Baltimore, where she enrolled at the Morgan College Preparatory School. She graduated in 1918 and entered Howard University, from which she received an Associates Degree in 1920. The following year, her first published story, "John Redding Goes to Sea," appeared in the college literary magazine *The Stylus*. "Drenched in Light" (1924) and "Spunk" (1925) were published in *Opportunity*, the magazine edited by Charles S. Johnson, who subsequently urged Hurston to come to New York. She arrived, as she tells it, with "$1.50, no job, no friends, and a lot of hope."

Hurston also had brilliance and scholarly ambitions, however. In 1925, she won a scholarship to Barnard College to study with the anthropologist Franz Boas, and two years later, she undertook anthropological field research in Alabama, Louisiana, the West Indies, and Eatonville, Florida. She received her B.A. in 1928. She meanwhile continued to write: a play, *Great Day*, was published in 1927, followed in 1930 by "Dance Songs and Tales from the Bahamas" and the third act of *Mule Bone: A Comedy of Negro Life in Three Acts*, a play written in collaboration with Langston Hughes; "Hoodoo in America" was published in 1931.

In New York City, at the center of the Harlem Renaissance in 1926, Hurston published "Muttsy" and, with Langston Hughes and Wallace Thurman, founded the avant-garde literary magazine *Fire!!*

"The Gilded Six-Bits" appeared in 1933, and her first novel, *Jonah's Gourd Vine*, loosely based on the life of her parents, was published the following year. With a Rosenwald Fellowship in 1934, Hurston traveled throughout the South collecting folklore. The result of her research was the publication of *Mules and Men* (1935), an anthropological study of black American folklore that was praised as a major contribution but criticized for its lack of political perspective. Guggenheim Fellowships in 1936 and 1938 enabled Hurston to study folklore in the West Indies, and she is the first black American woman to have collected and published such work. In later years, her interest in anthropology took her to several Caribbean and Latin American countries, including Jamaica, Haiti, and Honduras.

Hurston's most artistically successful fiction is *Their Eyes Were Watching God* (1937), a novel about a woman who tells a story of identity and love. In 1939, Hurston published *Moses, Man of the Mountain;* her autobiography, *Dust Tracks on a Road*, was published in 1942 and won the 1943 Annisfield Award. She also wrote many articles during this period, including "Fannie Hurst," "Story of Harlem Slang," "Negroes Without Self-Pity," and "Black Ivory Finale." In 1948, *Seraph on the Suwanee* was published, her final novel and the only one depicting the lives of whites.

Hurston wrote for various magazines in the 1950s, but her increasingly conservative views concerning race relations alienated her from black intellectual circles. A recluse in her later years, she died on January 28, 1960, in a welfare home in Fort Pierce, Florida.

CRITICAL EXTRACTS

MARGARET WALLACE

Jonah's Gourd Vine can be called without fear of exaggeration the most vital and original novel about the American Negro that has yet been written by a member of the Negro race. Miss Hurston, who is a graduate of Barnard College and a student of anthropology, has made the study of Negro folklore her special province. This may very well account for the brilliantly authentic flavor of her novel and for her excellent rendition of Negro dialect. Unlike the dialect in most novels about the American Negro, this does not seem to be merely the speech of white men with the spelling distorted. Its essence lies rather in the rhythm and balance of the sentences, in the warm artlessness of the phrasing.

No amount of special knowledge of her subject, however, could have made *Jonah's Gourd Vine* other than a mediocre novel if it were not for Miss Hurston's notable talents as a storyteller. In John, the big yellow Negro preacher, and in Lucy Potts, his tiny brown wife, she has created two characters who are intensely real and human and whose outlines will remain in the reader's memory long after the book has been laid aside. They are part and parcel of the tradition of their race, which is as different from ours as night from day; yet Miss Hurston has delineated them with such warmth and sympathy that they appeal to us first of all as human beings, confronting a complex of human problems with whatever grace and humor, intelligence and steadfastness they can muster.

John was a "yaller nigger," hated by his dusky foster-father because of the white blood in his veins. "His mamma named him Two-Eye John after a preacher she heered, but dey called him John Buddy for short." When he was too big to be beaten or bullied the share-cropping Ned Crittenden turned him off the farm. John got a job on Mr. Alf Pearson's place, and created with his big young body and his rich voice a great stir among the brown maidens in Mr. Pearson's service, and fell in love with Lucy Potts, a bright-eyed little girl who could run faster and recite longer pieces than anybody else in school. In the interests of his ardent courtship, John learned to read, and when Lucy attained her fifteenth birthday they were married.

John really loved Lucy and intended to be true to her, but he was totally unable to resist the open and insistent blandishments of other women. Even after he felt a "call" to the ministry he was always mixed up with some woman or other, frequently to the point of an open breach with his horrified and interested congregation. John's long and futile struggle with his lusty appetites, Lucy's cleverness and devotion in protecting him from the consequences, his entanglement after Lucy's death with the magic-making Hattie, his public ruin and public regeneration all make an extraordinarily absorbing and credible tale.

Not the least charm of the book, however, is its language—rich, expressive and lacking in self-conscious artifice. From the rolling and dignified rhythms of John's last sermon to the humorous aptness of such a word as "shickalacked," to express the noise and motion of a locomotive, there will be much in it to delight the reader. It is to be hoped that Miss Hurston will give us other novels in the same colorful idiom.

—Margaret Wallace, "Real Negro People," *The New York Times Book Review* (6 May 1934), excerpted in *Twentieth-Century American Literature*, ed. Harold Bloom (New York: Chelsea House Publishers, 1986), 1952–53

RICHARD WRIGHT

Their Eyes Were Watching God is the story of Zora Neale Hurston's Janie who, at sixteen, married a grubbing farmer at the anxious instigation of her slave-born grandmother. The romantic Janie, in the highly charged language of Miss Hurston, longed to be a pear tree in blossom and have a "dust-bearing bee sink into the sanctum of a bloom; the thousand sister-calyxes arch to meet the love-embrace." Restless, she fled from her farmer husband and married Jody, an up-and-coming Negro business man who, in the end, proved to be no better than her first husband. After twenty years of clerking for the self-made Jody, Janie found herself a frustrated widow of forty with a small fortune on her hands. Tea Cake, "from in and through Georgia," drifted along, and, despite his youth, Janie took him. For more than two years they lived happily; but Tea Cake was bitten by a dog and infected with rabies. One night in a canine rage Tea Cake tried to murder Janie, thereby forcing her to shoot the only man she had ever loved.

Miss Hurston can write; but her prose is cloaked in that facile sensuality that has dogged Negro expression since the days of Phillis Wheatley. Her dialogue manages to catch the psychological movements of the Negro folk-mind in their pure simplicity, but that's as far as it goes.

Miss Hurston *voluntarily* continues in her novel the tradition which was *forced* upon the Negro in the theater, that is, the minstrel technique that makes the "white folks" laugh. Her characters eat and laugh and cry and work and kill; they swing like a pendulum eternally in that safe and narrow orbit in which America likes to see the Negro live: between laughter and tears.

[Waters] Turpin's faults as a writer are those of an honest man trying desperately to say something; but Zora Neale Hurston lacks even that excuse. The sensory sweep of her novel carries no theme, no message, no thought. In the main, her novel is not addressed to the Negro, but to a white audience whose chauvinistic tastes she knows how to satisfy. She exploits that phase of Negro life which is "quaint," the phase which evokes a piteous smile on the lips of the "superior" race.

—Richard Wright, "Between Tears and Laughter," *New Masses* (5 October 1937), excerpted in *Twentieth-Century American Literature*, ed. Harold Bloom (New York: Chelsea House Publishers, 1986), 1954

DARWIN S. TURNER

Because ⟨*Jonah's Gourd Vine*⟩ derives its movement from the action of John Buddy, the plot is logically structured until the second marriage. At that point, desiring to provide poetic justice for her father vicariously, Miss Hurston resorted to melodrama, most apparent in the discovery of the voodoo symbols which motivated John Buddy to divorce his second wife and in the restoration of his fortune.

Although Miss Hurston delineated her protagonists credibly, she exaggerated minor figures. Because she hated her stepmother, Miss Hurston caricatured Hattie, John Buddy's second wife, as a vituperative, ignorant, immoral, vindictive monster. Miss Hurston designed a black girl, Mehaley, as a comic foil for Lucy. Whereas Lucy is intelligent, educated, affectionate, and relatively obedient to her mother's rigid morality, Mehaley is slothful, sensual, and amoral. The contrast reaches a farcical climax in the difference between Lucy's marriage and Mehaley's. Lucy marries John Buddy in a simple, decorous ritual performed with the reverence customary for a sacrament of the church. Mehaley's wedding is delayed first by the tardiness of the bridegroom. It is further delayed by her father, a self-appointed preacher, who refuses to permit an ordained minister to perform the ceremony. After the father prevails and after the bridegroom again imprisons his aching feet in his new shoes, the marriage vows are recited by the illiterate father, who pretends to read the words from a book which he believes to be the Bible but which is actually an almanac. That evening, the bride postpones consummating the marriage until she has satisfied her craving for snuff.

Miss Hurston's predilection for farcical statement frequently distorts the tone of the novel. For instance, while Ned and Amy Crittenden are arguing about the merits of mulattoes, Amy rebukes Ned's argument that Negroes cannot faint:

> "Dass awright. Niggers gwine faint too. May not come in yo' time
> and it may not come in mine, but way after while, us people is gwine
> faint just lak white folks."

The statement ceases to amuse when one realizes that, by attributing it to ex-slaves, Miss Hurston, for the sake of a laugh, denied the existence of slaves who fainted from exhaustion, hunger, and pain.

Exploitation of the exotic weakens the dialogue, which constitutes both the major strength and the major weakness of the novel. Effectively, Miss Hurston created a dialect, or dialects, which, if not authentic, nevertheless suggest a particular level of speech without ridiculing the speaker. The language also exhibits the rural Southern blacks' imaginative, vivid use of metaphor, simile, and invective:

> God was grumbling his thunder and playing the zig-zag lighting thru
> his fingers.

> "De chickens is cacklin' in de rice and dey say 'Come git it whilst iss fitten' cause t'morrer it may be frost-bitten!'"
> "Seben years ain't too long fuh uh coudar tuh wear uh ruffled bosom shirt."
> "Ah means to beat her 'til she rope lak okra, and den agin Ah'll stomp her 'til she slack lak line."

The verisimilitude of the language is intensified not merely by the dialect and idiom but even by words, such as "lies," "jook," "piney wood rooters," which require definition in the glossary.

But exploiting the appeal of this language, she piled up metaphorical invective to a height difficult for any mortal to attain ⟨. . . .⟩

Miss Hurston's attitude toward interracial relationships in the South seems curiously ambivalent if a reader does not know her social philosophy. On the "poor" side of the creek, John's mother, Amy Crittenden, bitterly denounces slavery, sharecropping, and abusive, unjust white "trash." On the other side of the river, however, John and even Lucy unquestioningly accept Alf Peterson's paternalism. Thus, Miss Hurston imputes all abuses of blacks to lower-class Southern masters, a sentiment which is commercially expedient but false. Except for these opening scenes in Alabama, however, the action of *Jonah's Gourd Vine* is confined to Eatonville, Florida, where the black inhabitants are unaffected by the white people of neighboring communities.

In the novel, Miss Hurston experimented with symbols with varying degrees of success. The image of "Jonah's gourd vine" does not seem to represent John effectively because no Jonah exists. The fact that John Buddy is created by God and is smitten by God furnishes merely a strained analogy. Miss Hurston, however, used a railroad train more effectively. One of the first objects which John sees after he had crossed the creek, the railroad locomotive impresses him as the most powerful, potentially dangerous force he has ever known. More than a machine or even an agent for transportation, however, it symbolizes his sexual awareness. Coming into his consciousness when he first enters a world of heterosexual relationships, it dominates his thoughts and finally destroys him.

—Darwin S. Turner, "Zora Neale Hurston: The Wandering Minstrel," in *In a Minor Chord* (1971), excerpted in *Twentieth-Century American Literature*, ed. Harold Bloom (New York: Chelsea House Publishers, 1986), 1953–54

JUNE JORDAN

A few years back, Hoyt Fuller posed the primary functions of Protest and Affirmation as basic to an appreciation of Black Art. Wright's *Native Son* is widely recognized as the prototypical Black protest novel. By comparison,

Hurston's novel, *Their Eyes Were Watching God*, seems to suit, perfectly, the obvious connotations of Black affirmation.

I would add that the functions of protest and affirmation are not, ultimately, distinct: that, for instance, affirmation of Black values and lifestyle within the American context is, indeed, an act of protest. Therefore, Hurston's affirmative work is profoundly defiant, just as Wright's protest unmistakably asserts our need for an alternative, benign environment. We have been misled to discount the one in order to revere the other. But we have been misled in other ways. Several factors help to explain the undue contrast between the careers of Wright and Hurston. ⟨. . .⟩

Zora Neal Hurston was born and raised in an all-Black Florida town. In other words, she was born into a supportive, nourishing environment. And without exception, her work—as novelist, as anthropologist/diligent collector and preserver of Black folktale and myth—reflects this early and late, all-Black universe that was her actual as well as her creative world.

You see her immovable, all-Black orientation in *Their Eyes Were Watching God*: whites do not figure in this story of Black love; white anything or anybody is not important. What matters is the Black woman and the Black man who come together in a believable, contagious, full Blacklove that makes you want to go and seek and find, likewise, soon as you finish the book.

Since white America lies outside the Hurston universe, both in fact and in her fiction, you do not run up on the man/the enemy. Protest, narrowly conceived, is therefore beside the point; rhythm or tones of outrage or desperate flight would be wholly inappropriate in her text. Instead, you slip into a total, Black reality where Black people do not represent issues: they represent their own, particular selves in a Family/Community setting that permits relaxation from hunted/warrior postures, and that fosters the natural, person-postures of courting, jealousy, ambition, dream, sex, work, partying, sorrow, bitterness, celebration, and fellowship.

Unquestionably, *Their Eyes Were Watching God* is the prototypical Black novel of affirmation; it is the most successful, convincing, and exemplary novel of Blacklove that we have. Period. But the book gives us more: the story unrolls a fabulous, written-film of Blacklife freed from the constraints of oppression; here we may learn Black possibilities of ourselves if we could ever escape the hateful and alien context that has so deeply disturbed and mutilated our rightful efflorescence—*as people*. Consequently, this novel centers itself on Blacklove—even as *Native Son* rivets itself upon white hatred.

But: because Zora Neale Hurston was a woman, and because we have been misled into devaluating the functions of Black affirmation, her work has been derogated as romantic/the natural purview of a woman (*i.e.*, unimportant), "personal" (not serious) in its scope, and assessed as *sui generis*, or idiosyncratic accomplishment of no lasting reverberation or usefulness.

All such derogation derives from ignorance and/or callow thinking we cannot afford to continue.

—June Jordan, "On Richard Wright and Zora Neale Hurston: Toward a Balancing of Love and Hatred," *Black World* (August 1974), excerpted in *Twentieth-Century American Literature*, ed. Harold Bloom (New York: Chelsea House Publishers, 1986), 1956

SHERLEY ANNE WILLIAMS

The image of the black woman as the mule of the world ⟨voiced by Janie's grandmother, Nanny⟩ becomes a metaphor for the roles that Janie repudiates in her quest for self-fulfillment and the belief against which the book implicitly argues. Love, for the old ex-slave, is "de very prong all us black women gits hung on": that is, as Nanny goes on to explain, wanting a dressed-up dude who can't keep himself in shoe leather, much less provide for someone else; his women tote that burden for him. Love doesn't kill; it just makes a black woman sweat. Nanny dies believing that the only armor against this fate is money or the protection of good white people.

Janie holds onto her vision of a fulfilled and fulfilling love through two loveless marriages. Nanny arranges Janie's first marriage, to Logan Killicks, an older farmer whose sixty acres ought to provide Janie with the security Nanny has been able to achieve only through working for white families. Killicks, however, can't see any further than his plow, and Janie is stifled by his plodding nature. Realizing that Janie doesn't return his love, he tries to destroy her spirit by threatening to make her help with the back-breaking labor of the farm. Nanny's metaphor is almost actualized, but Janie rebels. She runs away with Joe Starks, an ambitious go-getter who pauses on his way to becoming "a big voice" in the world (mayor and postmaster, principal landowner and businessman in Eatonville) to marry Janie. Joe stops making "speeches with rhymes" to Janie almost as soon as the wedding ceremony is over. Instead of love talk, he buys her the best of everything.

Joe provides Janie with the "front porch" existence of Nanny's dreams, but in doing so, he isolates her from direct participation in any life except his own. His stranglehold on her life and definition of self is symbolized in his prohibition against her participation in the tale-tellings, mock flirtations, and other comic activities that center around or emanate from the porch of his general store. Despite his own pleasure in these sessions, he charges that the people who gather at them are "trashy," and Janie is Mrs. Mayor Starks. They don't even own their own houses, and a woman of Janie's respectability shouldn't want to pass the time of day with them. Thus, "when Lige or Sam or Walter or some of the other big picture talkers were using a side of the world for a canvas, Joe would hustle her off inside the store to sell something." The link between selling and Joe's attempt to isolate Janie from authentic membership in the community is striking and deliberate: Janie is Joe's personal possession, "de mayor's wife." It is an image that, as Hurston says of their marriage, is soon deserted by the spirit. But it is not only class that Joe uses as a means of browbeating Janie into submission. She is a woman; her place is in the home (or wherever he tells her to be, like the store, where he forces her to clerk because her many mistakes give him another opportunity to belittle her intelligence). Someone has to think for women, children, chickens, and cows. The instances of Joe's chauvinism are obvious and many. The metaphor of the mule is further reified in Joe's insistence that Janie tote his narrow, stultifying notions of what behavior is appropriate to her class and sex. Rooted at first only in the specificity of the Afro-American female experience, the metaphor has been transformed into one for the female condition; Janie's individual quest for fulfillment becomes any woman's tale.

Joe dies of a kidney ailment after some years of marriage. Janie, now a widow with property and still a very attractive woman, meets and marries Vergible "Tea Cake" Woods, an itinerant laborer and gambler much younger than herself. Tea Cake is love and laughter and talking in rhymes. However, he fulfills Janie's dreams because he requires only that she be herself. At home with himself, he has no need to dominate Janie or curb her self-expression in order to prove his masculinity. In contrast to the social status that her previous marriages gave her (and the book is filled with contrasts), Janie's place in her relationship with Tea Cake is on the muck, a booming farming area, picking beans at his side. Janie has come *down*, that paradoxical place in Afro-American literature that is both a physical bottom and the setting for the character's attainment of a penultimate self-knowledge (think of Ellison's Invisible Man in his basement room or the hero of Baraka's *The System of Dante's Hell* in the Bottoms). Down on the muck, Janie's horizons are expanded by the love and respect she shares with Tea Cake. She becomes a participant in the life that Nanny, Logan, Joe, and other friends and advisors would have her believe is beneath her. "The men held big arguments here like they used to do on the store porch. Only here, she could listen and laugh and even talk some herself if she wanted to. She got so she could tell big stories herself from listening to the rest." Janie comes at last into her own, at home with herself, her man, and her world. This unity is symbolized in a final play on the black-woman-as-mule image. Tea Cake asks and Janie consents to work in the fields with him, because neither wants to be parted from the other even during the working day. Their love for each other makes the stoop labor of bean picking seem almost play. The differences between the image and the reversal of that image are obvious: Tea Cake has asked, not commanded; his request stems from a desire to be with Janie, to share every aspect of his life with her, rather than from a desire to coerce her into some mindless submission. It isn't the white man's burden that Janie carries; it is the gift of her own love.

—Sherley Anne Williams, "Janie's Burden," originally "Foreword" to *Their Eyes Were Watching God* (University of Illinois Press, 1978), excerpted in *Zora Neale Hurston*, ed. Harold Bloom (New York: Chelsea House Publishers, 1986), 100–2

Mary Helen Washington

In her first novel, *Jonah's Gourd Vine*, ⟨. . .⟩ Zora Hurston continued to use the folk life of Eatonville as the essential experience ⟨as she had in *Mules and Men*⟩. Loosely based on the lives of her parents, *Jonah's Gourd Vine* presents one of Hurston's many powerful women characters—Lucy Pearson, wife of the town's philandering preacher, John Pearson. On her deathbed, Lucy Pearson is such a strong-willed woman that John is afraid to be in the same room with her, and with the advice she gives Isis (probably Zora), she bequeaths the spirit to her daughter: "You always strain tuh be de bell-cow, never be de tail uh nothin'." With these publications and the ones that were to follow in the thirties, Zora Hurston had begun to take her work in directions that would earn her both high praise and severe censure. In an era when many educated and cultured blacks prided themselves on removing all traces of their rural black origins, when a high-class "Negro" virtue was not to "act one's color," Zora not only celebrated the distinctiveness of black culture, but saw those traditional black folkways as marked improvements over the "imaginative wasteland of white society."

Then, in 1937, came the novel in which Hurston triumphed in the art of taking the imagery, imagination, and experiences of black folk and making literature—*Their Eyes Were Watching God*. Hurston says in her autobiography that she wrote the novel in seven straight weeks in the Caribbean after a love affair ended, and, though the circumstances were difficult, she tried to "embalm" the novel with all of her tenderness for this man.

Perhaps because the novel's main character, Janie Woods, has a succession of husbands and finally finds joy and fulfillment in her third marriage, the novel has generally been thought of as a love story about love. On a much deeper and more important level, however, its theme is Janie's search for identity, an identity which finally begins to take shape as she throws off the false images which have been thrust upon her because she is both black and woman in a society where neither is allowed to exist naturally and freely. Hurston uses two images from nature to symbolize Janie's quest: the horizon and the blossoming pear tree. One, the horizon, suggests that the search is an individual quest; the other, the pear tree in blossom, suggests a fulfillment in union with another. Janie describes the journey to find herself in a language that takes us deep into black folk traditions:

> Ah been a delegate to de big 'ssociation of life. Yessuh! De Grand Lodge, de big convention of livin' is just where Ah been dis year and a half y'all ain't seen me.

Folk language, folkways, and folk stories work symbolically in the novel as a measure of a character's integrity and freedom. Those characters whose self-esteem and identity are based on illusion and false values are alienated from the black folk community, and, conversely, those, like Janie herself, who struggle against those self-alienating values toward a deeper sense of community, experience wholeness. Janie is both humiliated and angered by the attempts of her first two husbands to win her with materialistic gifts and to make her subservient to them. Thus the dramatic tension of the novel takes place on two levels: Janie has to resist both male domination and the empty materialism of white culture in order to get to the horizon.

Janie (née Crawford) Killicks Starks Woods is one of the few—and certainly the earliest—heroic black women in the Afro-American literary tradition. Critic Robert Stepto says that the primary voice in a literary tradition is "the personal, heroic voice, delineating the dimensions of heroism by aspiring to a heroic posture . . . or expressing an awareness of that which they ought to be." Janie assumes this heroic stature by her struggles for self-definition, for autonomy, for liberation from the illusions that others have tried to make her live by or that she herself has submitted to. Moreover, she is always the aware voice, consciously undergoing the most severe tests of that autonomy.

In *Their Eyes Were Watching God*, Hurston the creative artist and Hurston the folklorist were perfectly united. Zora Neale Hurston went on to publish two more books in the next two years—*Tell My Horse* (1938), a book of folklore from her experiences in Haiti, and another novel, *Moses, Man of the Mountain* (1939), a re-creation of the Moses myth with black folk characters. By the end of the thirties, she deserved her title: the best and most prolific black woman writer in America.

—Mary Helen Washington, "A Woman Half in Shadow," originally "Introduction: Zora Neale Hurston: A Woman Half in Shadow," in *I Love Myself When I Am Laughing . . . and Then Again When I Am Looking Mean and Impressive: A Zora Neale Hurston Reader*, ed. Alice Walker (New York: The Feminist Press, 1979), excerpted in *Zora Neale Hurston*, ed. Harold Bloom (New York: Chelsea House Publishers, 1986), 130–31

BLYDEN JACKSON

In all of Hurston's major fiction, in both its content and its rhetoric, Hurston's experience with black folklore affects commendably what she does. In none of that fiction is her experience with black folklore more of a positive force than in *Moses*. For in *Moses* Hurston's folklore goes beyond a mere contribution to the atmosphere of a tale—where, indeed, it does work no less advantageously than it does in either *Jonah's Gourd Vine* or *Their Eyes Were Watching God*. In *Moses* Hurston's folklore enters crucially into Hurston's whole conception of her novel as well as its execution at every point. Here, in this novel, Hurston is writing an allegory, telling the story, at one level of her narration, of some Hebrews caught in Egypt and their march to a promised land. And her story at this level is repetitive. It does not deviate by one essential whit from the same story as it is told in the Bible. Yet, from beginning to end, her novel is also, on a second level of narration, a story about black America, not because Hurston anywhere says that it is, but because Hurston's folklore everywhere happily transports Hurston's readers to a position from which every Jew in Goshen is converted into an American Negro and every Egyptian in Old Pharaoh's Egypt into a white in the America where Hurston's folk Negroes live.

Moses, then, is Hurston's most ambitious work. It requires from her a bold essay into a demanding display of superlative virtuosity. And it cannot be called a failure. Rather, it is possible to read it simply for the excellence with which it preserves its allegory and find it a genuinely astounding success. Yet, Hurston also conducts, simultaneously, an absorbing investigation of a theme. Hardly less than Machiavelli in *The Prince*, she discusses power—the kind of power, political in its nature, which is the prime object of concern for the Florentine in his famous treatise on statesmanship. Magic accounts for much of the power released by Moses in his contest with the Pharaoh. The plagues Moses brings to bear against the Pharaoh and his people cannot be credited to some particular skill or wisdom Moses has acquired in the difficult business of managing people. They are at best, when most charitably interpreted as an element in Hurston's allegory, a linking of the *Exodus* with voodoo and thus a splendid opportunity, which Hurston does not miss, for Hurston to live again some of her intense, unforgettable moments of sharing hallowed practices of the occult in New Orleans and the Caribbean. But magic does not obtrude in the picture Hurston presents of Moses's relations with the Hebrews, whom he must move from their subjugation in Egypt to a control of their own destinies in some place where Hebrew word is law. It could not obtrude in the thought of anyone contemplating the Negro minority in America and a program of leadership that might suffice to solve the problem of bringing this minority into a new and better relation with the white majority all too literally over them in a caste-bound social order sustained by a status quo apparently as impervious to change as the seasons and the hills. Faith healers, conjurors, medicine men, sorcerers of whatever kind obviously could not produce such a program. Not that Hurston's Moses is solely explicable in terms of factors such as training and experience that can be divorced from chance and other influences beyond human ken. Such influences exist. They always have. Conceivably they always will. Thus, Hurston's Moses is a leader partly because he was born to be a leader, with a capacity in his mighty hands for controlling people and natural phenomena that is indubitably a gift from God. Moreover, Moses talks with God and speaks for God, so that the elements of the given and the chosen in his leadership are inescapable. Yet he is also guided in the steps he takes as a leader by his reflections on what has happened to him or seemed worthy of his attention when it happened to other men. He dislikes war because he has seen so much of it as the commanding general of Pharaoh's army. He has grown sick of intrigue at the top of a social pyramid because he has lived in the Pharaoh's palace. And he has grown to love common humanity because of such developments in his own life as his affection for his servant, Mentu. A blend of the human and the extra-human make him what he is. Molded by that blend he shapes anew the history of the Hebrews.

If there was meant to be a lesson for the black leadership of Hurston's day in *Moses*, it is difficult to say of what that lesson was intended to consist. Hurston was no social visionary. She was neither another Percy Shelley nor another Karl Marx hypothesizing terms, loose or precise, for an earthly paradise. It was much more of the guild of Aristophanes and Gilbert and Sullivan —all, like her, conservatives—to which she belonged. Consequently, allegory though it is, *Moses* is also satire. Both witty and profound are Hurston's observations about black America with its, as it seemed to her, regrettably wide and deep division in loyalties among its upper class, its black bourgeoisie, and the Negro masses from whom her folklore came. The prominence of mulattos in the black bourgeoisie had not escaped Hurston's sardonic eye. And she appears to make her Moses a mulatto, although his non-Egyptian blood is Assyrian rather than Hebrew. But it is not Moses after all, of whom she is as critical as a representative of Negro leadership as it is Miriam and Aaron. These two, it appears, are black bourgeoisie who have made their way up into the leadership class from the ranks of the Negro masses. Of Miriam and Aaron she has many unkind things to say. Nor is she always kind to the ordinary Hebrews who must be, in her allegory, the rank and file of the Negro folk. Pettiness and ingratitude, especially, she notes in them. Yet she is more balanced than biased in what she says in *Moses* of both her leaders and those whom her leaders too often do not lead. If she is not a prophet, a seer, using her fiction to prescribe, more or less in specific detail, the hopeful pilgrim's path to a new and finer social order, she is, at least, a historian sufficiently non-dogmatic and nonideological to present her panorama of a human scene in a truly engaging way. Let others hymn, she seems to say, utopian tracts. Her *Moses* is, as it was meant to be, only life, actual, imperfect, sometimes difficult, and always true.

    —Blyden Jackson, *"Moses, Man of the Mountain*: A Study of Power," originally "Introduction" to *Moses, Man of the Mountain* (University of Illinois Press, 1984), excerpted in *Zora Neale Hurston*, ed. Harold Bloom (New York: Chelsea House Publishers, 1986), 152–54

HENRY LOUIS GATES, JR.

Hurston's achievement in *Dust Tracks* is twofold. First, she gives us a *writer's* life—rather than an account of "the Negro problem"—in a language as "dazzling" as Mr. ⟨Robert⟩ Hemenway says it is. So many events in the book were shaped by the author's growing mastery of books and language, but she employs both the linguistic rituals of the dominant culture and those of the black vernacular tradition. These two speech communities are the sources of inspiration for Hurston's novels and autobiography. This double voice unreconciled—a verbal analogue of her double experiences as a woman in a male-dominated world and as a black person in a non-black world—strikes me as her second great achievement.

    Many writers act as if no other author influenced them, but Hurston freely describes her encounter with books, from Xenophon in the Greek through Milton to Kipling. Chapter titles and the organization of the chapters themselves reflect this urge to testify to the marvelous process by which the writer's life has been shaped by words. "The Inside Search" and "Figure and Fancy" reveal the workings of the youthful Hurston's mind as she invented fictional worlds, struggled to find the words for her developing emotions and learned to love reading. "School Again," "Research" and "My People! My People!"—printed in the original form for the first time—unveil social and verbal race rituals and customs with candor that shocks even today. Hurston clearly saw herself as a black woman writer and thinker first and as a specimen of Negro progress last. What's more, she structured her autobiography to make such a reading inevitable.

    —Henry Louis Gates, Jr., "'A Negro Way of Saying,'" *The New York Times Book Review* (21 April 1985): 43, 45

JENNIFER JORDAN

Despite her lack of veracity, critics like Alice Walker, Robert Hemenway, and Mary Helen Washington have managed to maintain both a certain objectivity about Hurston's weaknesses and a respectful fondness for her daring and talent. This same openmindedness and tolerance for ambivalence are not always reflected in the critical responses to her greatest work, *Their Eyes Were Watching God*. Hurston's independence, her refusal to allow her love interests and marriages to hamper her career, and her adventuresomeness in confronting the dangers of anthropological research in the violent turpentine camps of the South and in the voodoo temples of Haiti make her a grand candidate for feminist sainthood. Difficulties arise, however, when critics transfer their narrow conception of Hurston's personal attitudes and history to their readings of *Their Eyes Were Watching God*, a novel that reflects Hurston's ambiguity about race, sex, and class. The result is the unsupportable notion that the novel is an appropriate fictional representation of the concerns and attitudes of modern black feminism. ⟨. . .⟩

Their Eyes Were Watching God is a novel that examines with a great deal of artistry the struggle of a middle-class woman to escape the fetters of traditional marriage and the narrow social restrictions of her class and sex. But Janie Killicks Starks Woods never perceives herself as an independent, intrinsically fulfilled human being. Nor does she form the strong female and racial bonds that black feminists have deemed necessary in their definition of an ideologically correct literature. The novel fails to meet several of the criteria defined by black feminist criticism. Perhaps the acceptance and glorification of this novel as the bible of black women's liberation speak to the unconscious conflicts about emotional and financial dependence, sexual stereotyping, intraracial hostilities, and class interests inherent within the black feminist movement. In its very ambivalences Hurston's *Their Eyes Were Watching God* may serve as a Rorschach test by which these conflicts are revealed and thus is an appropriate manifesto for black feminism.

But the novel's success or failure as an ideological document does not diminish its aesthetic worth. It remains one of the great novels of black literature—a novel that is laughing out-loud funny, that allows black people to speak in their own wonderful voices, and that portrays them in all their human nobility and pettiness.

—Jennifer Jordan, "Feminist Fantasies: Zora Neale Hurston's *Their Eyes Were Watching God*," *Tulsa Studies in Women's Literature* 7, no. 1 (Spring 1988): 106–7, 115

NELLIE MCKAY

Unlike the solitary but representative hero of male autobiography, Janie Starks and Zora Neale Hurston join voices to produce a personal narrative that celebrates an individual and collective black female identity emerging out of the search for an autonomous self. Although the structure of this text is different, the tradition of black women celebrating themselves through other women like themselves began with their personal narratives of the nineteenth century. Female slave narratives, we know, generally had protagonists who shared their space with the women who instilled pride of self and love of freedom in them. The tradition continued into the twentieth century. For instance, much of the early portion of Hurston's autobiography, *Dust Tracks on a Road*, celebrates the relationship she had with her mother and the lessons she learned, directly and indirectly, from other women in the community. Thus, Hurston's structure for Janie's story expands that already existing tradition to concretize the symbolic rendering of voice to and out of the women's community by breaking away from the formalities of conventional autobiography to make Janie's text an autobiography about autobiographical storytelling, in the tradition of African and Afro-American storytelling. Hurston, struggling with the pains and ambivalences she felt toward the realities of a love she had to reject for the restraints it would have placed on her, found a safe place to embalm the tenderness and passion of her feelings in the autobiographical voice of Janie Crawford, whose life she made into a very fine crayon enlargement of life.

    —Nellie McKay, "'Crayon Enlargements of Life': Zora Neale Hurston's *Their Eyes Were Watching God* as Autobiography," in *New Essays on* Their Eyes Were Watching God, ed. Michael Awkward (New York: Cambridge University Press, 1990), 68–69

BIBLIOGRAPHY

Color Struck; A Play in Four Scenes. 1926.

Great Day. 1927.

Mule Bone: A Comedy of Negro Life in Three Acts. 1930.

Jonah's Gourd Vine. 1934.

Mules and Men. 1935.

Their Eyes Were Watching God. 1937.

Tell My Horse. 1938.

Moses, Man of the Mountain. 1939.

Dust Tracks on a Road: An Autobiography. 1942.

Caribbean Melodies for Chorus of Mixed Voices and Soloists. Ed. William Still. 1947.

Seraph on the Suwanee. 1948.

I Love Myself When I Am Laughing and Then Again When I Am Looking Mean and Impressive: A Zora Neale Hurston Reader. Ed. Alice Walker. 1979.

The Sanctified Church. 1981.

Spunk: The Short Stories of Zora Neale Hurston. 1984.

SHIRLEY JACKSON
1919-1965

SHIRLEY ANNE JACKSON was born in San Francisco on December 14, 1919, the first of two children of Leslie Jackson and Geraldine Bugbee Jackson. She was a loner, interested mostly in reading and writing poetry and disdainful of her family's affluence and values. In 1933, the Jacksons moved to Rochester, New York, where Shirley attended the University of Rochester. She withdrew after one year, however, because of severe depression. She later enrolled at Syracuse University, receiving a B.A. in 1940. There she met the author and literary critic Stanley Edgar Hyman (1919–1970), whom she married in 1940.

The two collaborated on literary magazines at Syracuse until moving to New York City, where Jackson worked as a department store clerk; she described these years in "My Life with R.H. Macy." After the birth of their first two children, the family moved to North Bennington, Vermont. There Hyman taught at Bennington College and Jackson found more time to write. Her short story "Come Dance with Me in Ireland" appeared in *The New Yorker* in 1943 and was included in the collection *The Best American Short Stories: 1944*.

Four years later, *The New Yorker* published "The Lottery," which would become Jackson's most famous short story and created an immediate sensation. The ordinariness and shocking horror of this story about a small American town that practices an annual sacrifice induced more readers to send letters to *The New Yorker* than anything the magazine had previously published. The story was made into a screenplay in 1950 and has been recorded, recently by actress Maureen Stapleton. Hyman would later observe that "The Lottery" and Jackson's subsequent works that show her "fierce visions of dissociation and madness, of alienation and withdrawal, of cruelty and terror, have been taken to be personal, even neurotic fantasies. Quite the reverse: They are a sensitive and faithful anatomy of our times, fitting symbols for our distressing world of the concentration camp and The Bomb" (*Saturday Evening Post*, 18 December 1965).

Most of Jackson's works deal with terror, both supernatural and psychological, and often with the tenuousness of identity. Her first novel, *The Road Through the Wall* (1948), is about disturbed adolescents and is set in her childhood hometown of Burlingame, California. Her next two novels, *Hangsaman* (1951) and *The Bird's Nest* (1954), are about

28

adolescents and schizophrenia. *The Sundial* (1958) depicts a mad family awaiting the end of the world on a New England estate. *The Haunting of Hill House* (1959), a tale of the occult, and *We Have Always Lived in the Castle* (1962), about the collusion of two sisters in the poisoning of their family, became modest best-sellers. The gothic quality of Jackson's work has been compared to that of Nathaniel Hawthorne and Flannery O'Connor, while her depiction of evil in the everyday has been compared to the work of Paul Bowles and Truman Capote. Deeply interested in black magic, Jackson owned hundreds of books on the subject and was regarded—by herself, her family, and her friends—as a witch; she was consequently unwelcome among her neighbors in Vermont.

To the surprise of many of her readers, Jackson wrote two humorous books about domestic life and her own children: *Life Among the Savages* (1953) and *Raising Demons* (1957). She also wrote several works for children: *The Witchcraft of Salem Village* (1956), *The Bad Children: A Play in One Act for Bad Children* (1959), *Nine Magic Wishes* (1963), and *Famous Sally*, published posthumously in 1966. In 1961, Jackson won the Edgar Allan Poe Award for her story "Louisa, Please Come Home"; she would win the award again four years later for "The Possibility of Evil." *Come Along with Me*, a collection that includes part of a novel, 16 stories, and three lectures, was published posthumously in 1968.

Shirley Jackson died of heart failure while taking a nap at her home in North Bennington, Vermont, on August 8, 1965.

CRITICAL EXTRACTS

ROBERT B. HEILMAN

Miss Jackson's story ⟨"*The Lottery*"⟩ is remarkable for the tremendous shock produced by the ending. Let us ignore the problem of meaning for the moment and see how the shock is created. In general, the method is quite easily recognized. Up to the last six paragraphs the story is written in the manner of a realistic transcript of small-town experience: the day is a special one, true, but the occasion is familiar, and for the most part the people are presented as going through a well-known routine. We see them as decent, friendly, neighborly people; in fact, most of the details could be used just as they are in a conventional picture of idyllic small-town life. Things are easily, simply told, as if in a factual chronicle (note the use of date and hour). Suddenly, in the midst of this ordinary, matter-of-fact environment, there occurs a terrifyingly cruel action, official, accepted, yet for the reader mysterious and unexplained. It is entirely out of line with all the terms of actual experience in which the story has otherwise dealt. It is as if ordinary life had suddenly ceased and were replaced, without warning, without break, and without change of scene, by some horrifying nightmare. Hence the shock, which the author has very carefully worked up to. Note how the shock is enhanced by the deadpan narrative style, which in no way suggests that anything unusual is going on.

In one sense the author has prepared for the ending. A few slight notes of nervousness, the talk about giving up the tradition, and the emotional outburst by Mrs. Hutchinson all suggest some not entirely happy outcome. Still more important in building up an unusually strong sense of expectation is the entire absence of explanation of the public ceremony. (At the end, the reader recalls the gathering of stones earlier in the story. This unobtrusive introduction of stage properties for later use exemplifies the well-made kind of construction.) But all these preparations still look forward to an outcome which will fall within the realistic framework that the author has chosen to use. Yet the ending is not realistic: it is symbolic. We may summarize the method of the story by saying that it suddenly, without notice, shifts from a realistic to a symbolic technique. This is another way of describing the shock.

Here we come to the problem of meaning. The experienced reader will recognize immediately what Miss Jackson has done: she has taken the ancient ritual of the scapegoat—the sacrificing of an individual on whom the evils of the community are ceremonially laid (by looking up "scapegoat" in Frazer's *Golden Bough* the student can find accounts of many such practices)—and plunged it into an otherwise realistic account of contemporary American life. What the story appears to be saying, then, is that though ancient rituals die out, the habits of mind which brought them into being persist; that we still find scapegoats and "innocent victims."

The critical question is: Does the effect of shock really serve the symbolic intention of the story? Ideally, shock should have the effect of shaking up the accustomed habits of mind and, therefore, of compelling a more incisive observation of familiar ways of life. But shock may disturb as well as stimulate the mind and may leave the reader only feeling shaken up. The question here is whether the shock "seizes stage," so to speak, and so crowds out the revelation to which it should be secondary. It is difficult to shift from genial chatter—even with some overtones of fear—to ritual murder without leaving a sense of an unclosed gap. The risk would have been greatly lessened if atmosphere, instead of being used intentionally to emphasize the sense of the ordinary, had been used earlier in the story to introduce an element of the sinister. It would clearly have been most difficult to suggest the coexistence of the sinister and the innocuous from the start. But this would have been an ideal method, since that coexistence is really the human fact with which the story is concerned. But the story gives us the sinister after the innocuous, instead of the two simultaneously. To put it in other terms, the symbolic intention of the story could have been made clear earlier so that throughout the story we would have been seeking the symbolic level instead of being driven to look for it only retrospectively, after it has suddenly become apparent that a realistic reading will not work. (In ⟨Kafka's⟩ "The Hunger Artist," for instance, we have the symbolic figure—the hunger artist—as the center of attention from the start; we know immediately that the story goes beyond realism, and so we always read with an eye on the underlying meaning.) To set us immediately on the track of the symbolism would probably reduce the shock, but it might result in a more durable story.

—Robert B. Heilman, "Shirley Jackson, 'The Lottery': Comment," in *Modern Short Stories: A Critical Anthology*, ed. Robert B. Heilman (New York: Harcourt, Brace Jovanovich, 1950), 384–85

L. A. G. STRONG

Hangsaman does not reach the level of "The Lottery," which had a murderous impact, but it confirms the belief that Miss Jackson is an exceptional writer. In the longer form, she loses tension, and her repeated glimpses into her heroine's mind, clear and sharp though they are, give somehow the effect of taking her eye off the ball. The brilliantly objective vision at which she excels makes almost anything else seem like a loss of power. The theme of *Hangsaman* is simple and unoriginal. Natalie, seventeen-year-old daughter of a priggish but not unlikeable writer who not only thinks he understands her, but uses her as compensation for his wife's dislike, escapes from home to college. Her English tutor and his wife get on little better than her parents, she makes no real contact with the other girls, and finally becomes involved in an obscure adventure with the only girl who attracts her. The end of the book suggests that the hangman has "stayed his hand awhile," but does not tell us what will happen to Natalie; and I wanted to know.

The merits of this exciting and suggestive story stare at us from the page: the defects that blur its brilliance are less easy to analyse. Looking back to Miss Jackson's short stories, I think the answer is that her power to suggest intangible terrors derives directly from her power to see and to describe *objects*. Thus, when she analyses, there is a loss of clarity, of immediacy. The best in her writing is the enemy of the good. There is a self-consciousness about the early chapters of *Hangsaman* which was hardly ever apparent in the short stories. If Miss Jackson had not written those stories, *Hangsaman* would be a triumph. As she did, it is merely an astonishingly good first novel.

—L. A. G. Strong, [Review of *Hangsaman*], *Spectator* (5 October 1951): 452

HARVEY SWADOS

Miss Jackson's newest ghost story ⟨*The Sundial*⟩ is laid in a luxurious New England estate inhabited by a rather choice collection of creeps. A senile old gentleman, whose nanny reads him *Robinson Crusoe;* his power-hungry mate, dreaming of ruling the estate at any cost; their asthmatic daughter-in-law, mourning for her husband who has apparently been pushed down the stairs by mommy to ensure her control; and their sweet little granddaughter, happily defacing grandma's portraits and sticking significant pins in waxen dolls. There is also Aunt Fanny, given to receiving minatory visions of her deceased father, founder of the line and builder of the mansion. The family is rounded out with a bounder supposedly cataloguing the books in the library and a sissy nursemaid.

They are all mad, of course, which makes it somewhat easier for them to accept batty Aunt Fanny's disturbing report from her father that the world is soon to come to an end. Taking the apocalyptic tidings in stride, they are modestly consoled by the revelation that the estate itself is to be spared. There follows what might be called a period of adjustment, with the domineering Mrs. Halloran deciding which guests and relatives are to be permitted to stay on, and thus be allowed to enter the new world that is to be born after the destruction of the old, and which are to be consigned to the cataclysm. Not unpredictably, some of the younger, more earthbound members of the establishment, even though they are more than half-sold on Aunt Fanny's warnings of the ineluctable, yearn for the fleshpots of the dying outer world and attempt to return to it.

The inference is obvious. Miss Jackson takes ample advantage of it, and of the entire situation, to utter a number of acerbic and sibylline comments on our world and what are laughingly known as its inhabitants. The title itself refers to the sundial of the Halloran garden, on which is inscribed WHAT IS THIS WORLD? In a sense, the novel itself can be read as Miss Jackson's partial answer to the cosmic question, embroidered with comic embellishments.

The household expends a good deal of energy in laying in a store of supplies for the new life to come. "There was a carton of anti-histamine preparations. . . . There were cartons of plastic overshoes and rubbers, in assorted sizes, of instant coffee, of cleansing tissue and sunglasses. Suntan lotion, salted nuts in cans, paper napkins, soap, both bar and flaked, toilet paper (four cartons). . . ." Of course the logical place to store these essential ingredients of the brave new world is the library; after the books have been removed to the yard and burned, the breakfast foods and citronella seem to fit quite nicely on the shelves.

Miss Jackson does not miss too many opportunities. Negotiations are undertaken between the residents of the fortress-to-be and the leadership of a religious sect which also believes in the approaching destruction of the globe, but plans a relocation on another planet. Refugees are accepted as guests of the estate on the basis of their qualifications as seers or breeding machines. And hints are dropped from time to time that those of us who enjoy doing so may read the characters as symbols, either of the seven deadly sins or as other ecto-plasm manifestations, with the emphasis on the irony of survival of the worst.

Why is it then that the book finally leaves such a small impression? For one reader it is primarily because, while Miss Jackson is an intelligent and clever writer, there rises from her pages the cold fishy gleam of a calculated and carefully expressed contempt for the human race.

Pleasure in the vilenesses that human beings can commit one upon the other soon palls, particularly if it is unaccompanied by any imaginary representation of the specific moral gravity of a good human being. The result is that the figures in this literary landscape become less and less human and more and more simply the vehicles for an extended bitter joke that ends after several hundred pages by being merely tedious.

—Harvey Swados, "What Is This World?" *New Republic* (3 March 1958): 19–20

MAXWELL GEISMAR

Shirley Jackson's forte, as everybody knows, is the projection of a certain kind of psycho-supernatural horror. In the remote past our legitimate fear of the evil shapes and forms in nature was matched by the fantasies of evil which man himself invented. And which was which? Is nature mad, or are we? That is the central problem in *The Haunting of Hill House*, as it was in "The Lottery," and to Miss Jackson's credit there are brilliant episodes in her new book which give you the shivers and the shakes.

The story develops slowly, however, and it is just about reaching the midway point when we get caught up by it. The opening sections may seem almost banal, or certainly very familiar, in the tradition of the Gothic novel. Hill House is haunted, surely, and Dr. Montague, a professional figure with a weakness for psychic investigation, hires three "assistants" to help him make a study of the place. Two of these assistants are women who have had earlier experiences with the "other world." The third is Luke, an engaging young scoundrel, who has been forced upon the good doctor by the absentee owners of Hill House. So far so good, or rather, so bad.

If Miss Jackson is proficient in describing the alarums and excursions of human pathology, she is correspondingly weak on the "normal" world of human relations, or even of ordinary social gossip. The two women in the story, Eleanor and Theodora, engage in a curious kind of infantile Lesbian affection that is meant to be sophisticated, but is usually embarrassing. There is too much of this whimsy in the earlier parts of the novel; eventually it turns out that both women have an eye on Luke, and that their real relation is one of love-hate. While all this goes on, the doctor lectures us intermittently on the role played by haunted houses in the annals of magic.

It is only when the monster at Hill House strikes at last (and how!) that Miss Jackson's pen becomes charmed, or rather demonic, and the supernatural activity is really chilling. Why or what is it that closes every door in this "masterpiece of architectural misdirection"; that has the smell of putrefaction, the cold breath of death; that writes on the wall, pounds at the doors, whimpers and snickers, and leaves its tracks in a substance indistinguishable from blood? Our suspicion falls in turn upon each member of the little group, and then in particular upon one of the girls, Eleanor, who has been selected, it appears, as the special "victim" of the monster.

In fairness to Miss Jackson's readers, I can say no more than this—though my own conviction is that the author is not altogether fair with us. After the crime tales of a William Roughead, or the mystery tales of Henry James himself, we are bound to expect a "rationale" of even the supernatural. Miss Jackson never deigns to offer this to us. She is concerned only with the effect of a terrifying atmosphere—which she calls "reality"—upon a mind already rather preoccupied with horrors. But in this rather restricted and peculiar medium Shirley Jackson is, I must say, very eloquent.

—Maxwell Geismar, "Annals of Magic," *Saturday Review* (31 October 1959): 19, 31

IHAB HASSAN

I have always felt that some writers should be read and never reviewed. Their talent is haunting and utterly oblique; their mastery of craft seems complete. Even before reading Shirley Jackson's latest novel ⟨*We Have Always Lived in the Castle*⟩, I would have thought her case to be clear: she is of that company. And now Miss Jackson has made it even more difficult for a reviewer to seem pertinent; all he can do is bestow praise.

Yet praise can take many forms. Perhaps the best thing one can say of this author is that she offers an alternative to the canonical view of "seriousness" in literature. Like the late Isak Dinesen, she is a meticulous storyteller who can evoke the reality of the times without invoking its current, cloying clichés. Her work moves on the invisible shadow line between fantasy and verisimilitude; it also hovers between innocence and dark knowledge. Above all, her work never averts itself from the human thing, which it quickens with chilly laughter or fabulous imaginings.

We Have Always Lived in the Castle is not as eerie as some of Miss Jackson's other works, but it is every bit as deviate and gripping. There are three people who live in the ancestral home of the Blackwoods, up on a hill. Their life is a hermetic one, shut against the fearful and railing villagers below, and overcast by the memory of a mass murder, by arsenic, of most of the Blackwood family. The three are Constance Blackwood, who cooks and cares lovingly for the others, acquitted somehow of the murder; Uncle Julian, a survivor of that grim event, now an invalid, and Constance's younger sister, Mary Katherine, better known as "Merricat," who is still in her teens. Merricat is the shy, wild narrator of the story: the significance of that literary fact is one of the grisly discoveries that every reader must make for himself.

Yet the effect of the book does not only depend on mystery or suspense; nor on the casual intimations of evil that Miss Jackson can put in a phrase like "the falseness of spring." The effect depends rather on her ability to specify a real world which is at once more sane and more mad than the world we see. It is a feminine world—men tread lightly in it—full of bewitched or magical heirlooms, but also full of clean crockery, rhubarb jam and dandelion pies. The other side of that world is "the moon," the safe, dream space in which Merricat lives:

"On the moon we have everything," Merricat intones. "Lettuce, and pumpkin pie and *Amanita phalloides*. We have cat-furred plants and horses dancing with their wings. All the locks are solid and tight, and there are no ghosts."

The "ghosts," the intruder, is Cousin Charles, a greedy, insensitive man lured to the Blackwood mansion by rumors of a buried fortune. The havoc he wreaks, and the unsuspected dénouement of the action, bring into soft focus the human ambivalences of guilt and atonement, love and hate, health and psychosis. There is nothing illusory about these ambivalences, and also nothing final. Shirley Jackson has once again effected a marvelous elucidation of life in the ageless form of a story full of craft and full of mystery.

—Ihab Hassan, "Three Hermits on a Hill," *The New York Times Book Review* (23 September 1962): 5

CHESTER E. EISINGER

Many of the short stories in Shirley Jackson's *The Lottery, or The Adventures of James Harris* (1949) resemble closely the kind of new fiction written by ⟨Paul⟩ Bowles, and by Capote too. Where Bowles is strident and melodramatic, she manages a low-keyed and quiet nihilism which is nonetheless almost as pervasive as his. Where both men force us to look into the uncovered face of evil, she quite matter of factly assumes its presence everywhere; indeed, her healthy-looking, apparently normal children reveal a particular appetite for contemplating violence and horror. Seemingly content to deal with ordinary experience in an ordinary way, she is always aware of the other side of consciousness, of the lurking figure, real or imagined, who leads her characters out into a strange nowhere. Her unpretentious and rather colorless prose is a suitable vehicle for the laconic expression of an equation of disintegration: as the culture seems to be going to pieces in some of these stories, so does the human personality. Her fiction is created out of this play on the incongruity between the ordinariness of her manner and the unreality of the reality that she perceives. Her dedication to a pessimistic view of experience is everywhere explicit, but occasionally it is obscured by the manipulation of her paradoxes.

> —Chester E. Eisinger, "The New Fiction," *Fiction of the Forties* (1963), excerpted in *Twentieth-Century American Literature*, ed. Harold Bloom (New York: Chelsea House Publishers, 1986), 1995–96

HELEN E. NEBEKER

In the fourth paragraph ⟨of "The Lottery"⟩, Mr. Summers, who ironically runs the "coal" business, arrives with the postmaster, Mr. Graves, who carries the three-legged stool and the black box. Although critics have tended to see the box as the major symbol, careful reading discloses that, while the box is referred to three times in this paragraph, the stool is emphasized four times and in such strained repetition as to be particularly obvious. Further, in the next two paragraphs it will be stressed that the box rests upon, is supported by, the *three-legged stool*. It would thus seem that the stool is at least as important as the box: in my opinion, it is the symbol which holds the key to Jackson's conclusive theme. In the interest of structure and coherence, this point must be developed later in the article.

Returning to the symbol of the box, its prehistoric origin is revealed in the mention of the "original wood color" showing along one side as well as in the belief that it has been constructed by the first people who settled down to make villages here (man in his original social group). The chips of wood, now discarded for slips of paper, suggest a preliterate origin. The present box has been made from pieces of the original (as though it were salvaged somehow) and is now blackened, faded, and stained (with blood perhaps). In this box symbol, Jackson certainly suggests the body of tradition—once oral but now written—which the dead hand of the past codified in religion, mores, government, and the rest of culture, and passed from generation to generation, letting it grow ever more cumbersome, meaningless, and indefensible. ⟨. . .⟩

⟨As⟩ Tessie stands at bay and the crowd is upon her, the symbols coalesce into full revelation. "Tessie Hutchinson," end product of two thousand years of Christian thought and ritual, Catholic and Puritan merged, faces her fellow citizens, all equally victims and persecutors. Mrs. "Of-the-Cross" lifts her heavy stone in response to ritual long forgotten and perverted. "Old Man Warner" fans the coals (not fires) of emotions long sublimated, ritualistically revived once a year. "Mr. Adams," at once progenitor and martyr in the Judeo-Christian myth of man, stands with "Mrs. Graves"—the ultimate refuge or escape of all mankind—in the forefront of the crowd.

Now we understand the significance of the three-legged stool—as old as the tripod of the Delphic oracle, as new as the Christian trinity. For that which supports the present day box of meaningless and perverted superstition is the body of unexamined tradition of at least six thousand years of man's history. Some of these traditions (one leg of the stool if you like), are as old as the memory of man and are symbolized by the season, the ritual, the original box, the wood chips, the names of Summers, Graves, Martin, Warner (all cultures have their priesthoods!). These original, even justifiable, traditions gave way to or were absorbed by later Hebraic perversions; and the narrative pursues its "scapegoat" theme in terms of the stones, the wooden box, blackened and stained, Warner the Prophet, even the Judaic name of Tessie's son, David. Thus Hebraic tradition becomes a second leg or brace for the box.

Superimposed upon this remote body of tradition is one two thousand years old in its own right. But it may be supposed the most perverted and therefore least defensible of all as a tradition of supposedly enlightened man who has freed himself from the barbarities and superstitions of the past. This Christian tradition becomes the third support for the blood-stained box and all it represents. Most of the symbols of the other periods pertain here with the addition of Delacroix, Hutchinson, Baxter and Steve.

With this last symbolic intention clearly revealed, one may understand the deeper significance of Jackson's second, below-the-surface story. More than developing a theme which "deals with 'scapegoating', the human tendency to punish 'innocent' and often accidentally chosen victims for our sins" ⟨Virgil Scott, *Studies in the Short Story*, 1968, 20⟩ or one which points out "the awful doubleness of the human spirit—a doubleness that expresses itself in blended good neighborliness and cruelty . . ." ⟨Cleanth Brooks and Robert Warren, *Understanding Fiction*, 1959, 76⟩, Shirley Jackson has raised these lesser themes to one encompassing a comprehensive, compassionate, and fearful understanding of man trapped in the web spun from his own need to explain and control the incomprehensible universe around him, a need no longer answered by the web of old traditions.

Man, she says, is a victim of his unexamined and hence unchanged traditions which engender in him flames otherwise banked, subdued. Until enough men are touched strongly enough by the horror of their ritualistic, irrational actions to reject the long-perverted ritual, to destroy the box completely—or to make, if necessary, a new one reflective of their own conditions and needs of life—man will never free himself from his primitive nature and is ultimately doomed. Miss Jackson does not offer us much hope—they only talk of giving up the lottery in the north village, the Dunbars and Watsons do not actually resist, and even little Davy Hutchinson holds a few pebbles in his hands.

—Helen E. Nebeker, "'The Lottery': Symbolic Tour de Force," *American Literature* (March 1974), excerpted in *Twentieth-Century American Literature*, ed. Harold Bloom (New York: Chelsea House Publishers, 1986), 2003–5

LYNETTE CARPENTER

When Mary Katherine Blackwood, at the age of twelve, poisoned her family by putting arsenic in the sugar, she was careful not to endanger her sister Constance, whom she calls "the most precious person in my world, always." Now, six years later, with everyone dead but the invalid and feeble-minded Uncle Julian, Constance has become head of the Blackwood family, which consists of Constance, Mary Katherine (affectionately called Merricat by her sister), Uncle Julian, and Jonas the cat. When the events at the beginning of Mary Katherine's narrative take place, they live in seclusion in the Blackwood house, surrounded by extensive Blackwood property, barricaded against the intrusion of the outside world. They might have continued to live contentedly enough, had their neighbors allowed it. But female self-sufficiency, Jackson suggests, specifically women's forceful establishment of power over their own lives, threatens a society in which men hold primary power and leads inevitably to confrontation.

Jackson's last completed novel and a best seller, *We Have Always Lived in the Castle* is her most radical statement on the causes and consequences of female victimization and alienation, a theme that runs throughout her work. The novel may represent a personal culmination for Jackson, who suffered a nervous breakdown shortly after its publication in 1962; her journal from that period records longings for "freedom and security," "self-control," and "refuge" that echo the novel's central concern with the self-determination of women in a safe environment. ⟨. . .⟩

Readers and critics have struggled to explain the effect that *We Have Always Lived in the Castle* has on them. . . . ⟨Many⟩ express discomfort at being made to identify with a madwoman, but is Merricat mad? If paranoia depends upon delusion, Merricat is not paranoid because the hostility she perceives in the villagers is real. Like most of Jackson's protagonists, she seems young for her age, but immaturity is not madness.

Perhaps the aspect of Merricat's character that is most difficult to accept, however, is the violence. Early in the book, the violence of Merricat's fantasies is horrifying; while confronting hostile villagers in the grocery store, she says, "I would have liked to come into the grocery some morning and see them all, even the Elberts and the children, lying there crying with the pain and dying."

The villagers' hostility, although misdirected if they believe the poisoner to be Constance and not Merricat, might at first seem a justifiable response to a daughter's particularly cruel murder of four members of her family. Readers' sympathy with Merricat remains uneasy, even though they may feel, as Stuart Woodruff has suggested, that "parricide on such a scale is certainly regrettable, but the real horror in Miss Jackson's novel originates elsewhere." Yet the villagers' own violence invalidates once and for all their moral judgment of the sisters and indicates that the poisoning is only one violent action in a world where violence threatens to erupt at any moment, a world familiar to readers of Jackson's fiction. Thus Merricat's belief that she is literally embattled is confirmed, and her rage against the villagers is justified. Within the context of feminist psychology, rage is the most appropriate response to oppression. In Jackson's time as now, it was also the most dangerous, the most likely to be labeled madness and treated by institutionalization.

Merricat's rage against her family and the murders that resulted from it are less justifiable on the basis of the scant information her narrative provides; apart from sketchy descriptions of the victims and their treatment of Merricat, the reader has only Constance's word that "those people deserved to die." Because the danger to Merricat in this case seems to be one of psychological or emotional violence rather than physical violence, many readers feel uncomfortable with her response. Ihab Hassan has written that the novel addresses "the human ambivalences of guilt and atonement, love and hate, health and psychosis." By identifying Charles with Father and with the villagers, Jackson relates physical and psychological violence; both can destroy human beings.

—Lynette Carpenter, "The Establishment and Preservation of Female Power in Shirley Jackson's 'We Have Always Lived in the Castle,'" *Frontiers: A Journal of Women's Studies* 8, no. 1 (1984): 32, 37

BIBLIOGRAPHY

The Road Through the Wall. 1948.
The Lottery, or, The Adventures of James Harris. 1949.
Hangsaman. 1951.
Life Among the Savages. 1953.
The Bird's Nest. 1954.
The Witchcraft of Salem Village. 1956.
Raising Demons. 1957.
The Sundial. 1958.

The Bad Children: A Play in One Act for Bad Children. 1959.
The Haunting of Hill House. 1959.
We Have Always Lived in the Castle. 1962.
Nine Magic Wishes. 1963.
Famous Sally. 1966.
The Magic of Shirley Jackson. 1966.
Come Along with Me. 1968.

NELLA LARSEN
1891-1964

NELLA MARIE LARSEN was born in New York City on April 13, 1891, the second and youngest daughter of a Danish woman, Mary Hansen. Her father was a West Indian chauffeur, but there is no birth certificate to verify either the date and place of her birth or the identity of her father, except through records of other family members. Her half-sister, Anna, whose father was white, was born less than a year earlier. Mary Hansen married Peter Larsen on February 7, 1894; Nella was raised in an all-white household and attended school in the suburbs of Chicago. There is speculation that Nella was removed from the household when she was 9 or 10 years old; in the 1910 census, when Nella was 19, Mary Larsen is recorded as having only one child. After Nella's death, her half-sister remarked that she had not known that she had a sister. The pain and pattern of this enormous rejection led Nella to rewrite her childhood when she became an adult and would reverberate throughout her writing.

Larsen traveled through many educational institutions and in 1915 received a nursing degree from the Lincoln Hospital of Nursing. She was briefly a nurse at Tuskegee Normal and Industrial Institute in Alabama but then returned to New York City, where she worked at Lincoln Hospital and at the Department of Health. She excelled in her profession and was highly regarded by her colleagues, but by 1924 she had begun a new career as a librarian, in charge of children's books at the Harlem branch of the New York Public Library.

In 1919, Larsen married Dr. Elmer S. Imes, a physicist and notorious womanizer. The marriage would end in scandal in 1932, but the couple was part of the 1920s Harlem Renaissance, friends of W. E. B. Du Bois, Jessie Fauset, James Weldon Johnson, Jean Toomer, Carl Van Vechten, and Walter White. In the midst of this period of black artistic creativity and the rise of what was called the New Negro, Larsen began to write fiction. In 1920, as Nella Larsen Imes, she wrote two pieces for *The Brownies' Book*, a magazine for black children edited by Jessie Fauset: introductory remarks to "Three Scandinavian Games" and "Danish Fun" tell of her childhood spent in Denmark, a fiction Larsen would often repeat. Six years later, she published two short stories for adults that may be characterized as pulp fiction: "The Wrong Man" and "Freedom" appeared in *Young's Magazine* under the inverted name Allen Semi.

41

In 1926, Larsen also began writing the first of her two novels: *Quicksand*, which was published by Alfred A. Knopf in 1928, draws heavily upon Larsen's own experience and describes the psychological conflict of an educated, middle-class woman of mixed European and African blood. The book was critically acclaimed and received a Bronze Award for Literature from the Harmon Foundation. *Passing*, published in 1929, is another powerful depiction of the lives of middle-class black women.

In 1930, Larsen became the first black American woman to be awarded a Guggenheim Fellowship; she spent most of the year in Mallorca and southern Europe working on a new novel, *Mirage*. Charges of plagiarism were made the same year regarding her story "Sanctuary," published in *Forum* in January. Given her writerly strengths and seriousness it seems probable that any plagiarism was not deliberate. Worse than this, however, was the rejection of *Mirage* by Knopf. Two of her other novels were also rejected. At the same time, the Depression had stilled both the exuberance of the Harlem Renaissance and the emergence of the New Negro: times and fashions had changed. Finally, her marriage disintegrated. The combined rejections by her husband and by her publisher and the charges of plagiarism threw Larsen into a depression that lasted several years.

Larsen abandoned writing and returned to nursing in 1941. Before retiring in 1962, she was supervisor of nurses at Metropolitan Hospital. Nella Larsen was found dead in her apartment on March 30, 1964.

CRITICAL EXTRACTS

ROARK BRADFORD

The real charm of ⟨*Quicksand*⟩ lies in Miss Larsen's delicate achievement in maintaining for a long time an indefinable, wistful feeling—that feeling of longing and at the same time a conscious realization of the impossibility of obtaining—that is contained in the idea of Helga Crane. (Helga is an idea more than she is a human being: drawing character does not seem to be one of Miss Larsen's major accomplishments.) ⟨. . .⟩

It leads directly to a splendid emotional climax. The brief scene is at a party in Harlem. Helga is alone for a moment with the man who first understood that strange emotions swelled within her bosom. (That was years before at Naxos. Now he is the husband of her best friend.) Her nerves are tuned to a high pitch; her soul is stirred; savagery tears at her heart; the black blood chokes the white, and Africa rumbles through her veins. And the man—suddenly the veneers of civilization crackle about him and—well, the reader is as tense as the two actors in the drama.

But alas! Without knowing just where it comes from, the reader suddenly catches a faint odor of talcum powder. And from that point on the book—in this reviewer's opinion—suffers from odors . . . Burnt cork, mostly.

In spite of its failure to hold up to the end, the book is good. No doubt it will be widely read and discussed. The reader, to get the maximum enjoyment, should begin with a mind as free as possible of racial prejudices and preconceived notions and conclusions. Miss Larsen seems to know much about the problems that confront the upper stratum of Negroes, and happily, she does not get oratorical about what she knows. She is quite sensitive to Negro life, but she isn't hysterical about it. There is a saneness about her writing that, in these hysterical literary times, more than compensates for her faults.

—Roark Bradford, "Mixed Blood," *New York Herald Tribune Books* (13 May 1928): 22

Eda Lou Walton

To tell the story of a cultivated and sensitive woman's defeat through her own sex-desire is a difficult task. When the woman is a mulatto and beset by hereditary, social and racial forces over which she has little control and into which she cannot fit, her character is so complex that any analysis of it takes a mature imagination. This, I believe, ⟨is why⟩ Miss Larsen is too young to have the book, *Quicksand*, as a first novel. The attempt is to present Helga Crane not as a young colored woman, but as a young woman with problems unique to her temperament, and her background one largely of her own choice. Supposedly, save for a deep-rooted weakness, she has the vitality to manipulate the machinery of her days. But of this we are never quite convinced. As portrayed, the character is not quite of one pattern. Now it is Helga, the aesthete, the impulsively intelligent girl whom we feel; now it is Helga, the mulatto, suffering from an inferiority complex about her mixed ancestry, her lack of social status. Since she is supposedly complex, her character should be turned to us as a jewel of many facets. Instead we get it as a piece of bright red glass or as smoke-colored.

Besides the difficulty of incomplete characterization there is the fault of fine-writing in the worst sense of that word. The opening paragraph is a good example of that elaborateness of uninteresting detail into which Miss Larsen plunges in order to assure us that her Helga is cultured and modern.

Miss Larsen writes a little too carefully of the objective evidences of culture and too carelessly of the refinement within the woman herself. We are told again and again that Helga is restless, unhappy, passionate, but we don't believe it until, arbitrarily, Miss Larsen introduces proofs of action.

Quicksand is, for all this comment, a good tale, and a good first novel. Miss Larsen's prettiness of style may, with more writing, become power. She will undoubtedly learn a more effectual working out of laws of cause and event within characters. She has already the ability to interest us in her people and their problems.

But she has not in this first book anything of the usual richness and fullness of character presentation, or the zestful interest in life in Harlem that other novelists of Negro life have given us.

—Eda Lou Walton, [Review of Quicksand], Opportunity 6, no. 7 (July 1928): 212–13

ROBERT BONE

The key to the narrative structure of Quicksand is contained in a passage toward the end of the novel in which Helga Crane rebels against her lot as a brood mare: "For she had to admit it wasn't new, this feeling of dissatisfaction, of asphyxiation. Something like it she had experienced before. In Naxos. In New York. In Copenhagen. This differed only in degree." Helga's quest for happiness has led her, floundering, through a succession of minor bogs, until she is finally engulfed by a quagmire of her own making. The basic metaphor of the novel, contained in its title, is supported throughout by concrete images of suffocation, asphyxiation, and claustrophobia. Associated always with Helga's restlessness and dissatisfaction, these symbols of a loathsome, hostile environment are at bottom projections of Negro self-hatred: "It was as if she were shut up, boxed up with hundreds of her race, closed up with that something in the racial character which had always been, to her, inexplicable, alien. Why, she demanded in fierce rebellion, should she be yoked to these despised black folk?"

On one level, Quicksand is an authentic case study which yields readily to psychoanalytic interpretation. Each of the major episodes in Helga's life is a recapitulation of the same psychological pattern: temporary enthusiasm; boredom, followed by disgust; and finally a stifling sense of entrapment. Then escape into a new situation, until escape is no longer possible. Race is functional in this pattern, for it has to do with Helga's initial rejection and therefore with her neurotic withdrawal pattern. Her tendency to withdraw from any situation which threatens to become permanent indicates that she is basically incapable of love or happiness. No matter how often she alters her situation, she carries her problems with her.

Deserted by her colored father and rejected by her white stepfather, Helga's quest may be viewed as the search for a father's love. The qualities of balance and security which she finds so appealing in Danish society; her attraction for Dr. Anderson, an older married man; her desire for "nice things" as a substitute for the security of parental love; and her belated return to religion can all be understood in these terms. Her degrading marriage to a jack-leg preacher who "fathers" her in a helpless moment plainly has its basis in the Oedipal triangle. Her unconscious need to be debased is in reality the need to replace her mother by marrying a "no-account" colored man not unlike her gambler father. ⟨. . .⟩

The dramatic tension of the novel can be stated in terms of a conflict between Helga's sexuality and her love for "nice things." Her desire for material comfort is static; it is the value premise on which the novel is based: "Always she had wanted . . . the things which money could give, leisure, attention, beautiful surroundings. Things. Things. Things." Helga's sexuality, on the other hand, is dynamic; its strength increases until she is overwhelmed and deprived of the accouterments of gracious living forever. ⟨. . .⟩

⟨. . .⟩ Helga's tragedy, in Larsen's eyes, is that she allows herself to be declassed by her own sexuality. The tone of reproach is unmistakable. It is this underlying moralism which differentiates *Quicksand* from the novels of the Harlem School. It is manifested not in Helga's behavior, which is "naturalistic" and well motivated, even inevitable, but in the symbols of luxury which are counterposed to the bog, in the author's prudish attitude toward sex, and in her simple equation of "nice things" with the pursuit of beauty.

—Robert Bone, *The Negro Novel in America* (New Haven: Yale University Press, 1958), 103–6

CLAUDIA TATE

Race ⟨. . .⟩ is not ⟨*Passing*'s⟩ foremost concern, but is merely a mechanism for setting the story in motion, sustaining the suspense, and bringing about the external circumstances for the story's conclusion. The real impetus for the story is Irene's emotional turbulence, which is entirely responsible for the course that the story takes and ultimately accountable for the narrative ambiguity. The problem of interpreting *Passing* can, therefore, be simplified by defining Irene's role in the story and determining the extent to which she is reliable as the sole reporter and interpreter of events. We must determine whether she accurately portrays Clare, or whether her portrait is subject to, and in fact affected by, her own growing jealousy and insecurity. In this regard, it is essential to ascertain precisely who is the tragic heroine—Irene who is on the verge of total mental disintegration or Clare whose desire for excitement brings about her sudden death.

Initially, *Passing* seems to be about Clare Kendry, inasmuch as most of the incidents plot out Clare's encounters with Irene and Black society. Furthermore, Irene sketches in detail Clare's physical appearance down to "[her] slim golden feet." Yet, she is unable to perceive the intangible aspects of Clare's character, and Larsen uses Irene's failure as a means of revealing disturbing aspects of her own psychological character. ⟨. . .⟩

Irene is literally obsessed with Clare's beauty, a beauty of such magnitude that she seems alien, impervious, indeed inscrutable. ⟨. . .⟩ Irene repeatedly describes Clare in hyperbole—"too vague," "too remote," "so dark and deep and unfathomable," "utterly strange," "incredibly beautiful," "utterly beyond any experience. . . ." These hyperbolic expressions are ambiguous. They create the impression that Clare is definitely, though indescribably, different from and superior to Irene and other ordinary people.

Irene's physical appearance, on the other hand, is drawn sketchily. We know that she has "warm olive skin" and curly black hair. Though Irene is not referred to as a beauty, given her confidence and social grace, we are inclined to believe that she is attractive. Despite the fact that little attention is given to Irene's physical portrayal, her encounter with Clare provides the occasion for the subtle revelation of her psychological character. Hence, the two portraits are polarized and mutually complementary—one is purely external, while the other is intensely internal.

—Claudia Tate, "Nella Larsen's *Passing*: A Problem of Interpretation," *Black American Literature Forum* 14, no. 4 (Winter 1980): 143–44

MARY HELEN WASHINGTON

Larsen's failure in dealing with ⟨. . .⟩ marginality is implicit in the very choice of "passing" as a symbol or metaphor of deliverance for her women. It is an obscene form of salvation. The woman who passes is required to deny everything about her past—her girlhood, her family, places with memories, folk customs, folk rhymes, her language, the entire long line of people who have gone before her. She lives in terror of discovery—what if she has a child with a dark complexion, what if she runs into an old school friend, how does she listen placidly to racial slurs? And more, where does the woman who passes find the equanimity to live by the privilege status that is based on the oppression of her own people?

Larsen's heroines are all finally destroyed somewhere down the paths they choose. Helga Crane loses herself in a loveless marriage to an old black preacher by whom she has five children in as many years. She finally retreats into illness and silence, eventually admitting to herself a suppressed hatred for her husband. *Passing*'s Irene Redfield suspects an affair between her friend

Clare (recently surfaced from the white world) and her black physician husband. This threatens her material and psychological security. In the novel's melodramatic ending, she pushes Clare off the balcony of a seventeenth-floor apartment and sinks into unconsciousness when she is questioned about Clare's death.

And Nella Larsen, who created Helga and Irene, chose oblivion for herself. From the little we know of the last 30 years of her life, she handled the problem of marginality by default, living entirely without any racial and cultural identity. Her exile was so complete that one of her biographers couldn't find an obituary for her: "I couldn't even bury Nella Larsen," she said.

But unlike the women in her novels, Larsen did not die from her marginality. She lived 70 years, was an active part of the high-stepping Harlem Renaissance, traveled abroad, and worked as a nurse for 40 years. She was an unconventional woman by 1920s standards: she wore her dresses short, smoked cigarettes, rejected religion, and lived in defiance of the rules that most black women of her education and means were bound by. She lived through the conflicts of the marginal woman and felt them passionately. Why didn't she leave us the greater legacy of the mature model, the perceptions of a woman who confronts the pain, alienation, isolation, and grapples with these conundrums until new insight has been forged from the struggle? Why didn't she continue to write after 1929? ⟨. . .⟩

She did not solve her own problems, but Larsen made us understand as no one did before her that the image of the middle-class black woman as a coldly self-centered snob, chattering irrelevantly at bridge club and sorority meetings, was as much a mask as the grin on the face of Stepin Fetchit. The women in her novel, like Larsen, are driven to emotional and psychological extremes in their attempts to handle ambivalence, marginality, racism, and sexism. She has shown us that behind the carefully manicured exterior, behind the appearance of security is a woman who hears the beating of her wings against a walled prison.

—Mary Helen Washington, "Nella Larsen: Mystery Woman of the Harlem Renaissance," *Ms.* 9, no. 6 (December 1980): 50

CHERYL A. WALL

The novels ⟨Larsen⟩ left behind prove that at least some of her promise was realized. Among the best written of the time, her books comment incisively on issues of marginality and cultural dualism that engaged Larsen's contemporaries, such as Jean Toomer and Claude McKay, but the bourgeois ethos of her novels has unfortunately obscured the similarities. However, Larsen's most striking insights are into psychic dilemmas confronting certain black women.

To dramatize these, Larsen draws characters who are, by virtue of their appearance, education, and social class, atypical in the extreme. Swiftly viewed, they resemble the tragic mulattoes of literary convention. On closer examination, they become the means through which the author demonstrates the psychological costs of racism and sexism.

For Larsen, the tragic mulatto was the only formulation historically available to portray educated middle-class black women in fiction. But her protagonists subvert the convention consistently. They are neither noble nor long-suffering; their plights are not used to symbolize the oppression of blacks, the irrationality of prejudice, or the absurdity of concepts of race generally. Larsen's deviations from these traditional strategies signal that her concerns lie elsewhere, but only in the past decade have critics begun to decode her major themes. Both *Quicksand* and *Passing* contemplate the inextricability of the racism and sexism which confront the black woman in her quest for a wholly integrated identity. As they navigate between racial and cultural polarities, Larsen's protagonists attempt to fashion a sense of self free of both suffocating restrictions of ladyhood and fantasies of the exotic female Other. They fail. The tragedy for these mulattoes is the impossibility of self-definition. Larsen's protagonists assume false identities that ensure social survival but result in psychological suicide. In one way or another, they all "pass." Passing for white, Larsen's novels remind us, is only one way this game is played.

—Cheryl A. Wall, "Passing for What? Aspects of Identity in Nella Larsen's Novels," *Black American Literature Forum* 20, nos. 1–2 (Spring–Summer 1986): 97–98

DEBORAH E. MCDOWELL

Although Irene is clearly deluded about her motives, her racial loyalty, her class, and her distinctness from Clare, the narrative suggests that her most glaring delusion concerns her feeling for Clare. ⟨. . .⟩ The narrative traces this developing eroticism in spatial terms. It begins on the roof of the Drayton hotel (with all the suggestions of the sexually illicit), intensifies at Clare's tea party, and, getting proverbially "close to home," explodes in Irene's own bedroom. Preoccupied with appearances, social respectability, and safety, however, Irene tries to force these emerging feelings underground. The narrative dramatizes that repression effectively in images of concealment and burial. Significantly, the novel's opening image is an envelope (a metaphoric vagina) which Irene hesitates to open, fearing its "contents would reveal" an "attitude toward danger." ⟨. . .⟩ Irene tries to preserve "a hardness from feeling" about the letter, though "brilliant red patches flamed" in her cheeks. Unable to explain her feeling for Clare, "for which she could find no name," Irene dismisses them as "Just somebody walking over [her] grave." The narrative suggests pointedly that Clare is the body walking over the grave of Irene's buried sexual feelings.

Lest the reader miss this eroticism, Larsen employs fire imagery—the conventional representation of sexual desire—introducing and instituting this imagery in the novel's opening pages. Irene begins her retrospective account of her reunion with Clare, remembering that the day was "hot," the sun "brutal" and "staring," its rays "like molten rain." Significantly, Irene, feeling "sticky and soiled from contact with so many sweating bodies," escapes to the roof of the Drayton Hotel where she is reunited with Clare, after a lapse of many years. (Irene is, ironically, "escaping" to the very thing she wants to avoid.) ⟨. . .⟩

Although the ending is ambiguous and the evidence circumstantial, I agree with Cheryl Wall that, "Larsen strongly implies that Irene pushes Clare through the window." ⟨. . .⟩ To suggest the extent to which Clare's death represents the death of Irene's sexual feelings for Clare, Larsen uses a clever objective correlative: Irene's pattern of lighting cigarettes and snuffing them out. Minutes before Clare falls from the window to her death, "Irene finished her cigarette and threw it out, watching the tiny spark drop slowly down to the white ground below." Clearly attempting a symbolic parallel, Clare is described as "a vital glowing thing, like a flame of red and gold" who falls from (or is thrown out of) the window as well. Because Clare is a reminder of that repressed and disowned part of Irene's self, Clare must be banished, for, more unacceptable than the feelings themselves is the fact that they find an object of expression in Clare. In other words, Clare is both the embodiment and the object of the sexual feelings that Irene banishes.

Larsen's becomes, in effect, a banishing act as well. Or put another way, the idea of bringing a sexual attraction between two women to full narrative expression is likewise, too dangerous a move. ⟨. . .⟩ Larsen's clever narrative strategies almost conceal it. In *Passing* she uses a technique found commonly in narrative by Afro-American and women novelists with a "dangerous" story to tell: "safe" themes, plots, and conventions are used as the protective cover underneath which lie more dangerous subplots. Larsen envelops the subplot of Irene's developing if unnamed and unacknowledged desire for Clare in the safe and familiar plot of racial passing. Put another way, the novel's clever strategy derives from its surface theme and central metaphor—passing. It takes the form of the act it describes. Implying false, forged, and mistaken identities, the title functions on multiple levels: thematically, in terms of the racial and sexual plot; and strategically, in terms of the narrative's disguise.

—Deborah E. McDowell, "Introduction" to Quicksand *and* Passing (New Brunswick, NJ: Rutgers University Press, 1986), xxvi–xxvii, xxix–xxx

HAZEL V. CARBY

Social relations which objectified the body permeate ⟨*Quicksand*⟩. Helga herself was represented as a consumer, a woman who defined a self through the acquisition of commercial products, consumer goods, and commodities. As a woman, she is at the center of a complex process of exchange. Money was crucial to Larsen's narrative, structuring power relations, controlling social movement, and defining the boundaries of Helga's environment. Money replaces kinship as the prime mediator of social relations: Helga's white uncle sent her money as he could not afford to acknowledge her relationship to him. This money allowed her social movement; she bought her way out of a Jim Crow car and eventually out of Harlem. In Chicago, Helga spent money, buying and consuming rather than facing her desperate conditions. While the possession of money disguises her real social predicament, the lack of money forced degradation and the recognition that in the job market her social position as a black woman was narrowly defined as domestic worker.

Although money permitted Helga's movement within the text, the direction of her journey reproduces the tensions of migration into a structure of oppositions between country and city. Helga's first movement in the text is from South to North, from the rural outskirts of Atlanta to industrial Chicago. Immediately upon arrival in Chicago, Helga became one of a crowd. Her initial identification was with the anonymity of the city, where she had the appearance of freedom but no actual home or friends. This anonymity brought brief satisfaction and contentment, while Helga could maintain her position as consumer, but she discovered her vulnerability as an object of exchange when her money ran out. Larsen represented the city as a conglomeration of strangers, where social relations were structured through the consumption of both objects and people. The imagery of commerce and this process of exchange dominated the text as it moved to New York and Copenhagen. This polarity between rural and urban experience frames the text; in the closing pages, all cities are finally abandoned and Helga is metaphorically and, the reader is led to assume, literally buried in the rural South. ⟨. . .⟩

⟨. . .⟩ Larsen's representation of both race and class are structured through a prism of black female sexuality. Larsen recognized that the repression of the sensual in Afro-American fiction in response to the long history of the exploitation of black sexuality led to the repression of passion and the repression or denial of female sexuality and desire. But, of course, the representation of black female sexuality meant risking its definition as primitive and exotic within a racist society. Larsen attempted to embody but could not hope to resolve these contradictions in her representation of Helga as a sexual being, making Helga the first truly sexual black female protagonist in Afro-American fiction. Racist sexual ideologies proclaimed the black woman to be a rampant sexual being, and in response black women writers either focused on defending their morality or displaced sexuality onto another terrain. Larsen confronted this denial directly in her fiction. Helga consistently attempted to deny her sensuality and repress her sexual desires, and the result is tragedy. Each of the crises of the text centered on sexual desire until the conclusion of the novel, where control over her body was denied Helga and her sexuality was reduced to its biological capacity to bear children. Helga's four children represented her entrapment as she was unable to desert them; her fifth child represented her certain death.

—Hazel V. Carby, *Reconstructing Womanhood: The Emergence of the Afro-American Woman Novelist* (New York: Oxford University Press, 1987), 173–74

ELIZABETH AMMONS

Clearly, ⟨in *Passing*⟩ Irene and Clare are doubles. Clare represents for Irene the dangerous side of herself—foreign, outlawed—that she as a respectable middle-class black woman has successfully denied. Clare is sexual, daring, creative. She has moved out of African American bourgeois culture; she roams free of its demands for conformity and social service and endless attention to familial and community uplift.

But where has this "freedom" taken Clare? Her life as a white woman is hollow and self-destructive; it represents a pact with self-loathing, a project in self-erasure. Her true self is so unknown to the white man she has married and with whom she has had a child that she lives daily with his racist and hideously ironic nickname for her, "Nig." To tell him why the appellation is particularly offensive would be to lose the position of "freedom" she has created for herself. To remain silent is to acquiesce in the system of self-degradation that she has bought into. ⟨. . .⟩

Complicating these conflicting possibilities even further, Larsen allows us to know Clare's story only through another woman no less conflicted, dishonest, or cowardly than Clare. Dutiful, repressed, correct, Irene clearly *needs* Clare dead. ⟨. . .⟩ She pushes Clare out the window.

Or does Clare jump? We cannot say. We can surmise either possibility—or, paradoxically, in this novel about split and conflicting identities and possibilities—both. If Clare and Irene, finally, are alienated parts of one potentially whole identity, to say that Clare jumped is the same as to say that Irene pushed her, and vice versa. In either case, Larsen's story about the black woman artist in *Passing* ends in permanent silence. The divisions between respectable middle-class feminine status and the woman artist, between heterosexual and lesbian desire, and between acceptance in white and black America are unbridgeable.

—Elizabeth Ammons, *Conflicting Stories: American Women Writers at the Turn into the Twentieth Century* (New York: Oxford University Press, 1991), 190–91

Larsen, obviously aware of the traditions before her, chooses not to depict such serene returns ⟨to the African-American community⟩ for her ⟨mulatto⟩ characters in *Passing*. Even after returning back across the color line into the Black community, Clare Kendry finds no peace, rest, loyalty—or any real security. Clare's racial origins are revealed to her white racist husband at a party held at the Freelands' apartment. The "freeland" is free in one respect. Clare is finally "let out" of her marriage by the discovery. Earlier she had told her friend, Irene Redfield, "'But if Jack [her husband] finds out, if our marriage is broken, that lets me out. Doesn't it?'" The freeland Clare attains is finally ironic, however, since she promptly falls to her death, pushed by the same friend in whom she had so closely confided. In killing Clare off, Larsen does not depict any "freeland" or supportive community that will embrace Clare in her process of returning. Larsen undermines romantic convention, substituting ironic tragedy where there had been joy.

Even further, Larsen implies that there is no longer a Black community anywhere in the world to return to. Oddly enough, in *Passing*, Brazil, instead of Africa, is evoked as the quintessential text of racial equality and haven from North American white oppression. Irene Redfield, the narrative consciousness in *Passing*, reports that her husband Brian is enamored with Brazil and longs to escape there, away from racist Harlem, away from what he calls "'this hellish place.'" Even this vision, however, is ironized, showing the extent of Brian's romantic delusions. By the end of the twenties, the hopes of a Brazilian paradise, the "Eldorado" of the South, were shattered. Thus Larsen chose Brazil instead of Africa for a reason: By the time she wrote *Passing* in 1929, Brazil symbolized a deflated and ironic hope for an alternative community that was more a romantic dream than a reality. Larsen's irony, then, extends beyond the confines of her text to show how the weave of disillusionment runs through the global environment, and not just through bourgeois Black Harlem.

Larsen's letters (1925–1932) to Carl Van Vechten (to whom, along with his wife, Fania Marinoff, Larsen dedicated *Passing*) affirm the view of Larsen as a skeptic. Consistent with her distance from the cause of racial uplift shown in her novels, she wrote to Van Vechten that she "wanted very much the pleasure of refusing" an invitation to the Women's Auxiliary of the NAACP tea held in her honor in 1928. At the same time, however, she also attacked misguided and perhaps unintentionally racist white liberal thinking. ⟨. . .⟩

In her fiction and in her letters, Larsen does not offer any final messages or final Truth(s) that will clear away racial and social difficulties. This orientation prevents Larsen from portraying a triumphant character or social utopia. Every direction she offers is quickly undercut by a counter-dilemma—e.g., Brazil is no longer available as a social and racial utopia. Even the traditional

passing for white plot is undermined. There is no supportive "birthright" to which her passers may serenely return.
—Jonathan Little, "Nella Larsen's *Passing*: Irony and the Critics," *African American Review* 26, no. 1 (1992): 174–75

DAVID L. BLACKMORE

The implications of Larsen's "flirtation" ⟨in *Passing*⟩ with both female and male homosexuality are radical. For Irene, lesbianism offers an alternative to repressive middle-class marriages. As an African-American woman, Irene must inevitably confront the stereotype that women of her race are Jezebels. White American culture tells her that black female identity centers around desire, that in fact an African American woman is nothing but a beast driven by irrepressible sexuality. The key, then, to combating this stereotype lies in the repression of sexuality, in the confinement of desire to the constricted realm of the respectable marriage. Doing her part to dispel the Jezebel myth, Irene plays the role of the eminently respectable, asexual mother/wife. In focusing her energies and identity on her husband and sons, she deflects attention away from her own sexual nature. ⟨. . .⟩

It is unclear whether Larsen's suggestion of a lesbian relationship as an alternative to Irene's repressive marriage reflects a sexual decision she made or contemplated in her own life. However, her literary experimentation with non-traditional sexuality mirrors a larger trend in 1920s Harlem, where lesbianism and particularly female bisexuality received a great deal of attention as naughty but exciting options for adventurous, "modern" women. As Lillian Faderman details in her recent book *Odd Girls and Twilight Lovers*, a visible black lesbian subculture was established in Harlem early in the century. Furthermore, large numbers of whites flocked to Harlem in the '20's "to experience homosexuality as the epitome of the forbidden." The perception of upper Manhattan as a center of laissez-faire sexuality drew both blacks and whites who wished to observe or participate in sexual practices deemed immoral by the white establishment. ⟨. . .⟩

Just as a romance with Clare would provide an alternative to Irene's emotionally empty existence, so leading a homosexual life in Brazil would free Brian from his own unsatisfying role in bourgeois Harlem society. In Brazil he would face less pressure to "'care for ladies.'" He could express more openly his attraction to other men; he could, in fact, engage in sexual activity that would not be the "'joke'" that straight sex is to him. He would be free of his unwanted role as sexual overlord to his wife, and free to determine for himself the role a man should play in sexual and social relationships. No longer the "empowered" yet burdened provider for a family, he would also no longer be the segregated subordinate in a white man's world. Brian's Brazil provides an alternate vision of an Afro-centric sphere in which a man need not provide for a woman and where men may love each other freely. This, surely, is a radical vision on Larsen's part.

—David L. Blackmore, " 'That Unreasonable Restless Feeling': The Homosexual Subtexts of Nella Larsen's *Passing*," *African American Review* 26, no. 3 (1992): 478–79, 481

B I B L I O G R A P H Y

Quicksand. 1928.
Passing. 1929.
An Intimation of Things Distant: Collected Fiction. Ed. Charles R. Larson. 1992.

MARY McCARTHY

1912-1989

MARY McCARTHY was born in Seattle, Washington, on June 21, 1912, the first of four children of Roy Winfield McCarthy, a lawyer, and Therese Preston McCarthy. Her father was the son of wealthy Minneapolis Irish Catholics; her mother was the daughter of a prominent Episcopalian lawyer from Seattle and his Jewish wife. In the course of moving the family from Seattle to a new home in Minneapolis, both parents died in the 1918 influenza epidemic within a day of each other. Mary and her young siblings were placed in the care of indifferent relatives. The bleakness and emotional hardship of these years are recounted in two essays, "Yonder Peasant, Who Is He?" and "A Tin Butterfly," part of *Memories of a Catholic Girlhood* (1957).

In 1923, McCarthy was put under the guardianship of her maternal grandparents in Seattle. There she boarded at Forest Ridge Convent but spent weekends at her grandparents' home, where she discovered the works of Dickens, Tolstoy, Harte, Bulwer-Lytton, Mencken, and Huxley. After a year in a public high school, she entered an Episcopalian boarding school, the Annie Wright Seminary in Tacoma, where she was an excellent student particularly interested in Latin. The summer after her graduation in 1929, she enrolled in acting classes at the Cornish School in Seattle. In the fall she entered Vassar; she graduated with a B.A. four years later; and one week after graduating, she married Harold Johnsrud, an actor she had met in Seattle at the Cornish School. The first of four marriages, it ended in divorce in 1936.

During this time, McCarthy began to write short book reviews for *The Nation* and *The New Republic*. In her essays and novels, McCarthy would present acerbic and satirical views on marriage, sexuality, intellectualism, and the role of contemporary women. In 1936 and 1937, she worked at Covici Friede, a left-wing publishing house, and in 1937 she was listed among the editors of the revived anti-Stalinist *Partisan Review*. Her drama reviews for the magazine would later be collected in *Sights and Spectacles: 1937–1956*, expanded in 1963 and published as *Mary McCarthy's Theatre Chronicles*.

In 1938, McCarthy married the critic Edmund Wilson, and on Christmas Day that year her only child, Reuel Kimball Wilson, was born. Edmund Wilson encouraged her to write fiction, and the following year Robert Penn Warren published McCarthy's first story,

"Cruel and Barbarous Treatment," in the *Southern Review*. This story is the first in her collection of semiautobiographical pieces published in 1942 as *The Company She Keeps*, a collection that—with stories such as the sharp-witted and sexually frank "The Man in the Brooks Brothers Shirt"—demonstrated that McCarthy's razor wit could be directed at herself as well as at political or cultural subjects.

McCarthy taught literature at Bard College in 1945 and 1946, when she divorced Wilson and married Bowden Broadwater. In 1949, *Horizon* published and awarded a literary prize to her utopian philosophical tale *The Oasis*. Other works of this period include a collection of stories, *Cast a Cold Eye* (1950); *The Groves of Academe* (1952); *A Charmed Life* (1955); and two studies in art history, *Venice Observed* (1956) and *The Stones of Florence* (1959). McCarthy won a Guggenheim Fellowship in 1959, and two years later she divorced Broadwater and married a United States diplomat, James Raymond West. The same year, a collection of essays, *On the Contrary*, was published. *The Group* (1963), a best-selling novel about the lives of a group of Vassar graduates, brought McCarthy a national readership and reputation. In *Vietnam* (1967) and *Hanoi* (1968), McCarthy vehemently criticized United States involvement in Indochina.

In 1960 McCarthy moved to Paris, returning to her house in Maine each summer. In 1984 she was awarded the National Medal for Literature and the Edward MacDowell Medal. Mary McCarthy died in New York City on October 25, 1989.

CRITICAL EXTRACTS

ELIZABETH HARDWICK

Mary McCarthy! "'The Man in the Brooks Brothers Shirt'! That's my Bible!" I once heard a young woman exclaim. No doubt the famous short story is rightly understood as a sort of parable representing many a young girl's transgressions, even if it does not concern itself with the steps in the sinner's rehabilitation. It would be hard to think of any writer in America more interesting and unusual than Mary McCarthy. Obviously she wants to be noticed, indeed to be spectacular; and she works toward that end with what one can only call a sort of trance-like seriousness. There is something puritanical and perplexing in her lack of relaxation, her utter refusal to give an inch of the ground of her own opinion. She *cannot conform*, cannot often like what even her peers like.

She is a very odd woman, and perhaps oddest of all in this stirring sense of the importance of her own intellectual formulations. Very few women writers can resist the temptation of feminine sensibility; it is there to be used, as a crutch, and the reliance upon it is expected and generally admired. Mary McCarthy's work, from the first brilliant *The Company She Keeps* down to her latest collection of essays, *On the Contrary: Articles of Belief 1946–1961*, is not like that of anyone else and certainly not like that of other women. ⟨. . .⟩

Plot and dramatic sense are weak in Mary McCarthy's fiction. Taste and accuracy are sometimes substitutions. What people eat, wear, and read are of enormous importance. The reader follows the parade of tastes and preferences with a good deal of honest excitement and suspense, wondering if he can guess the morals of the kind of person who would cover a meat loaf with Campbell's tomato soup. He participates in a mysterious drama of consumption, in which goods are the keys to salvation. Taste is also used as the surest indication of character. "There were pieces of sculpture by Archipenko and Harold Cash, and the head of a beautiful Egyptian Queen, Neferteete." Accuracy, unusual situations documented with extreme care, mean for the reader a special sort of recognition. The story "Dottie Makes an Honest Woman of Herself" is about contraception in the way, for instance, Frank Norris's *The Octopus* is about wheat. "Dottie did not mind the pelvic examination or the fitting. Her bad moment came when she was learning how to insert the pessary herself. Though she was usually good with her hands and well-coordinated . . . As she was trying to fold the pessary, the slippery thing, all covered with jelly, jumped out of her grasp and shot across the room and hit the sterilizer. Dottie could have died." This story, *memorable* to put it mildly, could not have been written by anyone except Mary McCarthy. Reading it over again, the suggestion came involuntarily to mind that perhaps it was meant as a parody of the excesses of naturalistic fiction, a parody, too, of the brute, prosaic sexual details in, for instance, a writer like John O'Hara. There is an air of imparting information—like whaling in Melville or, more accurately, the examination of dope addiction in Gelber's play, *The Connection*. This aspect of *information* brings to memory the later story by Philip Roth in which a college girl suggests she knows all about contraception because she has read Mary McCarthy.

In a writer of this kind there is an urgent sense of the uses to which a vivid personal nature may be put by a writer's literary talent. There is very often an easily recognized element of autobiography and it is in autobiography that Mary McCarthy excels—that is, of course, if one uses the word in its loosest and largest sense. *The Company She Keeps* and *Memories of a Catholic Girlhood* are richer, more beautiful, and aesthetically more satisfying than, say, *A Charmed Life* or *The Groves of Academe*. The condition that made *The Oasis* somewhat still-born was that it was more biography than autobiography. In autobiography, self-exposure and self-justification are the same thing. It is this contradiction that gives the form its dramatic tension. To take a very extreme case, it is only natural that critics who find importance in the writings of the Marquis de Sade will feel that the man himself is not without certain claims on our sympathy and acceptance. In Mary McCarthy's case, the daring of the self-assertion, the brashness of the correcting tendency (think of the titles *Cast a Cold Eye* and *On the Contrary*) fill us with a nervous admiration and even with the thrill of the exploit. Literature, in her practice, has the elation of an adventure—and of course that elation mitigates and makes aesthetically acceptable to our senses the strictness of her judgments.

    —Elizabeth Hardwick, "Mary McCarthy" (1961), *A View of My Own* (1962), excerpted in *Twentieth-Century American Literature*, ed. Harold Bloom (New York: Chelsea House Publishers, 1986), 2361–62

ELIZABETH NIEBUHR

McCarthy: There may be something wrong with ⟨*A Charmed Life*⟩, I don't know. But it was always supposed to have a fairy tale element in it. New Leeds is *haunted*! Therefore nobody should be surprised if something unexpected happens, or something catastrophic, for the place is also pregnant with catastrophe. But it may be that the treatment in between was too realistic, so that the reader was led to expect a realistic continuation of everything going on in a rather moderate way. It was, to some extent, a symbolic story. The novel is supposed to be about doubt. All the characters in different ways represent doubt, whether it is philosophical or ontological doubt as in the case of the strange painter who questions everything—"Why don't I murder my grandmother?" and so on. Or the girl's rather nineteenth-century self-doubt, doubt of the truth, of what she perceives. In any case, everyone is supposed to represent one or another form of doubt. When the girl finally admits to herself that she's pregnant, and also recognizes that she must do something about it, in other words, that she has to put up a real stake—and she does put up a real stake—at that moment she becomes mortal. All the other characters are immortal. They have dozens of terrible accidents, and they're all crippled in one way or another, and yet they have this marvelous power of survival. All those drunks and human odds and ends. Anyway, the girl makes the decision—which from the point of view of conventional morality is a wicked decision—to have an abortion, to kill life. Once she makes this decision, she becomes mortal, and doesn't belong to the charmed circle any more. As soon as she makes it, she gets killed—to get killed is simply a symbol of the fact that she's mortal. ⟨. . .⟩

Niebuhr: ⟨Are there⟩ specific technical difficulties about the novel you find yourself particularly concerned with?

McCarthy: Well, the whole question of the point of view which tortures everybody. It's the problem that everybody's been up against since Joyce, if not before. Of course James really began it, and Flaubert even. You find it as early as *Madame Bovary*. The problem of the point of view, and the voice: *style indirect libre*—the author's voice, by a kind of ventriloquism, disappearing in and completely limited by the voices of his characters. What it has meant is the complete banishment of the author. I would like to restore the author! I haven't tried yet, but I'd like to try after this book, which is as far as I can go in ventriloquism. I would like to try to restore the author. Because you find that if you obey this Jamesian injunction of "Dramatize, dramatize," and especially if you deal with comic characters, as in my case, there is so much you can't say because you're limited by these mentalities. It's just that a certain kind of intelligence—I'm not only speaking of myself, but of anybody, Saul Bellow, for example—is more or less absent from the novel, and has to be, in accordance with these laws which the novel has made for itself. I think one reason that everyone—at least I—welcomed *Doctor Zhivago* was that you had the author in the form of the hero. And this beautiful tenor voice, the hero's voice and the author's—this marvelous voice, and this clear sound of intelligence. The Russians have never gone through the whole development of the novel you find in Joyce, Faulkner, et cetera, so that Pasternak was slightly unaware of the problem! But I think this technical development has become absolutely killing to the novel. ⟨. . .⟩

Niebuhr: In reading the Florence book, I remember being very moved by the passage where you talk of Brunelleschi, about his "absolute integrity and essence," that solidity of his, both real and ideal. When you write about Brunelleschi, you write about this sureness, this "being-itself," and yet as a novelist—in *The Company She Keeps* for instance—you speak of something so very different, and you take almost as a theme this fragmented unplaceability of the human personality.

McCarthy: But I was very young then. I think I'm really not interested in the quest for the self any more. Oh, I suppose everyone continues to be interested in the quest for the self, but what you feel when you're older, I think, is that—how to express this—that you really must *make* the self. It's absolutely useless to look for it, you won't find it, but it's possible in some sense to make it. I don't mean in the sense of making a mask, a Yeatsian mask. But you finally begin in some sense to make and to choose the self you want.

Niebuhr: Can you write novels about that?

McCarthy: I never have. I never have, I've never even thought of it. That is, I've never thought of writing a developmental novel in which a self of some kind is discovered or is made, is forged, as they say. No. I suppose in a sense I don't know any more today than I did in 1941 about what my identity is. But I've stopped looking for it. I must say, I believe much more in truth now than I did. I do believe in the solidity of truth much more. Yes. I believe there is a truth, and that it's knowable.

> —Elizabeth Niebuhr, "Mary McCarthy" [interview], *Paris Review* (Winter–Spring 1962), excerpted in *Twentieth-Century American Literature*, ed. Harold Bloom (New York: Chelsea House Publishers, 1986), 2363–64

BARBARA MCKENZIE

⟨A⟩ major theme that runs through *Memories* ⟨*of a Catholic Girlhood*⟩ concerns the contrast between outward appearance and internal reality. Like the recognition of hypocrisy (with which it is closely allied), this awareness has also affected Miss McCarthy's method as a writer. In "To the Reader," she recounts the first instance of her acknowledgment of the need to sustain outwardly acceptable behavior at the expense of inner truth. On the morning of her first Communion, she unthinkingly took a drink of water. To take Communion after having broken the fast would be, she knew, to accept the Holy Sacrament in a state of mortal sin. Not to take Communion, however, would incur her guardians' anger, the sisters' disapproval, and her classmates' disappointment. "So it came about: I received my first Communion in a state of outward holiness and inward horror, believing I was damned . . ." (20).

Subsequent moral crises in her life, Miss McCarthy affirms, have followed "the pattern of this struggle over the first Communion; I have battled, usually without avail, against a temptation to do something which only I knew was bad, being swept on by a need to preserve outward appearances and to live up to other people's expectations of me" (20-21). On that Communion morning, when she supposed herself damned, Miss McCarthy admits that in actuality she was fated "to a repetition or endless re-enactment of that conflict between excited scruples and inertia of will" (21).

This recognition of the difference between external and inner reality, or between the way things *seem* and the way things *are*, provides the disposition and subject matter of irony. The fiction (and for that matter, most of the non-fiction) of Mary McCarthy employs irony, which is to say that the form of her writing depends not only upon a need to expose and to ridicule, the objective of satire, but upon a deep and consistent awareness of the contradictions of human experience. In her fiction, Miss McCarthy often abandons the exaggeration and distortion of satire in favor of a level-headed, precisely worded presentation of the incongruities of what it is to be human. Irony, in other words, is seldom absent from Mary McCarthy's writing even though it does, at times, get lost amid the less profound trappings of satire. Resting on an awareness of the multiple levels and purposes of life, the ironical vision is, by definition, the result of a mature but resigned wisdom that counteracts the moments of self-indulgent contrariness that have made critics charge Mary McCarthy with precocity.

—Barbara McKenzie, *Mary McCarthy* (New York: Twayne Publishers, Inc., 1966), 31–32

ELAINE SHOWALTER

The dilemma of the woman writer in the second half of the twentieth century—struggling against convention to tell her own truth, and faced with male critics' contempt for it, and female critics' suspicion of it—is dramatized in the case of Mary McCarthy and *The Group*. Published in 1963, *The Group* is a subversive novel about women's roles and marriage, a deliberate exposure of the fantasy of the educated American woman's freedom. As McCarthy described it, the novel is about the failure of the idea of "progress in the feminine sphere." Nothing—not education, not politics, not technology, not sex—can jolt these somnolent young women, these sleeping beauties, from their Vassar tower, into dynamic growth. They are empty at the core, because they have never been free to experience themselves without the screen of male authority: cook books, sex books, child-rearing books, merge in their minds with their Vassar lectures, as infallible guides to the conduct of life.

In 1963 this message—McCarthy even makes the happiest woman in the book a lesbian—was not one America wished to recognize. While the book became a best-seller because of its allegedly sexy passages (sex from the woman's point of view seemed especially titillating and risqué) and because women readers responded to its underlying anger and accuracy, the male intellectuals hastened to attack this "trivial lady-writer's book" (Norman Podhoretz). John W. Aldridge thunderously banished McCarthy from the intellectual kingdom in an essay entitled "Princess among the Trolls." Now, he announced triumphantly, the masquerade was over. She was no great thinker; she gave herself airs; she felt superior to men; in fact, she hated men. *The Group*, according to Aldridge, was a kind of wish-fulfillment for her, enabling her to act out her self-deluding fantasies of intellectual dominance. "It is probably not surprising," he says wearily, "that Miss McCarthy's militant egotism should ultimately take the form of militant feminism and find its most satisfactory expression in the sexual contest between the brute male and the morally and intellectually superior female."

Norman Mailer, as one might guess, went wild. In a long essay called "The Case against McCarthy," he ranted against the detail of *The Group*, seeing in it what he calls the "profound materiality of women." In a classical Freudian analysis of his own metaphors and obsessions, Mailer describes this detail as the "cold lava of anality, which becomes the truest part of her group, her glop, her impacted mass." With sensitive critics like these, and best-sellerdom to boot, *The Group* virtually destroyed Mary McCarthy's literary and intellectual reputation. By the time Hollywood got hold of it, Pauline Kael reports in "The Making of *The Group*," McCarthy herself was regarded as "poison . . . she's competitive"; the book was interpreted as proof that higher education made women aggressive and neurotic.

Yet there is great irony in McCarthy's fall as a "militant feminist," for the chorus of women's voices in her fiction creates a veritable symphony of female self-hatred. McCarthy is only merciless with her own sex; it is to the women in her narratives that she directs her most relentless mockery. In her famous short story "The Man in the Brooks Brothers Shirt," the Babbitty man on the train emerges with considerable dignity and integrity, despite his crude middle-class tastes; it is the autobiographical arty heroine who is stripped of all self-respect and pretension. Similarly, in *The Group*, the female characters internalize all their aggressions against men. John Aldridge managed to find Amazons triumphant, but in truth, Kay, Noreen, Priss, and the rest pour their anger and frustration into bitchiness with each other, self-doubt, self-sacrifice, depression, madness, and suicide. They do not confront their men, much less defeat them.

Pauline Kael was more perceptive when she said that McCarthy's satire was an effort to protect herself against the horrible image of the castrating woman by "betraying other women. And of course women who are good writers succeed in betrayal but fail to save themselves." Since *The Group*, we have heard no more about women from McCarthy. Her subsequent books, a report from Vietnam, and a recent novel, *Birds of America*, narrated by an expatriate college boy obsessed with ecology, have found more favor.

—Elaine Showalter, "Killing the Angel in the House," *Antioch Review* (1973): 345–47

GORDON O. TAYLOR

'There is always one theme in Mary McCarthy's fictions', writes Alfred Kazin in *Bright Book of Life*: 'none of these awful people is going to catch *me*. The heroine is always distinctly right, and gives herself all possible marks for taste, integrity and indomitability. Other people are somehow material to be written up' ⟨*Bright Book of Life*, 1973, 188⟩. Whether or not one accepts this as fair, one *is* inclined to agree that a pattern of identification exists between the novelist and her fictional heroines. A reader of McCarthy's *non*-fiction is also often struck, particularly of late, by the extent to which self-portrayal can become central to her treatment of a subject. The inward play of her imaginative response is frequently as much the substance as the servant of her outwardly avowed literary purpose, or the onward momentum of her narrative line. The intellectual, aesthetic or moral assurance of her self-characterization exerts defining pressure on her materials, be they those of the critic or the polemicist, the autobiographer or the reporter. This pressure of personality indeed relates more than it distinguishes, sometimes even fuses, these various literary roles, along with a number of their respective techniques.

This seems particularly true of *Vietnam* (1967), *Hanoi* (1968) and *Medina* (1972), McCarthy's short books about the American presence in South Vietnam, the impact of the war on the North and the psychic as well as legal aftermath in America of the killing at My Lai. Materials originally written for magazine publication, each set of articles reworked and enlarged into pamphlet form before the next set was composed, constitute a rather fragmented basis for generalization concerning a writer's methods and effects. Yet read as a continuous sequence (the author herself has come to view them as one) these volumes convey a coherent narrative of experience absorbed as much as observed by McCarthy, and of her shaping personality correspondingly shaped. The circumference of her attention progressively contracts (as her titles suggest) from the abstract illusions underlying American involvement in Vietnam, to a more geographically and humanly specific consideration of the view from Hanoi, finally finding in Captain Medina a 'juncture-point' of the war's contradictions, more accessible to the novelist's than to the professional reporter's eye. So, too, one's sense of McCarthy's personal investment in her accounts progressively intensifies.

'Facts', those she accepts as given at the outset and reaffirms at the end, together with those she discovers or revises along the way, gradually become internalized, their secure possession by the reader increasingly a matter of McCarthy's *self*-possession. The 'integrity' of the novelist-heroine impugned by Kazin is in these works to be understood as a process through which the author-protagonist integrates the factuality of her material with her sense of herself, strives to complete herself in relation to it. This process, moreover, depends for rhetorical and moral persuasiveness on McCarthy's willingness to risk through self-questioning that safe certainty which Kazin suggests is an *un*questioned premise of her fictional self-projections. She *is* in these books, whatever the case in her novels, 'caught' in situations in which her *own* 'awfulness' or innocence eventually becomes a central issue, one determinant among many of the 'truthfulness' of her reportage. In order to 'write up' others she must, in the literary situation evolving around her here, write up herself.

—Gordon O. Taylor, "Cast a Cold 'I': Mary McCarthy on Vietnam," *Journal of American Studies* (April 1975): 103

WENDY MARTIN

In "The Woman Writer and the Novel," written in 1922, H. L. Mencken asserts that women novelists have been hindered by a "lingering ladyism—a childish prudery inherited from their mothers." Women will succeed in the novel as they "gradually throw off inhibitions that have hitherto cobwebbed their minds" ⟨103⟩. In *The Group*, McCarthy certainly succeeds in shredding inhibitions when she writes about sex, birth control, and childbirth. In *Cast a Cold Eye*, she succeeds in "killing the angel in the house" as she discusses the private lives of her heroines from their college days to their lives as young matrons, wives, and mothers. *The Group* is the novel which Mencken forecasts will be written by the woman of the future: "If I live to the year 1950, I expect to see a novel by a woman that will describe a typical marriage under Christianity, from the woman's standpoint. . . . That novel, I venture to predict will be a cuckoo. . . . It will seem harsh, but it will be true. And, being true, it will be a good novel. There can be no good one that is not true." ⟨104⟩.

In addition to exploring taboo subjects and presenting a view of the other side of patriarchy—a view of the world behind dominant men—the novel deflates romantic illusions based on the mythology of love as a benevolent force, and exposes the limitations and absurdities of bourgeois individualism. The novel enraged reviewers who dismissed it as trivial or bitchy. But it is Norman Mailer who complained most bitterly, insisting that McCarthy is insufficiently daring: "She simply is not a good enough woman to write a major novel. . . . She suffers from a lack of reach. She chooses not to come close enough to the horror of the closet . . . nice girls live on the thin, juiceless crust of the horror beneath" ⟨"The Case against McCarthy," 1966, 82⟩. Yet, *The Group* contains the essentials of life; it begins with a wedding and ends with a funeral. In the course of the novel, free love, adultery, cruelty, divorce, insanity are confronted squarely—the horror beneath social surfaces *is* exposed, and McCarthy's courage to examine these issues gives the novel its power. *The Group* is the pivotal point in McCarthy's career: in this work, she successfully fuses private lives with political issues.

In general, McCarthy's writing evolves from personal subjects, such as her childhood memories, to public events, such as the Vietnam war and the Watergate trials. But when her whole work is viewed in its totality, a distinction between private and public cannot be made—what happens to individuals happens to social groups, as well as to nations. *Birds of America* (1965), dedicated to Hannah Arendt, is a novel about the difficulty and dangers of allowing an idea to dominate perceptions so that it obscures the diversity and variety of nature and impairs the capacity for virtue and vice. It is also a satire about the rape of nature by technological society. ⟨. . .⟩

In *The Mask of State: Watergate Portraits* (1973), the corrective impulse in the form of social satire is a necessary and healthy response to greed and corruption in public life. Viewing national politics with the same discerning judgment she uses in *Memories of a Catholic Girlhood*, she untangles the threads of a national scandal just as she puzzled through the confused memories of her childhood. Instead of satiric portraits of Uncle Myers, the Man in the Brooks Brothers Shirt, the Yale Intellectual, Mr. Sheen, or Mulcahy, there are biting descriptions of Maurice Stans, Jeb Magruder, Mitchell, Haldeman, Ehrlichman, John Dean, and Gordon Liddy. Again, McCarthy uses the technique of correlating moral qualities with physical appearance, and the Watergate Group is ridiculed for being as self-indulgent, arrogant, domineering as any of their fictional counterparts in Mary McCarthy's rogues' gallery; "With his white fluffy celebrity sideburns, small well-cut features, smart suit accessorized with tie-clasp and cuff links bearing the presidential seal, Maurice Stans resembled a successful actor, a combination of Claude Rains in *Caesar and Cleopatra* and Claude Dauphin" ⟨9–10⟩. Mitchell is described as "sour, old, rancid, terse," and the portrait of Ehrlichman vividly recalls her description of the ape-like Uncle Myers: "Everything about his features and body movements is canted, tilted, slanting, sloping, askew. The arms swing loosely; the left hand with a big seal ring, like a brass knuckle, moves in a sweeping gesture. The broad head is too round—pygmyish" (94–95).

These men are self-important, bombastic, and pompous, and McCarthy's portraits of them as unthinking beasts expose them to public ridicule. Stripping away illusions of their reliability and competence as public leaders, her satire does not remedy the underlying pathology of their lives, but it does reveal the effects of their distorted values on a nation.

Like the satire of her eighteenth-century counterpart, Jane Austen, McCarthy's writing judges as well as chronicles a complex social and economic reality, exposing the pretensions of men and the illusions of women in patriarchal society. Finally, McCarthy's work substantiates the effort of the modern woman to erode the encrusted traditions which prevent her from being heard. She is our contemporary Ann Hutchinson, who looks her judges in the eye and refuses to let them tamper with her reality.

—Wendy Martin, "The Satire and Moral Vision of Mary McCarthy," *Comic Relief: Humor in Contemporary American Literature*, ed. Sarah Blacher Cohen (1978), excerpted in *Twentieth-Century American Literature*, ed. Harold Bloom (New York: Chelsea House Publishers, 1986), 2365–66

ROSALIE HEWITT

The Company She Keeps begins with a foreword by Mary McCarthy, the first of two reading, also judging, selves that appear ⟨also in *Cast a Cold Eye* and

Memories of a Catholic Girlhood). The "Foreword," of course, was written for the publications of *Company*, a work referred to by publishers and reviewers as a "novel." But in the "Foreword" McCarthy clearly wants the "novel" to be read as an autobiographical journey—a desire that was not communicated and could not have been communicated explicitly when the "episodes" first appeared separately. And McCarthy identifies herself in the "Foreword" with the reader, both of whom are to accompany the heroine back over her life's "itinerary" as the heroine searches for her lost identity. McCarthy closes with a statement that is an implicit controlling device to force the reader into a perspective similar to the one she herself has when she confronts the various personalities of the heroine in the "episodes" of *Company*: "For the search is not conclusive: there is no deciding which of these personalities is the 'real' one; the home address of the self, like that of the soul, is not to be found in the Book" (*Company*, 7). But McCarthy now is not only identifying with the reader but also with the heroine, for the third person emphasis in this last sentence merges the self of the heroine with McCarthy's own self who is the person who knows whether the self is really to be found in the book.

The "episodes" of *Company* indeed suggest, both in narrative technique and in thematic content, that the heroine is not a very integrated self, although in the last episode of "Ghostly Father, I Confess" there is a more direct movement toward self-understanding and wholeness of self. But again McCarthy uses the "Foreword" to tell the reader how to read, this time directions not for a philosophical reading, but for a technical reading—instructions on how to confront the linguistic signals, particularly the pronouns that establish point of view. As a reader, McCarthy says she revisits "points of view . . . the intimate 'she,' the affectionate, diminutive 'you,' the thin, abstract, autobiographical 'I'" and is moved to ask, as she imagines her reader will too, "Can all this be the same person?" (*Company*, 7). One thing McCarthy is doing here is trying to establish indirectly a rationale for calling this series of "stories"/"episodes" a "novel," but she is also less indirectly pondering the nature of the self and its contradictions and inconsistencies. That the self of the heroine is connected in McCarthy's mind with her own self and that she intended the heroine to be a fictional representation of her own self is implicitly signaled in the foreword and in the text itself, but these connections will not become explicitly apparent until some years after the 1942 publication.

⟨. . . Let⟩ us examine the text itself and the points of view as McCarthy has suggested. The first narrative in *Company* is "Cruel and Barbarous Treatment," a narrative related by an omniscient narrator in the third person, using "she" to refer to the heroine. No proper names are given in the narrative. The pronoun references as well as other references do not clearly establish the author McCarthy with the "she"; most readers would initially draw the conclusion that the narrative was fiction. The next narrative "Rogue's Gallery" shifts point of view to the "I," the heroine who, given McCarthy's instructions, we must equate with the unnamed "she" of "Treatment" even though other references do not necessarily establish that bond. "Gallery," however, focuses on a character study of the heroine's employer and only becomes autobiographical through the mirror of biography. It is in "Gallery," some distance into the narrative, that we are given the name of the heroine, "Miss Sargent," spoken by the employer, the first name "Margaret" appearing near the end. The next narrative "The Man in the Brooks Brothers Suit" again moves to third person, but this time center of consciousness, the "she" central. The "she" is very much a participant in the action, becoming infamous to McCarthy readers as the young wife who allowed herself to be seduced by a salesman on a cross-country train. Although the heroine's name is not mentioned in this narrative, and although the heroine and the author McCarthy are clearly separate, there is a sympathy built up between author and heroine and then transferred to the reader (much like the James-Strether-reader relationship in *The Ambassadors*.) In the next narrative "The Genial Host" the heroine becomes the "you," to be identified both with the narrator and the participant, but the identity established is one of type rather than individuality, a type representative of the "Trotskyite, bohemian intellectual." The next narrative "The Portrait of the Intellectual as a Yale Man" is identical to "The Genial Host" in its emphasis on type but it returns to the omniscient point of view of the first narrative, with the heroine a minor character who exists primarily in terms of her usefulness to the "Yale man." The last narrative "Ghostly Father, I Confess" is most autobiographical in mode; the internal identity of the heroine becomes defined by her development of a consciousness of self as she remembers past experiences. The point of view is center of consciousness moving to the "I" of interior monologue, the context a session between the heroine and her psychoanalyst. Here, for the first time in the narratives, the heroine refers to herself as "Meg," thinking of herself as an entity that can be named even though her sense of self is still, like the shifts of point of view in *Company*, one of unintegration.

When Meg tries to establish a sense of identity by returning to the past, recalling in some detail incidents that had long been suppressed, she is also creating for the first time her own autobiography, but it is a private, nonarticulated autobiography. The fact that some of the details of Meg's memories—the death of her mother in the flu epidemic, her being punished by her aunt for winning a literary prize, her loss of faith—again reappear in Mary McCarthy's avowed autobiography, *Memories of a Catholic Girlhood*, might prompt later readers to speculate that the double disguise in *Company* (Mary McCarthy's creation of a fictional heroine who cannot publicly articulate her past) testifies to McCarthy's own inability at that time to confront her own past directly. Yet, to read *Company* as it was intended, as fiction, there is, as the McCarthy of the "Foreword" would desire, a kind of coherence established by the heroine's search for self even if there are contradictions, inconsistencies, incoherences in the identity of self (this search for self would have not emerged during the reading of these narratives in periodical publication).

As readers of *Company*, we may also perceive the many selves as defined by de Man reflected in the heroine. Margaret Sargent reads the world, she judges the world and herself in the world, she writes (both in her occupational role as writer and in her metaphorical role as composer of the biographical narratives), and she reads herself (most consciously in the last narrative). And these same selves may be reflected in the author McCarthy as she writes, then reads and judges, and writes again. Yet to take the narrative texts alone, separate from the "Foreword," there is no linguistic evidence for concluding that McCarthy intends her self, her "real" self as intellectual, as bohemian, as wife, as writer, as divorcee, etc., to be directly identified with the heroine. And most of McCarthy's contemporary readers (at the time of publication) would not make any autobiographical connections. Only McCarthy's family, closest friends, and co-workers would have legitimately read the narratives as autobiographical fiction. However, as McCarthy becomes more famous, as she begins to write more overt autobiography, as she speaks in interviews of the connections between episodes of *Company* and her own life, new readers and former readers will read *Company* differently than it was read in 1942. But, though readers will read it as autobiographical fiction, it is still to be read as *fiction*. For McCarthy invented a character and invented a fictional world—the Meg Sargent figure is not to be equated with the real McCarthy self. In other words, McCarthy is not yet ready to write autobiography. The metaphor of search, of quest that McCarthy uses in the "Foreword" is revealing, for there isn't yet a "Mary McCarthy" to write the direct autobiography of self. There is only the Mary McCarthy who creates Margaret Sargent, both without a home address.

—Rosalie Hewitt, "A 'Home Address for the Self': Mary McCarthy's Autobiographical Journey," *Journal of Narrative Technique* (Spring 1982), excerpted in *Twentieth-Century American Literature*, ed. Harold Bloom (New York: Chelsea House Publishers, 1986), 2368–69

CAROL BRIGHTMAN

Her ability to hurt a friend through the medium of fiction was legendary. In later life, McCarthy sometimes tried to make amends for this, as she did after reading Mary Meigs's account of the pain the portrait of Dolly Lamb in *A Charmed Life* caused her when she read it in the 1950s. "She didn't understand that this was fiction, and that these criticisms of her work are expressions of another character," McCarthy insisted; but in 1982 she wrote Meigs: "It pains me awfully to think of you suffering all those years over these passages. Misread by you or not, they are still my doing," and she apologized for having "grossly invaded your privacy . . . even though I don't know how to rectify and never did. I *cannot* stop using real people in my fiction."

It was the old problem of the novelist's 'indebtedness to life.' To Mary Meigs, McCarthy quoted Hannah Arendt in her defense: "You are a critic, and so you must quote." But Mary McCarthy was indebted to "the ridiculous side of people," her French translator and friend Anjou Levi rightly observes; it was "her inspiration, the core of her humor, and her vision of things." It was this angle of vision, "a sort of distortion, a sort of writing on the bias," as McCarthy herself perceived, that sometimes hurt those friends who were not unaware of their ridiculous sides themselves but regretted the immortality McCarthy granted them.

The same angle of vision kept most of her fiction—though not necessarily her criticism—from reaching the first rank. Too often she wrote from the spoils of experience rather than out of a respect for its mysteries. "Freedom (the subjective) is in the fiction, and necessity is in the fact," she remarks sagely in "The Fact in Fiction," but her own fictional worlds are driven by necessity; her characters are usually not free to talk back to the author. Ultimately, her importance as a writer lies less in her ability to prize great secrets from the relatively narrow bands of experience she traverses than in her extraordinary sensitivity to the emotive power of language. It is her respect for words and their mysteries that makes her literary example worth pondering.

The peculiar intensity of McCarthy's prose, the authority one feels behind its observations and judgments, comes in part from a scrupulous commitment to accurate expression. "The McCarthy 'style' depends for its power on two things," the Maine poet Constance Hunting comments: "absolute precision of vocabulary and the pressing of literary substance to yield utmost immediacy of perception and clarity of emotion." No slackness, no vagueness, no "voluminous drapery," no waste. Perception, emotion, are 'felt' through the medium of language. McCarthy's commitment 'to the word' is something akin to a religious dedication. When all else fails, when the flesh weakens, the spirit falters, it is as if words, with their ancient moorings in deeds, are signal fires guiding the mind's eye to far horizons. Not only in literature but in life, a word tumbling out of a potential character's mouth 'sets' that person on a certain stage. What McCarthy calls, in an essay from the 1950s, "the natural symbolism of reality" is matched for her in the linguistic realm by a kind of natural symbolism in language, sometimes overheard, sometimes created.

Finding the right metaphor to illuminate something murky in the psychic drama is her forte; certainly it produced some of her most arresting images.

"Surrounded by friends, she rode like a solitary passenger on her train of thought," she writes of Hannah Arendt after the death of Arendt's husband. Of Hannah herself: "thought, for her, was a kind of husbandry, a humanizing of the wilderness of experience . . ."—which writing was for Mary McCarthy.

—Carol Brightman, *Writing Dangerously: Mary McCarthy and Her World* (New York: Clarkson Potter/Publishers, 1992), 634–35

BIBLIOGRAPHY

The Company She Keeps. 1942.
The Oasis. 1949.
Cast a Cold Eye. 1950.
The Groves of Academe. 1952.
A Charmed Life. 1955.
Sights and Spectacles: 1937–1956. 1956.
Venice Observed. 1956.
Memories of a Catholic Girlhood. 1957.
The Stones of Florence. 1959.
On the Contrary: Articles of Belief, 1946–1961. 1961.
Mary McCarthy's Theatre Chronicles, 1936–1962. 1963.
The Group. 1963.
Birds of America. 1965.
Vietnam. 1967.
Hanoi. 1968.
The Writing on the Wall and Other Literary Essays. 1970.
Medina. 1972.
The Mask of State: Watergate Portraits. 1974.
The Seventeenth Degree. 1974.
Cannibals and Missionaries. 1979.
Ideas and the Novel. 1980.
The Hounds of Summer and Other Stories. 1981.
Occasional Prose. 1985.
How I Grew. 1987.

CARSON McCULLERS

1917-1967

LULA CARSON SMITH was born on February 19, 1917, in Columbus, Georgia, the first of three children of Lamar and Marguerite Waters Smith. The young Carson studied music intensively and by the age of 13 was determined to become a concert pianist; during her high school years, however, she contracted rheumatic fever, and she instead decided to become a writer. She read extensively and soon completed several plays, a novel, and poetry "that nobody could make out, including the author."

In 1934, Carson went to New York and almost immediately lost all her money. To support herself, she took a series of odd jobs while studying creative writing at Columbia and New York universities in her spare time. Although often ill (she would be plagued by illnesses of sometimes great intensity throughout her life), she wrote prolifically during this period; her first work of fiction, "Wunderkind," was published in *Story* magazine in 1936. At about the same time, she began writing a story that would eventually become *The Heart Is a Lonely Hunter*. The novel appeared four years later and was reviewed favorably; it was soon followed by another novel, *Reflections in a Golden Eye*.

In 1937, Carson had married a fellow southerner and aspiring writer, James Reeves McCullers, Jr. Both, however, were bisexual, and by 1940 the emotional strain of their various relationships became overwhelming. Carson moved into February House, the famed Brooklyn writers' enclave. She divorced Reeves in 1942 and stayed in Brooklyn until 1945, spending summers at the Yaddo Colony writers' retreat. In 1945, she remarried Reeves and moved with him to Nyack, New York.

Throughout the 1940s, McCullers continued to write; to meet important writers (Eudora Welty, Katherine Anne Porter, and Tennessee Williams, among others); and to gather recognition for her work, including two Guggenheim Fellowships and a grant from the American Academy of Arts and Letters. She published articles and short stories in *Vogue, Harper's Bazaar, The Saturday Review, Decision,* and *The New Yorker;* she completed her novels *The Ballad of the Sad Café* in 1943 and *The Member of the Wedding* in 1946; both were great successes. At the suggestion of Tennessee Williams, McCullers later dramatized *The Member of the Wedding*, which began a long Broadway run in 1950 and was awarded the New York Drama Critics Circle and Donaldson prizes for best play of 1950.

Throughout the 1940s, however, McCullers's health declined: she suffered stabbing head pains, several bouts of pneumonia, and two strokes, the second of which left her partially blind and temporarily paralyzed. In 1948, she attempted suicide after a brief separation from Reeves, but she refused to participate in a double suicide as Reeves urged her to do before he killed himself five years later. McCullers's mother died in 1955; the loss sent her into prolonged grieving, which was complicated by further medical problems throughout the 1950s and 1960s, including breast cancer.

Despite her nearly debilitating health, however, McCullers continued to write, producing short stories and dramatizations of her fiction. Her work is considered largely autobiographical, with its recurring themes of isolation, gender confusion, and unrequited love. Her characters are nearly always "freakish" in some way: the deaf-mute John Singer and the mentally handicapped Antonapoulos in *The Heart Is a Lonely Hunter*, for example; the strong, mannish, cross-eyed businesswoman Miss Amelia in *The Ballad of the Sad Café*; or the sado-masochistic and voyeuristic characters of *Reflections in a Golden Eye*. All are society's misfits, outsiders struggling to overcome isolation through love.

In the last 10 years of her life, McCullers wrote *The Square Root of Wonderful* (1958), a story involving a premature death from leukemia, and *Clock Without Hands* (1961), her last novel. She continued to travel and lecture as her health permitted, but by 1962 she was mostly confined to a wheelchair. When she died of complications from a stroke on September 29, 1967, she left unfinished a journal work, tentatively named *Illuminations and Night Glare*.

CRITICAL EXTRACTS

WILLIAM P. CLANCY

It is a feeling of intense loneliness, Stephen Spender has written, which gives all great American literature something in common, and this feeling finds expression in its recurrent theme: "the great misunderstood primal energy of creative art, transformed into the inebriate . . . the feeling ox . . . the lost child."

Spender's insight seemed to me a particularly acute one when I first read it. Surely one is haunted by loneliness and longing in Hemingway, in

Fitzgerald, in Faulkner. When I was reading the collected novels and stories of Carson McCullers, his observation struck me with new force. Here is a young American talent of the very first order, and one leaves her work with an almost terrifying sense of the tragic aloneness of man. The symbol for this aloneness is always, as Spender has said, the sensitive, the dumb, the suffering, the lost child. In reading the work of Mrs. McCullers, we become aware of being in the presence of a great tragic spirit, and we ourselves become possessed of a great pity and fear.

This apprehension of loneliness, this pity and fear, is constant in Carson McCullers' work. The present volume, in addition to the title story 〈*The Ballad of the Sad Café*〉, contains her three novels, *The Heart Is a Lonely Hunter*, *Reflections in a Golden Eye*, and *The Member of the Wedding*, and six of her short stories. Through them all we move from one level of tragedy and terror to another: Miss Amelia, the fearsome and cross-eyed, hopelessly in love with an almost diabolical hunchback; Madame Zilensky, the musician, living vicariously through the pathological lie; the deaf-mute, finding his voice only through another mute; the inarticulate soldier, keeping secret vigil by the bed of a woman to whom he can never speak; all these and others probe depths of man's misery, depths to which few writers ever gain access. The art of Carson McCullers has been called "Gothic." Perhaps it is—superficially. Certainly her day-to-day world, her little Southern towns, are haunted by far more master-ful horrors than were ever conjured up in the dreary castles of a Horace Walpole. It seems to me, however, that the "Gothic" label misses the essential point. Because Carson McCullers is ultimately the artist functioning at the very loftiest symbolic level, and if one must look for labels I should prefer to call her work "metaphysical." Behind the strange and horrible in her world there are played out the most sombre tragedies of the human spirit; her mutes, her hunchbacks, speak of complexities and frustrations which are so native in man that they can only be recognized, perhaps, in the shock which comes from seeing them dressed in the robes of the grotesque. They pass us on the street every day but we only notice them when they drag a foot as they go by.

At the very opening of the title story, the face of Miss Amelia, the propri-etor of the "Sad Café," is described as a face ". . . like the terrible dim faces known in dreams . . . sexless and white, with two gray crossed eyes which are turned inwards so sharply that they seem to be exchanging with each other one long and secret gaze of grief." This description, remarkable for its meta-physical fusion of horror and compassion, might serve as a symbol of Carson McCullers' art. And this fusion, I would say, represents an achievement equalled by few other contemporary American writers.

—William P. Clancy, *Commonweal* (15 June 1951): 218

FRANK BALDANZA

The articulation of the truths about love and being which form the core of ⟨*The Member of the Wedding*⟩ comes out of a long twilit kitchen seminar, punctuated by the sounds of rats in the walls and the distant tuning of a piano, and culminating in tears on the parts of all three participants. Berenice reviews in her song-like chant her own erotic history, a direct duplication of the essentials of Aristophanes' speech in *Symposium*, but this time the theme is played in reverse, rather than "one octave lower" as in "A Tree . A Rock . A Cloud." It will be remembered that Aristophanes maintains that at one time each human being was a double creature with two heads, four arms and legs, and the like; and that Zeus, in a moment of fury, punished mankind by splitting each creature in two; Aristophanes interprets the frenzied search of humans for love simply as a pursuit of one's own other half-soul; as a consequence, obviously, success and failure in love are dependent on whether or not one actually finds the other half of his own soul in the beloved. Thus love is synonymous, almost mathematically, with wholeness. Berenice extols her ecstatic first marriage to Ludie Freeman as a transfiguring experience. After his death, however, repeated attempts to duplicate the relation failed; she took up with Jamie Beale because his thumb resembled Ludie's, and with Henry Johnson because he had come into possession of Ludie's coat, and so on for a whole series of husbands. She drives the lesson home to F. Jasmine thus: "'It applies to everybody and it is a warning. . . . Why don't you see what I was doing?' asked Berenice. 'I loved Ludie and he was the first man I ever loved. Therefore, I had to go and copy myself forever afterward. What I did was to marry off little pieces of Ludie whenever I come across them. It was just my misfortune they all turned out to be the wrong pieces. My intention was to repeat me and Ludie.'"

She was reversing the Platonic theory by continuing the search after Ludie's death because supposedly once she had found the other half of her soul in Ludie, there would be no second chance, short of his reincarnation. But Berenice is very wise in the ways of love, and knows all about its power and its variety: "'I have knew mens to fall in love with girls so ugly that you wonder if their eyes is straight. I have seen some of the most peculiar weddings anybody could conjecture. Once I knew a boy with his whole face burned off so that—!'" After a bite of cornbread, she continues: "'I have knew womens to love veritable Satans and thank Jesus when they put their split hooves over the threshold. I have knew boys to take it into their heads to fall in love with other boys.'" But the aim of her whole exposition is the exclamation that despite all her experience, she has never known someone to fall in love with a wedding. She soberly warns F. Jasmine against the obsession. However, Berenice's commitment to sensual love puts her in a category of lesser beings, and the real concern of the tale is with F. Jasmine's spiritual discoveries about love and being. She realizes that she is no longer the child who was hustled out of a movie for hooting at a showing of *Camille,* and now actually participates as an equal in the kitchen discussion of love. Berenice's warning about the troubles ahead for F. Jasmine may be well founded, to be sure, but it is the experience of people like her, Carson McCullers means to say, that embodies the most exquisite values.

What Frankie learns, and what Berenice knows only very fleetingly, is a nearly mystical conviction of "connections" with all sorts of random people seen casually on the street—precisely what Walt Whitman feels on the Brooklyn ferry and what Virginia Woolf's Mrs. Dalloway feels in her meanderings on London streets. In Platonic terminology, she had begun to experience love as an absolute. She can now exclaim with the tramp in the short story " 'All strangers and all loved!' "

—Frank Baldanza, "Plato in Dixie," *Georgia Review* (Summer 1958), excerpted in *Twentieth-Century American Literature,* ed. Harold Bloom (New York: Chelsea House Publishers, 1986), 2386

CARSON McCULLERS

A writer's main asset is intuition; too many facts impede intuition. A writer needs to know so many things, but there are so many things he doesn't need to know—he needs to know human things even if they aren't "wholesome," as they call it.

Every day, I read the New York *Daily News,* and very soberly. It is interesting to know the name of the lover's lane where the stabbing took place, and the circumstances which the *New York Times* never reports. In that unsolved murder in Staten Island, it is interesting to know that the doctor and his wife, when they were stabbed, were wearing Mormon nightgowns, three-quarter length. Lizzie Borden's breakfast, on the sweltering summer day she killed her father, was mutton soup. Always details provoke more ideas than any generality could furnish. When Christ was pierced in His *left* side, it is more moving and evocative than if He were just pierced.

One cannot explain accusations of morbidity. A writer can only say he writes from the seed which flowers later in the subconscious. Nature is not abnormal, only lifelessness is abnormal. Anything that pulses and moves and walks around the room, no matter what thing it is doing, is natural and human to a writer. The fact that John Singer, in *The Heart Is a Lonely Hunter,* is a deaf-and-dumb man is a symbol, and the fact that Captain Penderton, in *Reflections in a Golden Eye,* is homosexual, is also a symbol, of handicap and impotence. The deaf mute, Singer, is a symbol of infirmity, and he loves a person who is incapable of receiving his love. Symbols suggest the story and theme and incident, and they are so interwoven that one cannot understand consciously where the suggestion begins. I become the characters I write about. I am so immersed in them that their motives are my own. When I write about a thief, I become one; when I write about Captain Penderton, I become a homosexual man; when I write about a deaf mute, I become dumb during the time of the story. I become the characters I write about and I bless the Latin poet Terence who said, "Nothing human is alien to me."

When I wrote the stage version of *The Member of the Wedding*, I was at the time paralyzed, and my outward situation was miserable indeed; but when I finished that script, I wrote to a friend of mine, "Oh, how wonderful it is to be a writer, I have never been so happy. . . . "

When work does not go well, no life is more miserable than that of a writer. But when it does go well, when the illumination has focused a work so that it goes limpidly and flows, there is no gladness like it. ⟨. . .⟩

The writer's work is predicated not only on his personality but by the region in which he was born. I wonder sometimes if what they call the "Gothic" school of Southern writing, in which the grotesque is paralleled with the sublime, is not due largely to the cheapness of human life in the South. The Russians are like the Southern writers in that respect. In my childhood, the South was almost a feudal society. But the South is complicated by the racial problem more severely than the Russian society. To many a poor Southerner, the only pride that he has is the fact that he is white, and when one's self-pride is so pitiably debased, how can one learn to love? Above all, love is the main generator of all good writing. Love, passion, compassion are all welded together.

In any communication, a thing says to one person quite a different thing from what it says to another, but writing, in essence, is communication; and communication is the only access to love—to love, to conscience, to nature, to God, and to the dream. For myself, the further I go into my own work and the more I read of those I love, the more aware I am of the dream and the logic of God, which indeed is a Divine collusion.

    —Carson McCullers, "The Flowering Dream: Notes on Writing," *Esquire* (December 1959), excerpted in *Twentieth-Century American Literature*, ed. Harold Bloom (New York: Chelsea House Publishers, 1986), 2381, 2383

JOHN B. VICKERY

Clearly Carson McCullers is primarily interested in the drama that is enacted within the soul of the lover and which finds its source in the painful discovery of the self as a sharply defined and limited ego. The very act of loving implies a desire for some vital and immediate contact and hence a separation. As Berenice explains to Frankie Addams, one becomes conscious of the fact that "'me is me and you is you and he is he. We each one of us somehow caught all by ourself.'" The feeling of being trapped within one's own identity and unable to form a meaningful relationship with others leads to the idea of uniqueness and ultimately of freakishness. In its simplest form, this is apparent in the actual physical deformities of Amelia Evans and Cousin Lymon in *The Ballad of the Sad Café*. In subsequent books the freakishness is attributed to the characters either by the observers who see in Blount, for example, something deformed even though "when you looked at him closely each part of him was normal and as it ought to be" or by the characters themselves who, like Frankie, imagine and fear their own abnormality. ⟨. . .⟩

The archetypal pattern of love is presented in its clearest and simplest form in *The Ballad of the Sad Café*. For each of the three main characters is successively lover and beloved. Each, then, is in turn a slave and a tyrant, depending on whether he is loving or being loved. The refusal or inability of the characters to synchronize their changes of heart produces the interlocking romantic triangles which constitute the plot, while the grotesque comedy arises out of their each in turn conforming to a role they contemptuously rejected in another.

Chronologically Marvin Macy is the first to be subjected to the metamorphosis of love. Without rhyme or reason, this man, handsome and virile though insolent and wild in nature, falls passionately in love with Amelia Evans of the Amazonian figure and crossed eyes. In the process he is transformed into a love-sick calf, shorn of his masculine pride and inherent violence. As the villagers watch with malicious delight, he is unceremoniously ejected from the marriage bed and finally from the house itself. By refusing to accept him into her home and life, to call him by name, or even to speak of him save "with a terrible and spiteful bitterness," Amelia preserves her physical and emotional inviolateness. Thus Marvin's love simply reinforces her in her chosen isolation and complete self-sufficiency.

She herself, however, is not invulnerable. That passion which she incongruously awakened in Marvin is evoked in her by a pompous little hunchback. Cousin Lymon becomes the focus of her life, providing her with a whole new world and whole new set of relationships. For to her he is simultaneously the lover-husband she has rejected and the child she will never have. Furthermore, through him she establishes a precarious contact with the rest of the village insofar as the cafe, formed for Lymon's entertainment, becomes a meeting place for all who seek "fellowship, the satisfactions of the belly, and a certain gaiety and grace of behavior." But even as she escapes from that constricting loneliness of which Cousin Lymon makes her aware, she loses her cherished independence. As in the case of Marvin, by loving she herself creates the beloved tyrant who eventually repudiates and destroys her.

Although Lymon, unlike Marvin, is courted and does not court, yet in his first meeting with Amelia he too begs wordlessly, like a child, for her compassion. It is only later when this compassion has deepened into a grotesque love that he assumes his place as master and invites Marvin to stay in Amelia's house. Only when he becomes imbued with the masculinity which Marvin has regained in the world outside the town is he capable of straightforward self-assertion. Indeed he himself becomes a psychic projection of Marvin, and by stealing Amelia's love, he amply redresses the latter's failure. But if the hunchback comes to love the power resident in that violence of which Marvin is the symbol, he, nevertheless, began as the child of Amelia's heart. In relation to her he is a homuncular incubus, the product of a nightmare marriage and the dark, secret perversion of her own soul. And it is only with the flight of the hunchback and the victorious Marvin, who wins revenge by publicly humiliating her, that she grasps the solitary nature of love and accepts its suffering. It is this awareness which constitutes the first stage in the agon of experience which is human love.

—John B. Vickery, "Carson McCullers: A Map of Love," *Contemporary Literature* (Winter 1960), excerpted in *Twentieth-Century American Literature*, ed. Harold Bloom (New York: Chelsea House Publishers, 1986), 2376–77

IHAB HASSAN

In *The Member of the Wedding*, 1946, Carson McCullers exhibits the kind of formal unity which her first novel lacks. There is also a smarting sense of life in the work, a profound sense of change, and a quality of intense groping which the behavior of the central characters seeks continually to incarnate. The story is primarily that of Frankie Addams, a motherless, twelve-year-old girl engaged in a romance with the world. The agonies of growth, the search for identity, the paradoxical desire to escape, to experience, to belong, suddenly converge on Frankie on the occasion of her brother's wedding which becomes the intolerable symbol of all her longings and the focus of her perverse misunderstanding of the adult world. ⟨. . .⟩

Formally the novel is divided into three parts, each taking its character from the role Frankie assumes. We see her first as Frankie Addams, the tomboy, bored and restive. "Until the April of that year, and all the years of her life before, she had been like other people." Her actual world is defined by the kitchen which she shares with Berenice and John Henry. "The three of them sat at the kitchen table, saying the same things over and over, so that by August the words began to rhyme with each other and sound strange." The transformations begin when Frankie suddenly decides to become a member of the wedding: her heart divides like two wings. In the next section of the novel we see Frankie as the new, exotic personality, F. Jasmine, who is all pride and anticipation. Her flirtation with a soldier, her lengthy conversations with Berenice on the subject of love, her lone wanderings through town, reflect the mood of willfulness which is the prelude to disenchantment. It is in the last part of the novel that disenchantment—what else?—sets in. Mrs. McCullers, beautifully disposes of the wedding itself in a few lines and devotes the rest of the book to convert the initial bitterness of, not Frankie or F. Jasmine, but Frances now, to a final affirmation of youth's resilience. Frances, entitled at last to her full name, outgrows the humiliation of her first defeat. Unlike Mick Kelly, she moves beyond the acrid feeling that the world has cheated her. And with the heedlessness of youth she takes up new friends and other illusions, remotely conscious of the death of John Henry and the separation from Berenice. There is change; there is really no knowledge or confirmation. Guilt and anxiety are equally forgotten, only pathos remains. As the identity of Frankie changes from part to part, so do her images of "the spinning world," now fractured, now whole; and the seasons, keeping richly in step, change from spring to fall. ⟨. . .⟩

The style of the novel presents the blossoming of human feelings no less aptly than it presents the varying moods of nature. But it is a style of confession, or rather manifestation sensitive to the sudden epiphanies of daily life. It is not dramatic despite the inimitable tang and humor of its dialogue, and despite the plasticity of character which allowed the novel to be made into a successful play.

What drama the novel contains, it draws from the juxtaposition of three characters to one another—not from their interactions. Thus is Frankie caught between the violated innocence of John Henry and the viable experience of Berenice. Berenice is indeed the rock on which the novel rests. She calls to mind both Portia and Brannon, and calls forth a quality of existence as wholesome as our daily bread and as enduring. To all of Frankie's wild dreams, she stands as a silent modifier—for she is too wise to rebuke. With three husbands behind her and a fourth in the offing, she speaks as one who has known love and experienced loneliness. Her understanding of life is as tragic as Frankie's misunderstanding is pathetic. Without her, the tortured sensitivity of Frankie—a sensitivity, after all, which has no correlative but the wistfulness of puberty—would seem pointless and contrived. But between innocence and experience only illusions can lie. And the illusions of Frankie disguise the hopes of all mankind even if her destiny falls short of what our moment fully requires.

—Ihab Hassan, "Carson McCullers: The Aesthetics of Love and Pain," *Radical Innocence* (1961), excerpted in *Twentieth-Century American Literature*, ed. Harold Bloom (New York: Chelsea House Publishers, 1986), 2378–79

DONALD EMERSON

Although it exhibits Mrs. McCullers' best qualities, *Clock without Hands* is not her best work. Her gifts of understanding, tenderness and humor are evident once more; her love for her characters vitalizes even those whose actions are destructive. There is none of the cold irony which she used to show up the characters of *Reflections in a Golden Eye*. Mrs. McCullers is most herself as the novelist of inward experience, but in *Clock without Hands* she attempts to add another dimension by making her characters stand for the whole South. It is a mistake. The private and the symbolic roles are not fused; the individual and the representative do not merge. The result for the reader is confusion arising from what seems to have been Mrs. McCullers' uncertainty about her objective. There is also a looseness of structure which weakens the novel and which apparently came of her attempt to make it a far bigger book than she finally published.

A novelist who begins, "Death is always the same, but each man dies in his own way," must expect to remind her readers of a famous first sentence of *Anna Karenina*. The expectation of a novel of scope is reinforced when it becomes apparent that each of the chief characters has a symbolic role; nothing less than the entire Southern dilemma is to be represented through the tangled private histories of a restricted group in a small city. Mrs. McCullers allows the Supreme Court decision on integration of schools to reach the bedside of a dying man who has sunk beyond any concern with news, in a scene which makes sense only if the large implications are a chief intention. *Clock without Hands* does not live up to the intention, for the implications of the action undercut the symbolic roles assigned the chief characters.

The title is itself ambiguous. J. T. Malone, the druggist of Milan, Georgia, is under sentence of death from leukemia, a man confusedly watching his time run out on a clock without hands. But when in that last scene Malone's old friend Judge Clane bursts into the sickroom with news of the decision, the reader catches the suggestion that the Court's "all deliberate speed" is also to be measured by a clock without hands. Behind this scene and the other references to the clock there is the implied warning "It is later than you think," the legend which Baudelaire is supposed to have affixed to his own handless clock in the anecdote which possibly suggested Mrs. McCullers' title. ⟨. . .⟩

Besides failing to achieve the dimensions which Mrs. McCullers intended, the novel is structurally weak. Mrs. McCullers has customarily restricted the scope of her fictions, and she limits her cast in *Clock without Hands*. But there is no central character with whom all the others feel the sole relation they all experience, as with the deaf-mute Singer in *The Heart Is a Lonely Hunter*. There is no tight pattern of antipathies such as enmeshed the men, the women, and the horse in *Reflections in a Golden Eye*. No single character such as Frankie

Addams of *The Member of the Wedding* exists to give the novel a viewpoint. In her latest novel, Mrs. McCullers begins with Malone and the Judge, neglects this relation to concentrate on the Judge, Jester, and Sherman, and returns to it to put a period to the action. Malone is removed almost from significance in the lives of the others.

His significance for the novel is at the level where Mrs. McCullers excels: the depth of conscious being which exists below the hope of communication, where the self, however vaguely apprehended, is forever alone. Her penetration to this essential privacy is made possible by Mrs. McCullers' compassion, which goes as far beyond sympathy as understanding exceeds observation. Here she touches the characters of *Clock without Hands* with the tenderness she has shown even the grotesques in all her work save *Reflections in a Golden Eye*, in which the fantastic, jewel-like eye of Anacleto's peacock feather reflects coldly the ironies of troubled lives. Compassionate identification which reveals how Malone, the Judge, Jester and Sherman all grope toward a sense of identity is too far removed from awkward political symbolism for easy reconciliation; the distance explains the defects of the novel, the looseness of plot, and the failure of *Clock without Hands* to rank with Mrs. McCullers' best work. This same distance, however, justifies praise of Mrs. McCullers' best qualities, which appear even in the disappointing attempt to merge individual and typical roles for a timely social commentary.

The year of Malone's dying sets the period of the novel's action, but Malone is essentially cut off from men from the beginning, and he slips down rungs of despair past fear, rebellion, hope and acceptance into indifference. Except for the occasion when he protests against the plan to murder Sherman Pew, his last months of life touch others only tangentially. His inward life, however, is a leading motif in the counterpoint of Mrs. McCullers' real subject: the self, and its experience of love, frustration, and the isolation of defeat.

—Donald Emerson, "The Ambiguities of *Clock without Hands*," *Contemporary Literature* (Fall 1962), excerpted in *Twentieth-Century American Literature*, ed. Harold Bloom (New York: Chelsea House Publishers, 1986), 2379–80

IRVING MALIN

Reflections appear in Carson McCullers' fiction. In *The Heart Is a Lonely Hunter* each character ⟨. . .⟩ is a double—Biff, Mick, Blount, and Copeland are broken images of one another. Each is concerned with himself, unconsciously refusing to notice another person. As John B. Vickery writes: there is "a sense of terror aroused by the tragic fact that those who are seeking salvation through companions with whom they might create a community are in fact incapable of recognizing their fellows."

This central situation is reinforced by various images of fragmentation. On the first page we note that Singer and Antonapoulos, although linked arm in arm, are incomplete images of each other. The Greek has half-closed eyelids, a stupid smile. Singer, on the other hand, has "quick, intelligent" eyes. The two are in love, but the love implies cruel fragmentation. Their situation reflects the other relationships in the novel; it "mirrors as well as creates the larger scene in which the characters operate." This is immediately evident in the Biff-Alice relationship. Alice likes lying in bed; she enjoys religion; she knows how a business should be run. Biff is completely opposite. Again the relationship is fragmented, but this very fact reflects the mutes' relationship.

Distortion is evident in physical description. There are many things about Blount "that seemed contrary. His head was very large and well-shaped, but his neck was soft and slender as a boy's. The mustache looked false, as if it had been stuck on for a costume party and would fall if he talked too fast." Biff looks at Mick and sees a "gangling, towheaded youngster, a girl of about twelve. . . . She [is] dressed in khaki shorts, a blue shirt, and tennis shoes—so that at first glance she [is] like a very young boy." Later Biff thinks that in every person there is "some special physical part kept always guarded"—the body itself is fragmented. Biff thinks that for Singer it is the hands; for Mick her tender breasts; for Alice, her hair; and for himself, his genitals. Jake at one point looks in the mirror and sees "the same caricature of himself he had noticed so many times before." Already deformed, he seems even more so. Copeland's body fights his mind: his tuberculosis destroys his strong true purpose. The distortion is effectively presented in terms of sex by Biff: often old men acquire high voices and "mincing" walk; old women get "rough and deep voices" and grow dark mustaches. He himself wishes he could be a mother; after Alice dies, he uses her lemon rinse. The human being is a freak.

—Irving Malin, "Self-Love," *New American Gothic* (1962), excerpted in *Twentieth-Century American Literature*, ed. Harold Bloom (New York: Chelsea House Publishers, 1986), 2375–76

BARBARA A. WHITE

Honey Brown, who "just can't breathe no more," is Frankie's double in ⟨*The Member of the Wedding*⟩. Frankie feels a kinship with him because she senses that he is in the same divided state that she is. On the one hand, Honey works hard studying music and French; on the other, he "suddenly run[s] hog-wild all over Sugarville and tear[s] around for several days, until his friends bring him home more dead than living." Although he can talk "like a white schoolteacher," he often adopts his expected role with a vengeance, speaking in a "colored jumble" that even his family cannot understand. Honey spends only part of his energy trying to overcome or protesting the limitations placed on him; the rest of the time he accepts society's label of "inferior" and punishes himself.

Frankie exhibits this same psychology. She frequently "hates herself," and her attempts at rebellion against the female role are mainly symbolic. As Simone de Beauvoir puts it, the young girl "is too much divided against herself to join battle with the world; she limits herself to a flight from reality or a symbolic struggle against it." De Beauvoir mentions four common forms of "symbolic struggle": odd eating habits, kleptomania, self-mutilation, and running away from home. While Frankie never carries these behaviors to extremes, she indulges in all four types. She eats "greedily," pilfers from the five-and-ten, hacks at her foot with a knife, and tries to run away. It is characteristic of these acts that, like Honey's rampages, they are ineffective—the young girl is "struggling in her cage rather than trying to get out of it." At the end of the novel we find Honey in an actual prison and Frankie in a jail of her own.

Frankie's principal "flight from reality" is her creation of a fantasy world. The adult Honey laughs at her solution to racism, that he go to Cuba and pass as a Cuban. But Frankie still deals with her feeling of being trapped by escaping to the haven of her dreams where she can fly airplanes and see the whole world. Her favorite pastime with Berenice and John Henry is their game of criticizing God and putting themselves in the position of creator. Frankie agrees with the basic modifications Berenice would make. The world would be "just and reasonable": there would be no separate colored people, no killed Jews, and no hunger. Frankie makes a major addition, however. "She planned it so that people could instantly change back and forth from boys to girls, whichever way they felt like and wanted." This plan provides a neat symbolic solution to Frankie's conflicts.

To many commentators on McCullers's work, however, Frankie's dream is an "abnormal" one; a product of the author's "homosexual sensibility." ⟨. . .⟩ Leslie Fiedler initiated discussion of gender in McCullers's fiction when he referred to Frankie and Mick as "boy-girl" characters. This point might have led to recognition of McCullers's portrayal of the conflict between a woman's humanity and her destiny as a woman; but Fiedler went on, in a disapproving tone, to call the "tomboy image" "lesbian" and argue that McCullers is "projecting in her neo-tomboys, ambiguous and epicene, the homosexual's . . . uneasiness before heterosexual passion." Fiedler ends up in the absurd position of contending that Frankie and Berenice are having a "homosexual romance."

Some critics have tried to preserve Fiedler's basic argument by giving Frankie a more appropriate lover. They see her relationship at the end of the novel with her newfound friend, Mary Littlejohn, as "latently homosexual"; Mary's name fits conveniently with this theory—she is a "little John," a "surrogate male lover." Other critics influenced by Fiedler take Frankie's refusal to recognize "the facts of life" as evidence of different sexual "abnormalities." Perhaps she wants to join her brother's wedding so that she can commit incest; perhaps she is really "asexual" (to Ihab Hassan, McCullers's "men-women freaks" are "all bi-sexual, which is to say a-sexual"). The critics who have followed Fiedler's lead leave as many questions unanswered as he does. We never learn what a "homosexual sensibility" might be and how it is "abnormal," what the "tomboy image" has to do with lesbianism, how "bisexual" and "a-sexual" are the same. Because so many terms remain undefined, discussion of sex and gender in McCullers's fiction has been hopelessly confused.

At issue seems to be McCullers's endorsement of androgyny in her fiction. Frankie and Mick are only two among many androgynous characters, including Singer and Biff Brannon in *The Heart Is a Lonely Hunter*, Captain Penderton in *Reflections in a Golden Eye* (1941), and Amelia in *Ballad of the Sad Café* (1943). These characters are McCullers's most sympathetic, and they often seem to speak for her. ⟨. . .⟩

If McCullers implies any solution besides racial equality to the social injustice and personal isolation and despair she portrays in her novels, it is a move toward the loosening of conventional gender roles, toward the more androgynous world Frankie envisions when she wishes people could "change back and forth from boys to girls."

—Barbara A. White, "Loss of Self in *The Member of the Wedding*," *Growing Up Female: Adolescent Girlhood in American Fiction* (Greenwood Press, 1985), excerpted in *Carson McCullers*, ed. Harold Bloom (New York: Chelsea House Publishers, 1986), 133–35

SANDRA M. GILBERT AND SUSAN GUBAR

Since the terms of the psychodrama unfolding in McCullers's sad cafe ⟨1951⟩ are so inexorable, Miss Amelia is doomed from the start to lose the physical battle with Macy which constitutes the novella's climax. Because she has given up her bed to Lymon (who has given up his to Marvin Macy), her only bed has been an uncomfortable sofa, and perhaps, we are told, "lack of sleep . . . clouded her wits." But in itself, as McCullers makes clear, neither sleeplessness nor the stress of having her house invaded would necessarily have been enough to guarantee Miss Amelia's defeat. "A fine fighter," this powerful woman "know[s] all manner of mean holds and squeezes," so that "the town [is] betting on" her victory, remembering "the great fight between Miss Amelia and a Fork Falls lawyer who had tried to cheat her . . . a huge strapping fellow [who] was left three quarters dead when she finished with him. And it was not only her talent as a boxer that had impressed everyone—she could demoralize her enemy by making terrifying faces and fierce noises" (61). In spite of

Miss Amelia's unnatural strength, though, the sexual subtext represented by the grotesque triangle in which she is involved dooms her to defeat.

For as McCullers describes it, the spectacular fight in which Marvin Macy and Miss Amelia engage before a mass of spectators in the cleared cafe at seven P.M. on Ground Hog Day is not just a jealous struggle for power over Lymon, it is the primal scene of sexual consummation which did not take place on their wedding night. ⟨. . .⟩

Why is the hunchback the agent of Miss Amelia's symbolic defloration as well as her literal defeat and thus the instrument of Marvin Macy's sexual triumph? And why is his leap into the fray accompanied by a mysterious cry? McCullers's text is so complex that we have to read it as overdetermined. From one perspective, if we take the hunchback to represent the false phallus associated with Miss Amelia's presumptuous usurpation of masculine privilege— with, that is, what Freud would call her "penis envy" and her "masculinity complex"—then his intervention in the fight signals the moment when she must be forced to confront the delusional quality of her pseudo-virility. Deformed himself, Lymon lands on her back to dramatize the way in which his physical deformity echoes her sexual deformity. In this reading, then, as Miss Amelia is made to surrender her pretensions to power, true masculinity reasserts itself with a victorious war whoop that sends a shiver down the spines of the onlookers, who realize that they are present at a solemn cultural event.

From another perspective, if we see the hunchback as representing the "little man" that is the female clitoris or, in a more generalized sense, the authentic if truncated female libido that Miss Amelia has refused to acknowledge, then the intervention of the hunchback in the fight signals the moment when she has been forced to confront her desire for Marvin Macy. Certainly from the day Macy returned to town, her behavior has notably changed: abandoning overalls for a dress, feeding Macy at her table, and finally bedding him down in her private quarters, she might almost "[seem] to have lost her will" (53) because she is in a kind of erotic trance, and the hunchback's open flirtation with Marvin Macy might well express her own secret enthrallment. In this reading, therefore, the mysterious cry is a cry of female orgasmic surrender which sends a shiver down the spine of onlookers because they realize that they are voyeurs witnessing a ceremonial sexual event.

Finally, from yet a third perspective, if we define the hunchback not simply as an anatomical or allegorical aspect of Miss Amelia but rather as an autonomous male character, then his intervention in the fight signals the moment when, by eliminating Miss Amelia as a rival, he achieves a homosexual union with the man whom he has been trying to seduce since the moment when they exchanged their first gaze of secret complicity. In this reading,

then—a reading that supposes McCullers's text to be haunted by female anxiety about male social and sexual bonding—Miss Amelia is simply the medium
whose house and flesh provide the opportunity for Lymon and Marvin Macy
to come together, and the mysterious cry at the end of the fight expresses their
homoerotic orgasm while sending a shiver down the spines of onlookers
because they realize they are witnessing a perverse and subversive event.
Moreover, that the two men leave town together after destroying most of Miss
Amelia's property reiterates the point that she not only is no longer necessary
to them but that their union requires her obliteration.

Whether one subscribes to all or none of these readings, it is clear that at
the conclusion of "Ballad" Miss Amelia has been metamorphosed from a
woman warrior to a helpless madwoman. Her very body has shriveled, for she
is "thin as old maids are thin when they go crazy"; her eyes emphasize her isolation because they are "more crossed . . . as though they sought each other
out to exchange a little glance of grief and lonely recognition"; and her voice
is "broken, soft, and sad" (70). Bereft of her once legendary physical strength,
she has also lost her social, intellectual, and economic authority; her cafe is
closed; her house is boarded up and all her "wise doctoring" is over, for she
tells "one-half of her patients that they [are] going to die outright, and to the
remaining half she recommend[s] cures so far-fetched and agonizing that no
one in his right mind would consider them for a moment" (69–70).
Incarcerated in a wasteland of a town where "the soul rots with boredom," she
resembles not only such paradigmatic mad spinsters as Miss Havisham in
Dickens's *Great Expectations* and Miss Emily in Faulkner's "A Rose for Emily" but
also a female version of T.S. Eliot's wounded Fisher King.

Even the male prisoners in the novella's mysterious epilogue—a brief coda
entitled "THE TWELVE MORTAL MEN"—are happier on their chain gang than is
this prisoner of sex in her sad cafe, for as she sits in silence beside the one window of her house "which is not boarded" and turns toward the empty street "a
face like the terrible dim faces known in dreams," their voices swell together
"until at last it seems that the sound does not come from the twelve men on
the gang, but from the earth itself, or the wide sky" (3, 71). Even in the penitentiary, McCullers implies, men are sustained by their own community while
a woman like Miss Amelia—who, even at her most powerful, never had a community of women—has been inexorably condemned to the solitary confinement such a singular anomaly deserves.

—Sandra M. Gilbert and Susan Gubar, *No Man's Land: The Place of the Woman Writer in the
Twentieth Century*, vol. 1: The War of the Words (New Haven: Yale University Press, 1988),
108–12

BIBLIOGRAPHY

The Heart Is a Lonely Hunter. 1940.

Reflections in a Golden Eye. 1941.

The Ballad of the Sad Café. 1943.

The Member of the Wedding. 1946.

The Member of the Wedding: A Play. 1951.

The Ballad of the Sad Café: Novels and Stories. 1951.

Collected Short Stories and the Novel The Ballad of the Sad Café. 1955.

The Square Root of Wonderful. 1958.

Clock Without Hands. 1961.

Sweet as a Pickle, Clean as a Pig. 1964.

The Mortgaged Heart. Ed. Margarita G. Smith. 1971.

Short Novels and Stories. 1972.

Sucker. 1986.

MARGARET MITCHELL

1900-1949

MARGARET MUNNERLYN MITCHELL was born in Atlanta, Georgia, on November 8, 1900. She and an older brother, Stephens, born in 1896, were children of Eugene Muse Mitchell, a prominent attorney, and Mary Isabelle ("Maybelle") Stephens. On both sides of the family were soldiers in the American Revolutionary War, the Irish rebellions, and the Civil War. Relatives' accounts of war and battlefield tales told by Confederate veterans fascinated Margaret and shaped her talent for gripping narrative; she became a prolific writer at an early age. Between 1912 and 1917, she wrote and performed numerous plays and skits for her family.

Mitchell attended the Washington Seminary in Atlanta, a prestigious girls' finishing school. Although she loved mythology, she was an indifferent student; neither was she a social success. She did, however, upstage her more socially adept classmates in the school's theatrical productions, and she was named editor of the school's magazine her senior year. Mitchell entered Smith College in the fall of 1918, shortly after the United States entered World War I. Two personal events would then alter her life: her fiancé, Clifford Henry, was killed in action in France, and her mother died of influenza in January of 1919. In June, Mitchell returned to Atlanta to run the household for her father and brother.

She made her society debut in 1920, revealing a strong personality: she scandalized Atlanta society by performing a provocative "Apache dance" with a male Georgia Tech student at the season's final charity ball. Greater infamy followed when she took her place in the Atlanta Junior League, insisting upon performing her volunteer service among the black and charity wards in a local hospital. The League rejected her in 1922.

During the same years, however, Mitchell suffered further personal misfortunes. She seemed prone to accidents, illness, and physical disabilities: appendicitis, influenza, a foot broken first while swimming and again in a fall from a horse, and ribs twice broken marked the years from 1919 to 1921. Plagued by insomnia and the increasing weight of what she called her "black depression," Mitchell kept a diary, composed long letters to friends, and wrote short stories and other fiction, almost all of which she destoyed.

In 1922, Mitchell married Berrian Kinnard "Red" Upshaw, a man of bad temper and worse finances but with considerable charm. Mitchell decided to earn her own income by writing, at a salary of $25 per week, for *The Atlanta Journal Sunday Magazine*, where John R. Marsh, Upshaw's former rival for her affections, was an editor and her mentor. Mitchell subsequently divorced Upshaw in 1924 and married John Marsh the following year.

From 1923 until 1926, Mitchell wrote major bylined and unsigned pieces, book reviews, advice to the lovelorn, and gossip columns, and she edited serialized stories. Editor Angus Perkerson offered what he considered the highest praise possible for a woman within the journalistic fraternity: "She wrote like a man." Mitchell would never be paid like a man, however. As a reporter, she preferred to write, as she described it, a story "the way a woman would tell it," with a focus upon details and personal elements. Her stories were marked by her identification with her subject, no matter how lowly or obscure.

Mitchell's ailments forced her to quit her job, and Marsh encouraged her to devote herself to writing fiction. She continued to submit freelance articles to the *Journal* and wrote a novella, *'Ropa Carmagin*, a Southern gothic tale about a tragic love affair between the daughter of a ruined Southern family and a handsome mulatto; the manuscript has not survived. In 1926, Mitchell began writing the novel that would define her career. A project that few of her closest friends were even aware of, *Gone with the Wind*, a romantic epic treating the Civil War and one woman's extraordinary personality, was published in June 1936. It won the Pulitzer Prize for 1937, and to date its worldwide sales have been exceeded only by those of the Bible. The novel was adapted to an equally successful film in 1939—although the film, Mitchell would say, absurdly romanticized her vision of the South.

Beginning in 1941, Mitchell began a series of anonymous scholarship donations to Morehouse College for the tuition and fees of African-American medical students; she would make nearly 50 such gifts. She was not an integrationist, but at a time of brutal segregation and violent racism Mitchell was always concerned with matters of principal. Volunteering at the Atlanta penitentiary, she became interested in the prison magazine, *The Atlantan*. She organized and sponsored writing contests among the prisoners and encouraged the more talented writers after their release.

Crossing an Atlanta intersection in 1949, Mitchell was struck by a car. She died five days later on August 16, 1949.

CRITICAL EXTRACTS

STEPHEN VINCENT BENÉT

This is war, and the wreck and rebuilding that follows it, told entirely from the woman's angle. We have had other novels about the Civil War by women, including Mary Johnston's excellent ones and Evelyn Scott's remarkable "The Wave." But I don't know of any other in which the interest is so consistently centered, not upon the armies and the battles, the flags and the famous names, but upon that other world of women who heard the storm, waited it out, succumbed to it or rebuilt after it, according to their natures. It is in the diaries and the memoirs—in Letitia Macdonald and Mrs. Roger A. Pryor and a dozen more. But it has never been put so completely in fiction before. And it is that which gives "Gone With the Wind" its originality and its individual impact.

It is a long book and a copious one, crowded with character and incident, and bound together with one consistent thread, the strong greediness of Scarlett O'Hara who was bound to get her way, in spite of the hampering ideal of the Perfect Southern Gentlewoman and the ruin that follows men's wars. She didn't, quite, in the end, though she got a great many other things, including money and power—but the tale of her adventures and her struggles makes as readable, full-bodied, and consistent a historical novel as we have had in some time—a novel which, in certain passages, as in the flight from burning Atlanta, rises to genuine heights. Miss Mitchell knows her period, her people, and the red hill country of North Georgia—she knows the clothes and the codes and the little distinctions that make for authenticity. Tara is a working plantation, not a white-porched movie-set—and Atlanta is itself and an individual city, not a fabulous combination of all the first-family features of Richmond, Charleston, and New Orleans. The civilization of the antebellum South was something a little more than a picturesque gesture in gentility—and to a public a little surfeited with wistful reminiscence of the cape-jessamine side of it, Miss Mitchell's rather more realistic treatment should come as a decided relief.

For they are here, the duelists and the belles that we are accustomed to— but there is also Gerald O'Hara, the adventuring Irishman whose quick, restless vitality was able to build Tara into the pattern of a gentleman's plantation and whose charm, together with his finely-bred wife, got him accepted at last as one of the County. And there is his daughter Scarlett, who learned all the outward signs and symbols of the Perfect Gentlewoman, without ever, in the heart, subscribing to the code. We see her first in the raw blooming pride and ruthlessness of youth, with a most unladylike determination to marry the sensitive, appealing, rather dawdling Ashley Wilkes whether he happens to like it or not. We see her last, after three marriages, none of them to Ashley; bruised and hardened by life but still defiant, still with the strong, blind confidence of the dominant that tomorrow or the next day she will yet bend life completely to her will. It is a consistent portrait and a vivid one. And as consistent is the portrait of her opposite, Melanie Wilkes, who never had to think about being a lady because she was one, and who kept to the end the slight steel courage of the fine. The two women, their innate difference, and the curious bond between them are admirably characterized. And it is they, with Rhett Butler, the other nonconformist to the genteel code, who make the book—for Ashley, though ably sketched, is bound to be something of a walking gentleman and a romantic dream.

As background and accompaniment, there is the breakdown of a civilization and the first tentative steps at its rebuilding. Miss Mitchell, as I have said, attempts no battle-pieces, but the grind of the war is there, the patriotic fairs and the slow killing of friend and acquaintance, the false news and the true, the hope deferred and the end and the strangeness after the end. When Scarlett and Melanie, fleeing from Atlanta before the approach of Sherman's army, return to the O'Hara plantation, they return, quite literally, to a ruined world. That was the way it was, and Miss Mitchell's description of Scarlett's frenzied, tireless attempt to rebuild some semblance of life and vigor into Tara is one of the most fascinating sections of her novel. The young men were dead in the war, the land wasted, the field-hands gone. And a plantation, under those conditions, was about as easy a place to live in as a battleship in mid-ocean without its crew. But Scarlett bullied for it, slaved for it, and starved for it—and resolved, with bleak determination, that, come what might to the old code of gentility, she, Scarlett O'Hara, would never be hungry again.

How she made her determination good and what paths her determination led her through form the theme of the last sections of the book. I shall not spoil Miss Mitchell's plot by recounting it in detail, for it is a good one. But her picture of the early days of Reconstruction and the tainted society of scalawags and carpetbaggers through which Scarlett moved with Rhett Butler is quite as vivid as her picture of the war years. Throughout, she draws her distinctions with a sure hand. The extraordinary episode of the rescue of the ex-Confederates by the testimony of Belle Watling and her girls may not please Miss Mitchell's Atlanta audience but it has the convincing ring of folk-lore. And the post-war attitude of a dozen different types of human being, from Rhett Butler's to Ashley Wilkes's, is surely and deftly done—as is the amazing incident of Archie the ex-convict, who acted as chaperone and bodyguard to the ladies of Atlanta during Reconstruction days.

It is only one of a score of such incidents, for Miss Mitchell paints a broad canvas, and an exciting one. And, in spite of its length, the book moves swiftly and smoothly—a three-decker with all sails set. Miss Mitchell has lost neither her characters in her background nor her background in her characters, and her full-blooded story is in the best traditions of the historical novel. It is a good novel rather than a great one, by the impalpables that divide good work from great. And there is, to this reviewer, perhaps unjustly, the shadow of another green-eyed girl over Scarlett O'Hara—as Rhett Butler occasionally shows traces both of St. Elmo and Lord Steyne and Melanie's extreme nobility tends to drift into Ameliaishness here and there. Nevertheless, in "Gone With the Wind," Miss Mitchell has written a solid and vividly interesting story of war and reconstruction, realistic in detail and told from an original point of view—and, as the Book-of-the-Month selection for July, it should reach the wide audience it very genuinely deserves.

  —Stephen Vincent Benét, "Georgia Marches Through," *The Saturday Review of Literature* 14, no. 10 (4 July 1936): 5

ROBERT Y. DRAKE, JR.

Miss Mitchell's work has little of the subtlety of presentation that characterizes the more "literary" Civil War novels, little of the "awareness" of reality that one finds in a novel like Stark Young's *So Red the Rose*, little of the complexity of the imagination of William Faulkner or the art of Robert Penn Warren. And yet I am inclined to think that its very lack of subtlety and self-consciousness is in its favor. For the society it presents (in an epic sweep, covering both War and Reconstruction) was essentially unself-conscious, as the life of tradition always is, as opposed to the analytic and introspective. And it seems to me that in a treatment as broad in scope as Miss Mitchell's is, it is altogether proper that its style maintain the detachment of the folk tale or the epic. For Miss Mitchell's novel is primarily a *story*, in which things happen to people, not, as is the case with so much modern fiction, a *study*, in which people happen to things. I am oversimplifying, of course; but the point I wish to make is that *Gone With the Wind* is an epic treatment of an epic theme. And we must not look for the subtlety or conscious craftsmanship in it that we demand in more "literary" fiction. ⟨. . .⟩

  The chief focus of ⟨what forms the novel's main⟩ conflict between tradition and anti-tradition is, of course, within the character of Scarlett O'Hara. From the very beginning we see this conflict beginning to emerge, growing in intensity until it reaches its climax in the rundown fields of Twelve Oaks, only to have its direction completely reversed at the end of the book. We know that Scarlett has a "sharp intelligence," which, in accordance with the precepts of Southern ladyhood, she struggles to hide under a countenance "as sweet and bland as a baby's." To all outward appearances she is the daughter of a coastal aristocrat, her mother; but, as Rhett tells her, to her indignation, the current

that really flows in her vitals has its source in some not too remote Irish peasant ancestor. Pragmatic to the bone, she seems concerned with none of the
Southern "principles" which Ashley, Melanie, and even Rhett would fight and
die for. She is bent only on survival—at all costs. In the memorable climactic
scene in the devastated grounds of Twelve Oaks she vows solemnly that she
will never go hungry again. ⟨. . .⟩ And then when she toyed with the idea of
becoming Rhett's mistress in order to get the tax money for Tara, she shows
her disregard for the Church. She knew the Church forbade fornication on
pain of hell fire; but, if the Church thought that was going to keep her from
saving Tara, "well, let the Church bother about that." And later, during
Reconstruction, she flouts many of the proprieties of Southern ladyhood by
engaging in business. And yet she is always *outwardly* a Southerner. Though
she hobnobs with the carpetbag aristocracy, she goes out of her way to be
rude to men in the blue uniform. And she will do anything to save Tara and
what it means to her, though she does not grasp its full significance until the
end of the novel. She wants the strength of the Southern tradition, though she
does not realize it until the end; but she is not willing until then to bow to the
exactions of the tradition.

There is little subtlety or complexity in Scarlett's character, but that is
quite proper in the heroine of an epic. The conflict within Scarlett may well
be characterized as one between simplicity (anti-tradition) and complexity
(tradition), between her "romantic love" for Ashley and her real inclination
toward Rhett. But, as the novel moves toward its close, she gains progressively
in insight; and finally, at the death of Melanie, which is the book's "catastrophe," she learns what it is that she really wants, only to lose it at the moment
of this realization. And the insight, toward which the novel has been moving,
is thus achieved.

> She had never understood either of the men she had loved and so
> she had lost them. Now, she had a fumbling knowledge that, had she
> ever understood Ashley, she would never have loved him; had she
> understood Rhett, she would never have lost him. She wondered for-
> lornly if she had ever really understood anyone in the world.

In the death of Melanie, who embodies a "living" tradition, Scarlett realizes at last that it is only "dead" tradition which she has loved in Ashley. It is
only in Rhett that there is real vitality, as the dying Melanie makes her see. But
now it is too late. Scarlett, who is only beginning to see life in its complexity,
imagines that she can really start over again, that the past really can be wiped
out. "My darling," says Rhett, "you're such a child. You think that by saying,
'I'm sorry,' all the errors and hurts of years past can be remedied, obliterated
from the mind, all the poison drawn from old wounds. . . ." Ironically, it is now,

when she is closer to reality than she has ever been, that she loses Rhett, the "reality" she has really been seeking in the "idealistic" Ashley. But in that loss there is a gain in maturity and a growth in spirit. ⟨. . .⟩

And so at the novel's end Scarlett stands alone, having lost Melanie, "who had always been there beside her with a sword in her hands, unobtrusive as her own shadow, loving her, fighting for her with blind passionate loyalty, fighting Yankees, fire, hunger, poverty, public opinion and even her beloved kin." She has lost Ashley, whom she finds she has never really loved; and she has lost Rhett, on whose love she has unconsciously relied and whom she did not come to love until it was too late. But there is something left—Tara and all that it stands for, Tara and Mammy, "the last link with the old days." "We shall manage—somehow," she had told Ashley a few hours before when Melanie died. Now, again, she is ready to "manage," for "tomorrow is another day." But this catch-phrase is no longer a rationalization for a desire to escape the complexity of experience. She is now deliberately choosing to return to Tara and the life of tradition which she has loved all along, unconsciously, in Tara. Like Rhett, she has been redeemed into the life of tradition. In that context she will find solace and perhaps even some remedy for her griefs.

> She had gone back to Tara once in fear and defeat and she had emerged from its sheltering walls strong and armed for victory. What she had done once, somehow—please God, she could do again! How, she did not know. She did not want to think of that now. All she wanted was a breathing space in which to hurt, a quiet place to lick her wounds, a haven in which to plan her campaign. She thought of Tara and it was as if a gentle cool hand were stealing over her heart. She could see the white house gleaming welcome to her through the reddening autumn leaves, feel the quiet hush of the country twilight coming down over her like a benediction, feel the dews falling on the acres of green bushes starred with fleecy white, see the raw color of the red earth and the dismal dark beauty of the pines on the rolling hills.
>
> With the spirit of her people who would not know defeat, even when it stared them in the face, she raised her chin. She could get Rhett back. She knew she could. There had never been a man she couldn't get, once she set her mind upon him.

This, then, is what "happens" in *Gone With the Wind*, an epic treatment of the fall of a traditional society. It is structurally, by its very nature, one-sided. The Yankees are quite properly portrayed as deep-dyed villains, as in the case of General Sherman, whose machinations all occur off-stage but whose menace is distinctly and oppressively felt in the wartime chapters, or in the instance of Jonas Wilkerson, the former O'Hara overseer who marries the poor-white, Emmie Slattery, and ironically tries to become master of the acres he once rode as overseer. In this respect *Gone With the Wind* is no more non-partisan than the *Aeneid*. But it dramatically demonstrates, as the *Aeneid* did before it, that you cannot destroy a traditional society simply by destroying its machinery. The strength of such a society does not lie, ultimately, in outward forms or institutions but, rather, in the "knowledge carried to the heart," the intangibles by which it lives. *Gone With the Wind* states once more, in dramatic terms, the hoary truth that, though you may lick a people, you cannot "reconstruct" them.

I know of no other Civil War novel with as much "breadth" in conception as *Gone With the Wind*. What it lacks in "depth" and in "art" it compensates for in the clarity and vitality of its presentation of the diverse and yet unified issues involved, in sustained narrative interest, and in the powerful simplicity of its structure. The conflict which it dramatizes is as old as history itself. It has been presented more skillfully before, and no doubt will be again. But it will never be done more excitingly or appealingly than it is here.

—Robert Y. Drake, Jr., "Tara Twenty Years After," *The Georgia Review* 12, no. 2 (Summer 1958): 142, 146–50

ANNE GOODWYN JONES

Like many other Southerners of her generation, Margaret Mitchell spoke of William Faulkner and Erskine Caldwell in the same breath: both betrayed the South for Yankee bucks, feeding the Northern appetite for Southern decadence. But Faulkner has his own chapter in this history, and even *Tobacco Road* has landed in a more exclusive neighborhood. Mitchell (1900–1949) alone remains in "popular fiction," with her book that did not contain, in her words, a "single sadist or degenerate." And with reason. For rarely did popular fiction writers share with Faulkner the least desire for formal experimentation; only in the case of Faulkner's own brother did they exploit with Caldwell the distancing possibilities of the tradition of Southwest humor. Most of them tell plain stories—more than half of them historical novels—with old-fashioned plots of love and adventure. And they found a public that heard in their stories a voice it could understand and trust. Yet almost to a person, these writers use those conventions not to avoid but to express the motive energy of deeply felt concerns, concerns that in fact formed the great theme of the greater writers of the Southern Renascence: the meaning of the past for the present. ⟨. . .⟩

⟨. . .⟩ *Gone With the Wind* ⟨. . .⟩ sold a million copies in the first six months, and now endures in popular American mythology. Well it might, for *Gone With the Wind* merges its readers' interests in history and gender by means of a further revision of the female domestic literary traditions. Thus Mitchell self-consciously uses her experiment in gender to investigate the contemporary South's capacity for continuity with the past. She never clearly answers the questions she raises; yet leaving uncertain the relation of past to present—popularly expressed in the question, "Will Rhett ever come back?"—makes the novel interesting to almost everyone.

Mitchell uses the conventions of women's fiction. She pairs protagonists; Scarlett and Melanie present the varying difficulties of female self-assertion and self-sacrifice. She sends the men off to war to permit female autonomy and growth. And she gives Scarlett the final love recognition scene that conventionally offers the chance for a woman to have love as well as a voice. Mitchell's focus on the dark twin is not unusual; it follows the pattern set by Augusta Evans Wilson in the previous century. But ⟨. . .⟩ the field for her Scarlett's autonomous growth is, rather than the home, the plantation, or border worlds like teaching and writing, clearly the male, public, economic, competitive world. Scarlett, of course, runs a sawmill, hires and fires, and rides alone on business, taking the risks traditional to men; the "Gerald" in her heart emerges from the facade of ladyhood. Further, what conventionally would be a joyful love scene at the end becomes only Scarlett's recognition and articulation of her love for Rhett; he no longer gives a damn. The implications are considerable: Mitchell has given us a woman who has entered (traditional) history, and for whom love is not the reward.

This emergence of a "new woman" is related to questions of change and continuity, of history as subject, in two further ways. Mitchell fully intended Scarlett to symbolize Atlanta; in her strengths and weaknesses, in her continuities and breaks with the past, we are to see those of the New South. But unlike Ashley and Rhett, Scarlett never gains the analytic capacity to envision herself as a meaningful part of history. Thus as she challenges gender, as she enters history, and as she represents the South, she embodies Mitchell's meditation on history; but she herself will, at best, think about it all tomorrow.

With Ashley and Rhett, Mitchell explores a "new man" as well. In certain respects each is a Southern gender stereotype, like Melanie and Scarlett; Ashley is the Southern gentleman of culture and sensitivity, and Rhett the swashbuckling reincarnation of ⟨Inglis Fletcher's⟩ Sir Richard Grenville. Yet Rhett's choice of personal gain over regional piety, his directness, his challenges to codes of female behavior, all make him potentially new, a Grenville without his Virgin Queen. Because he stands for the Old South of his Charleston birth, Rhett embodies the possibility of continuity, of the South's incorporating new values into its tradition. But the thoroughness with which he rejects his new values at the end of the novel, in his unequivocal decision to return to the old ways, suggests the depth to which Mitchell despaired of that continuity, as expressed in a revision of Southern manhood. (Similarly, the ultimate weakness of both Ashley and Melanie suggests her abandonment of what had been a sustained effort to revitalize the idea of the Old South.)

Only with Scarlett, daughter of an aristocrat and an immigrant, raised in the red clay up-country, does the novel leave some ambiguity. On one hand, Scarlett's return to Tara means a return to the (now metaphoric) "gentle cool hand" of her mother Ellen and the "broad bosom" of Mammy, possibly then to a past of preautonomous childhood. Yet on the other hand, we as readers—knowing her history and presumably capable of analyzing it—might well anticipate that now, freed from the self defined in loving Ashley and then Rhett, back at private, agricultural, feminine, antebellum Tara with her skills and self learned in the public, business, masculine, postbellum world, she may manage to solve simultaneously the riddles of Southern womanhood and of Southern history by incorporating the new into the old. The question we should ask then is not "Will Rhett ever come back?" but "If he comes back, who will *he* be?"

Perhaps the failure of *Gone With the Wind* 〈. . .〉 to use the possibilities of language more fully than it does made it popular; perhaps that failure of language also keeps it from greatness. For under these bushels we find no brilliance like Faulkner's or Porter's. Nevertheless, the light these writers made helps us to see that the yearning for a stable past and the sense of its inadequacy, the excitement of liberation into the new and the anxiety of the shapes it was taking—in short, the conflict between monumentalist and modernizer—informed the works of popular as well as high culture writers, women as well as men, of the period 1920 to 1950. And a good number of these writers, even if it was at the cost of sentimentality or irresolution, imagine that neither tradition nor innovation must be forsaken.

—Anne Goodwyn Jones, "*Gone With the Wind* and Others: Popular Fiction, 1920–1950," in *The History of Southern Literature*, ed. Louis D. Rubin, Jr. (Baton Rouge: Louisiana State University Press, 1985), 363, 372–74

HELEN TAYLOR

In *Gone With the Wind*, the rather titillating and appealing gender confusions experienced by Scarlett are balanced by ominous suggestions of mingled racial identities. However uneasily feminine, Scarlett is indisputably white. As with other southern heroines, that whiteness is emphasised throughout the novel—from her magnolia-white skin to her small white hands (contrasted as they are with the 'huge black paws' of the family slaves, 299). But once the war and abolition have hit Tara, oh-so-white Scarlett is in danger of losing her dominant racial status. On the road back to Tara, she sleeps in the wagon 'like a field hand on hard planks' (385), and once back on the plantation, works on the land knowing she would 'never feel like a lady again until her table was weighted with silver and crystal and smoking with rich food . . . until black hands and not white took the cotton from Tara' (594). After the fire in the kitchen, Scarlett and Melanie laugh at each other's blackened faces, Melanie likening her friend's to 'the end man in a minstrel show' (459); and when Scarlett in her finery visits Rhett in jail, it is her blistered, red hands which show him that, far from idling, she's been 'working like a nigger' (564). This motif of the blackening of white skin, hence name and status, acts to exhort the reader to deplore the Confederacy's defeat, and to vindicate the violent tactics of the Ku Klux Klan and other southern whites to redeem that white supremacy which is sanctified as natural within the narrative.

There is a significant difference between *Gone With the Wind* and other romantic novels—namely, the happy ending involves not a man but a piece of property/land. While Rhett departs, declaring indifference to his wife, surprisingly Scarlett does not do what we all ache for—pursue him to bring about a final tempestuous reconciliation. No, the novel ends in a manner inconsistent with True Romances but entirely appropriate for the political and historical project to which the novel addresses itself throughout. Scarlett decides to return to the 'sheltering walls' of Tara in order to 'plan her campaign' of retrieving Rhett Butler. The thought of Tara comforts and strengthens her, and gives her renewed confidence in herself and her ability to do what she's always done—get a man on whom she's set her mind.

Her Irish father's home Tara is significantly named after the sacred place of early Celtic Ireland, the supreme seat of the monarch. In Irish mythology, land is described in terms of a woman's form; until the seventeenth century the land was imagined in terms of a woman old as the hills, restored endlessly to youth through union with the right mate. Woman earth outlives men and tribes; in Irish mythology women allow power to kings through a sexual/supernatural union. Thus it is fitting for Scarlett to return finally to Tara—as mythic natural home of woman, where she may both survive and be reborn, and also lure back and reconquer her king. Hence the militaristic language associated with the plantation—it is a virtual fortress from which Scarlett had once before 'emerged . . . strong and armed for victory' (1010). And hence the symbolic resonance of Tara on which the David Selznick film lingers: repeating as a refrain the silhouetted figure of Scarlett35 35/Woman against red sky, dark Tara/Mythological Haven or Stronghold, heightened by the swelling chords of Max Steiner's theme music.

But Tara is not (as in Irish mythology) defined simply as a female haven, a woman's place. It is explicitly a place for *upper middle class white women*, a site existing timelessly outside real social relations, and all class and race divisions and conflicts of interest. Tara is the embodiment of southern white femininity: the white-walled and white-curtained house and 'fleecy white' cotton bolls contrast reassuringly with the red earth, green pines and bushes. And most of all with the Blackness of Mammy, who of course 'would be there'. Scarlett's final longing is for the 'broad bosom on which to lay her head, the gnarled black hand on her hair', for it is only within Mammy's mute embrace that Scarlett can reassert her secure, dominant position in class and race terms: 'Mammy, the last link with the old days.' Scarlett is thus revived by the thought of Mammy, and the anticipated reconnection with her antebellum heritage, confirmed now by the return to Tara. The final page of the novel brings together into a metaphoric and symbolic harmony a naturalised vision of a reborn South, safely in the hands of strong, capable, property-owning white women, vindicated and supported by the passive, loving 'endurance' of Black womanhood which knows its (subordinate) place.

    —Helen Taylor, "*Gone With the Wind*: the mammy of them all," in *The Progress of Romance: The Politics of Popular Fiction*, ed. Jean Radford (New York: Routledge & Kegan Paul, 1986), 130–32

DARDEN ASBURY PYRON

Two initial problems hinder the appreciation of Margaret Mitchell's epic within this framework of Southern intellectual history, the first more esthetic and formal, the second more practical and immediate.

First, even as the most flattering reviewers noted, *Gone with the Wind* lacks art. Thus, typically, Henry Steele Commager wrote, "if not a work of art," *Gone with the Wind* is "a dramatic recreation of life itself." This distinction involves rather more than stylistic infelicities or ineptitude. It relates to the absence of self-conscious, esthetic intention. The idea of "the dramatic recreation of life itself" might suggest something of the distinction between art and journalism. Mitchell was a good journalist. She practiced the craft of novel-writing in a similar way, basically of ordering concrete facts about a page. She never claimed a higher revelation. She specifically disclaimed more elevated purpose. If her novel might still speak to something in the human spirit, Mitchell herself did not set out with this aim in mind. Yet her novel's very lack of artfulness and coherent esthetic vision makes it useful; it reveals more clearly many of the intellectual and social currents that lay behind 20th-century civilization, still more, regional intellectual history after World War I. If her novel does not belong in the literary canon, it does, however, inform that canon. As a document, if not a text, it merits serious inquiry.

A more practical problem of fixing Mitchell's epic within the interwar world lies in the novel's very close identification with the Old South romance, that central target of her generation's sharpest barbs. That identification has its own history. David Selznick's memorable film sealed the interpretation upon the novel. With its exaggeration of aristocracy and slavery and its omissions of yeomanry, his version amused the author. She "yelped with laughter" on seeing the Hollywood Twelve Oaks, for example, which she described whimsically as an impossible hybrid of Grand Central Station and the State Capitol at Montgomery.

Evoking the Old South ideal lay very far indeed from her mind. She consistently expressed dismay at being categorized "among those writers who picture the South as a land of white columned mansions whose wealthy owners had thousands of slaves and drank thousands of juleps," she wrote 〈. . . .〉

〈She insisted〉 that all her characters, "except for the Virginia Wilkes, were of sturdy yeoman stock." These same "Virginia Wilkes," however, provided the very opening for the other reading of her novel, for through them, she displays the full panoply of the plantation romance. Ashley in particular represents that myth, not least of all in his nostalgic profusions about moonlight, magnolias, mocking birds, and singing darkies. Mitchell certainly knew and used the conventions of the plantation South and the Lost Cause romance. To what end and effect, however, remains another matter.

Like others of her generation, Mitchell challenged the legend. She did so in various ways. Thus, while she presents the most sentimental notions about the Old South, she usually distances them from the auctorial voice. This is especially notable with Ashley Wilkes. She uses the device of letters within the text to isolate his most sentimental memories of the past's "golden glow." The two main characters in the novel, Rhett and Scarlett, served the same distancing function. At every puff of platitude or romantic convention, they deflate with words, deeds, or sometimes merely pointed gestures the pretentions of the myth. The famous barbecue and armory scenes demonstrate neatly these characters' purposes. Mitchell drew each scene to represent the traditional Southern world in microcosm. This makes her characters' debunking realism and commonsense skepticism all the more significant. With a few pointed questions, Rhett shatters the pretty harmony of the country picnic and reduces the Cavaliers to stammering rage. Scarlett's cynical reflections on the regional bellehood have similar effects. 〈. . .〉

Mitchell undermines the aristocratic idea in other ways. As opposed to the grace and easy harmony of the mythic social order, she depicts its conflicts and oppressions. If she ignored the oppression of slavery, she lost no occasion to show the restrictions upon women. Scarlett describes conventional society specifically as a prison, but the author shared these values, demonstrated, as Louis Rubin has argued, in the corset-lacing scene. Throughout the work, Mitchell bares the covert violence with which the social order compelled allegiance, as in Rhett's exclusion from polite society and rejection by his Charleston family. Whispers work effectively as whips in this regard.

Generational negativity colors her individual aristocrats as well as her aristocracy as a class. She denies them life and vitality. Ellen Robillard lacks any color or spontaneity. She is a ghost in the novel. Repressed herself, she

becomes a prime agent in her daughter's repression. While Mitchell employs traditional language to describe the class—aloof, ineffectual, passionless, and weak, she also associates them with illness and physical disfiguration, like spindly-legged, knock-kneed spavins and the sallow look of malaria. Her animal analogues are telling, too: The Wilkes-Hamiltons are lap dogs, does, and rabbits, while the Butlers are lumbering dinosaurs. Natural selection does the South a favor to weed them out. Like Faulkner's planter class with Benjy's castration at the end of the Compson line, Mitchell's aristocrats are impotent too.
   —Darden Asbury Pyron, "*Gone With the Wind* and the Southern Cultural Awakening," *The Virginia Quarterly Review* 62, no. 4 (Autumn 1986): 575–79

JOEL WILLIAMSON

Margaret Mitchell grew up in a white Georgia world very much pervaded by a fear of the black beast rapist. And yet in *Gone With the Wind* there is no potential black rapist worthy of mention in more than a few lines, and none at all important enough to be given a name. Indeed, there are no really self-interested, self-moving blacks at all in the story. Some blacks are badly used by scalawags and carpetbaggers, but the most important black people—like Mammy, Pork, Dilcey, Big Sam, and Peter—are well used by elite southern whites to keep the white world in good running order. In the mass, in *Gone With the Wind*, black people are simply shunted aside. There is no hint that Atlanta University and other black schools existed during much of the time period covered by the novel, nor that there was an emerging black elite in the city. Margaret Mitchell wrote a strikingly white novel, so white in fact that some of the white characters seem black. The most important of these is Rhett Butler.

   Seemingly, there are four evidences, compelling in greater or lesser degree, of Rhett's blackness. The first and least important is his coloring. The second and third relate to his attitudes and behavior in matters of work and sex. The fourth relates to the author herself.

   In her novel Margaret Mitchell painted Rhett Butler as exceedingly dark. Perhaps one day some patient scholar will do a description and analysis of color references to individual characters in *Gone With the Wind*. Without doubt, Rhett would be the front-runner on the dark side, with a great number of "blacks," "darks," and "swarthies" applied to him, all now and again accentuated by the whiteness of his teeth or the redness of his lips. Interestingly, at least twice he is an Indian, and once Scarlett calls him a hound, but caresses the word as she is saying it so that it sounds more like "darling." Surprisingly, the runner-up in dark coloring would probably be Melanie Wilkes, whose very name comes from the Greek word *melanos*, meaning black. Ironically, in terms of ideals Melanie is whiter than white. At the other end of the color spectrum is Ashley Wilkes, who is not only fair and blond, but represents the very essence of light. Margaret Mitchell describes him as "sunny haired."

Of course, heroes in America have often been dark, perhaps even usually so, and making Rhett Butler dark does not make him black. We can move somewhat further in that direction, however, by considering Rhett's attitudes and behavior in regard to work and sex. ⟨. . .⟩

The great depression of the 1890s had ⟨. . .⟩ cut black men, frequently young black men, away from the marginal lands of the agricultural South. Often enough they drifted toward the big cities such as New Orleans, Memphis, and Atlanta. There they found a world for which they had no preparation. Like Robert Charles, the protagonist in the New Orleans riot of 1900, they went from job to job, from address to address, from name to name, and had no wife. White people, looking on from the outside, saw the floating black man as choosing the life he seemed to live. They saw him as the run-away, the Negro loose, the Negro in the woods of previous times and other places. They saw him as the "hipster-trickster," an almost precisely counter-punctual anti-Victorian male who saw himself as too smart to work and too much man for one woman to hold.

Rhett Butler certainly fills that role in Margaret Mitchell's novel, and he is despised by white society for it. Rhett is the dark, mysterious, and slightly malevolent hero loose in the world. Like Red Upshaw in Mitchell's own life, he holds no job, has no profession and no clearly visible means of support—yet he has money and lots of it. Rhett is, in a sense, the "nigger loose." He is independent, cocky, and insufferably yet subtly insolent. He has an uncanny capacity for divining the thoughts of others and for popping up at the right place and time to promote his own interests. ⟨. . .⟩

Rhett himself confesses that he is too much man for one woman. The fact is also implied in his long-running intimacy with Belle Watling, the madame whose house often seems to be his home. Meeting Scarlett changes his life. She is, for him, in the turn-of-the-century phrase, "the one woman." He understands her perfectly, and bends his considerable energies toward having her love him. Appearances to the contrary notwithstanding, it's not nearly so much her body that he wants as it is her heart and mind. ⟨. . .⟩

⟨. . .⟩ In a scene that many students of *Gone With the Wind* call "the rape scene," Rhett makes a last desperate effort to possess Scarlett as a whole woman. In this instance, she has made a mess of things in another clumsy attempt to get Ashley to seduce her. Rhett is so frustrated by Scarlett's obsession with Ashley that he falls to drinking heavily in the dining room of their Peachtree Street mansion. In the southern white mind in the turn-of-the-century years, the black beast rapist was often associated with liquor. Scarlett approaches the dining room, but suddenly Rhett appears in the doorway, the light behind him, and he is "a terrifying faceless black bulk." Holding her captive in the dining room, he shows her his "large brown hands" and says, "I could tear you to pieces with them." Placing his hands on either side of her head, he declares to Scarlett that he could smash her skull "like a walnut." Struggling, she accuses him of being a "drunken beast" ⟨. . . .⟩

Perhaps the most compelling evidence that Rhett Butler represents blackness comes from Margaret Mitchell's own life. During the summer of 1926, when John Marsh was pressing his housebound wife to write a novel, she passed from several years of smoking, drinking, hard working, and good health to a sequence of injuries and illnesses. She had, she said, "several hundred novels in my mind," but somehow could write none of them. She procrastinated, but John persisted and in the fall she began a short story she called "'Ropa Carmagin." Three weeks later it was a 15,000-word novella. Europa Carmagin, the heroine, is the daughter of one of those failed planter families that Margaret's mother Maybelle had warned her about, the families that did not have "gumption" enough to meet the challenges of the Civil War and Reconstruction. The Carmagin plantation offers rotting fences, exhausted fields, and a garden choked with weeds. Far from pulling renewed life from this now "barren ground," 'Ropa, as Mitchell calls her, spends her energies loving a handsome mulatto man whose mother had been a slave on the Carmagin plantation. The scene of all this is Clayton County near Jonesboro, the same as that of Tara, but the time is the 1880s, and Europa, unlike Scarlett, puts love before money. In the end the dark lover is killed, and the neighbors force 'Ropa to leave her ancestral home.

Peggy Mitchell Marsh liked Europa Carmagin and she liked the story she had written. She thought it rich and accurate in historical detail, and especially, she relished the idea that the theme "miscegenation" would raise the story from "romance" to "literature." She showed the manuscript to John, as she did all she wrote, and waited for the close editing he always supplied. John was himself fascinated by the background, the period, and he even liked Europa Carmagin. But he thought that Peggy had not drawn a true portrait of the mulatto and that the work in general was not up to her talent. Most of all, he did not like the theme of miscegenation. He suggested she put the manuscript aside and think about it for a while before he attempted to make notes on it for her.

In 1926, it appears that Margaret Mitchell was about to write a book about miscegenation that was not vastly distant from the truly great novel that William Faulkner published a decade later under the title *Absalom, Absalom!* In that story the white girl, Judith Sutpen, loves and is fully set to marry a mulatto man, Charles Bon, before he is shot down and killed. Moreover, the mulatto man she would marry is her half brother—the son of her father. We do not know who Europa's lover's father was, but we do know that he was the son of a Carmagin slave woman. As we now understand patterns of miscegenation in the Old South, it would have been almost ordinary if Europa's white kin had been the father of her lover, and it would not have been unusual if her own father had been the father of her lover.

—Joel Williamson, "How Black Was Rhett Butler?" in *The Evolution of Southern Culture*, ed. Numan V. Bartley (Athens, GA: University of Georgia Press, 1988), 97–103

HELEN TAYLOR

⟨*Gone with the Wind*⟩ took Margaret Mitchell many years to complete. If her resentful letters are to be believed, the endless, insistent demands on her time by others made the writing of the novel tough going. There are scores of complaints by women writers of very different periods, recorded, often in diaries, journals or letters, that the duties and tasks expected of them as women, whether daughters, wives, mothers or friends, have made writing at best an intermittent, often an impossible task. The strong and determined—and healthy!—have persisted; the less assertive and physically or psychically fragile have become silent, or broken down in various ways. In an echo of complaints by women as disparate as Elizabeth Gaskell, Alice James, Virginia Woolf and Tillie Olsen, Margaret Mitchell expressed these sentiments in letter after histrionic letter. For instance:

> When I look back on these last years of struggling to find time to write between deaths in the family, illness in the family and among friends . . ., childbirths (not my own!), divorces and neuroses among friends, my own ill health and four fine auto accidents . . . it all seems like a nightmare. I wouldn't tackle it again for anything.

Although she pays little lip service to them and in her correspondence tends to encourage the idea of herself as a unique phenomenon, the Southern woman writer who explained the South to the world, nevertheless Margaret Mitchell owes a considerable debt to earlier and contemporary Southern writers. Many male critics assume that *GWTW* was heavily influenced by *Vanity Fair* and *War and Peace*; Margaret Mitchell assured many correspondents that she had never read either. More usefully, critic Kathryn Lee Seidel traces *GWTW* back to nineteenth-century male 'plantation fiction', locating Scarlett's origins in such figures as Bel Tracy, heroine of John Pendleton Kennedy's *Swallow Barn* (1832) and Virginia Beaufort in John W. DeForest's *The Bloody Chasm* (1881). And like dozens of women writers who wrote fiction which both mourned the loss of antebellum Southern society and celebrated the role of white women after the

Civil War in the restoration of the white South, Mitchell relied on the auto-biographical and fictional writing of other women for inspiration and chal-lenge. Her letters are scattered with brief references to such women: Mary Johnston, Georgia author of *The Long Roll* (1911) and *Cease Firing* (1912), whose novels her mother read to her, weeping all the while; Augusta Evans Wilson, whose *St Elmo* (1867) provided an early model for Rhett Butler; Ellen Glasgow and Caroline Miller, whose fiction about the Southern states made a great impression on her; and many Civil War diarists, published and unpublished—such as the Georgian Eliza Frances Andrews. Again, following in other Southerners' footsteps, she began her fiction-writing by experimenting in a well-worn genre. Her novella 'Ropa Carmagin', about a white girl in love with a former slave mulatto man, has the tragic ending of most of its kind: the mulatto lover is killed and Europa is forced to leave her ancestral home.

Mitchell was also clear from which women writers she wished to dissoci-ate herself. Like conservative Southern white women before her, she denounced the book which President Lincoln cited as the cause of the Civil War, *Uncle Tom's Cabin*. Replying to a Mr Alexander L. May who wrote to her from Berlin in 1938, she claimed to be 'very happy to know that "Gone With the Wind" is helping refute the impression of the South which people abroad gained from Mrs Stowe's work', a book she claimed 'had a good deal to do with the bitterness of the Abolition movement'. And of the Grimké sisters, who left the slave state South Carolina to go north and became distinguished figures in the Abolition and women's rights movements of the 1830s, Mitchell told an anecdote about family friends. According to her the Grimkés were distant fam-ily ancestors, but these friends were deeply embarrassed about it (being 'most unreconstructedest of Rebels imaginable') and claimed that the sisters were 'mentally unbalanced'. Mitchell enjoyed the joke on these women who were seen, outside liberal circles, as traitors to the white South.

Besides dissociating herself from certain women writers, to many of her correspondents Mitchell was anxious to deny any didactic intention in writing the novel. In one of the few letters that admit to a conscious purpose, she claims she was tired of Jazz Age fiction and wanted to write something which did not use the term 'son of a bitch' and in which 'no one was seduced and there wouldn't be a single sadist or degenerate'. In this letter she is anxious to assure Mrs Harris that it was not prissiness or shock at Jazz Age fiction, and she had no desire to write 'a sweet, sentimental novel of the Thomas Nelson Page type'. Page was the classic writer of moonlight-and-magnolia romances which celebrated the white-dominated South and by the 1920s were regarded as presenting an outdated version of the region. What Mitchell wanted to do in her novel was to create a central female character (as well as some minor characters) who 'does practically everything that a lady of the old school should not do'.

—Helen Taylor, *Scarlett's Women:* Gone With the Wind *and Its Female Fans* (New Brunswick, NJ: Rutgers University Press, 1989), 72–75

B I B L I O G R A P H Y

Gone with the Wind. 1936.

Margaret Mitchell's "Gone with the Wind" Letters: 1936–1949. 1976.

ANAÏS NIN

1903-1977

ANAÏS NIN was born on February 21, 1903, in Neuilly-sur-Seine, near Paris. Her mother, Rosa Culmell Nin, was a singer of Danish and French ancestry, and her father, Joaquin Nin, was a composer and musician of Catalan heritage. Both parents, however, were Cuban—and this mixture of nationality would fit neatly into Anaïs's own view of herself as a being of multiple selves. When her father left the family—a singularly devastating event for the young girl—her mother brought Anaïs and her two brothers to New York City, in 1914. Anaïs attended public schools until 1918, when she dropped out and began educating herself in the public libraries. From the age of 11, she began a diary both as a letter to her lost father and as a personal haven. The diaries were also literarily self-conscious, and in them Nin would begin to address the question of the fragmented self.

At 21, Nin married Hugh Guiler, who as Ian Hugo became known as a filmmaker, engraver, and illustrator of her books. They moved to Paris, where she remained until the outbreak of World War II. In France her literary career began with the publication of the critical work *D. H. Lawrence: An Unprofessional Study* in 1932. American author Henry Miller took an interest in the book, and with him Nin would develop a lifelong attachment that was both professional and passionate. During the 1930s she assisted Miller in the publication of his first book, *Tropic of Cancer* (1934), and he advised her on her surrealistic prose poem *House of Incest* (1936). The surrealist movement and the influence of Nin's study of psychoanalysis under Otto Rank may be detected throughout her work. Her literary and artistic circle in Paris included writers Lawrence Durrell, Antonin Artaud, and Michael Fraenkel. Many of those in her circle, however—including Durrell and Miller—objected to Nin's self-exploratory writing, which she herself considered particularly female: a writing from the womb. She would dedicate herself to this project.

Nin returned to New York City at the beginning of World War II. Unable to find a publisher for her work, she established the Gemor Press (her second such press) and, at her own expense, printed copies of her novels and short stories. *Winter of Artifice*, a collection of three novelettes, was published in 1939, followed by two collections of stories, *Under a Glass Bell* (1942) and *This Hunger* (1945), and by her first novel, *Ladders to Fire* (1946). Although they received no critical attention at the time, her works were highly regarded by many leading literary figures. Nin became friends with the young Gore Vidal, who would later write about her in his novel *Two Sisters* (1970).

Not until 1961 did all of Nin's fiction become available. She had a small following of readers for over 30 years, but only with the publication of her diaries, beginning in 1966, did she become known as a significant writer. The success of her *Diary* (1966–1980) and *Linotte* (1978), an account of her life between the ages of 11 and 17, sparked interest in her earlier work. *Cities of the Interior* (1959), Nin's most ambitious work, is a five-volume continuous novel containing her short fiction, *Ladders to Fire* (1946); *Children of the Albatross* (1947); *The Four-Chambered Heart* (1950); her most popular novel, *A Spy in the House of Love* (1954); and *Solar Barque* (1958). Nin lectured frequently after the publication of the diaries and wrote introductions to books by other authors.

Other works by Anaïs Nin are *Seduction of the Minotaur* (1961), a collection of short stories; *Collages* (1964), a collection of character portraits loosely structured as a novel; the critical works *Realism and Reality* (1946), *On Writing* (1947), *The Novel of the Future* (1968), *A Woman Speaks* (1975), and *In Favor of the Sensitive Man* (1976). *Delta of Venus: Erotica*, published posthumously in 1977, collects Nin's previously unpublished erotica written on commission during the early 1940s.

Anaïs Nin died in Los Angeles on January 14, 1977.

CRITICAL EXTRACTS

HENRY MILLER

As I write these lines Anaïs Nin has begun the fiftieth volume of her diary, the record of a twenty-year struggle towards self-realization. Still a young woman, she has produced on the side, in the midst of an intensely active life, a monumental confession which when given to the world will take its place beside the revelations of St. Augustine, Petronius, Abelard, Rousseau, Proust, and others.

Of the twenty years recorded half the time was spent in America, half in Europe. The diary is full of voyages; in fact, like life itself it might be regarded as nothing but voyage. The epic quality of it, however, is eclipsed by the metaphysical. The diary is not a journey towards the heart of darkness, in the stern Conradian sense of destiny, not a *voyage au bout de la nuit*, as with Céline, nor even a voyage to the moon in the psychological sense of escape. It is much more like a mythological voyage towards the source and fountain head of life—I might say an *astrologic* voyage of metamorphosis. ⟨. . .⟩

There is a very significant fact attached to the origin of this diary, and that is that it was begun in artistic fashion. By that I do not mean that it was done with the skill of an artist, with the conscious use of a technique; no, but it was begun as something to be read by some one else, as something to influence some one else. In that sense as an artist. Begun during the voyage to a foreign land, the diary is a silent communion with the father who has deserted her, a gift which she intends to send him from their new home, a gift of love which she hopes will re-unite them. Two days later the war breaks out. By what seems almost like a conspiracy of fate the father and child are kept apart for many years. In the legends which treat of this theme it happens, as in this case, that the meeting takes place when the daughter has come of age.

And so, in the very beginning of her diary, the child behaves precisely like the artist who, through the medium of his expression, sets about to conquer the world which has denied him. Thinking originally to woo and enchant the father by the testimony of her grief, thwarted in all her attempts to recover him, she begins little by little to regard the separation as a punishment for her own inadequacy. The difference which had marked her out as a child, and which had already brought down upon her the father's ire, becomes more accentuated. The diary becomes the confession of her inability to make herself worthy of this lost father who has become for her the very paragon of perfection.

In the very earliest pages of the diary this conflict between the old, inadequate self which was attached to the father and the budding, unknown self which she was creating manifests itself. It is a struggle between the real and the ideal, the annihilating struggle which for most people is carried on fruitlessly to the end of their lives and the significance of which they never learn. ⟨. . .⟩

One thinks inevitably of the manifestoes of the Surrealists, of their unquenchable thirst for the marvellous, and that phrase of Breton's, so significant of the dreamer, the visionary: 'we should conduct ourselves as though we were really *in the world!*' It may seem absurd to couple the utterances of the Surrealists with the writings of a child of thirteen, but there is a great deal which they have in common, and there is also a point of departure which is even more important. The pursuit of the marvellous is at bottom nothing but the sure instinct of the poet speaking, and it manifests itself everywhere in all epochs, in all conditions of life, in all forms of expression. But this marvellous pursuit of the marvellous, if not understood, can also act as a thwarting force, can become a thing of evil, crushing the individual in the toils of the Absolute. It can become as negative and destructive a force as the yearning for God. When I said a while back that the child had begun her great work in the spirit of an artist I was trying to emphasize the fact that, like the artist, the problem which beset her was to conquer the world. In the process of making herself fit to meet her father again (because to her the world was personified in the Father) she was unwittingly making herself an artist, that is, a self-dependent creature for whom a father would no longer be necessary. When she does encounter him again, after a lapse of almost twenty years, she is a full-fledged being, a creature fashioned after her own image. The meeting serves to make her realize that she has emancipated herself; more indeed, for to her amazement and dismay she also realizes that she has no more need of the one she was seeking. The significance of her heroic struggle with herself now reveals itself symbolically. That which was beyond her, which had dominated and tortured her, which *possessed* her, one might say, no longer exists. She is de-possessed and free at last to live her own life.

Throughout the diary the amazing thing is this intuitive awareness of the symbolic nature of her role. It is this which illuminates the most trivial remarks, the most trivial incidents she records. In reality there is nothing trivial throughout the whole record; everything is saturated with a purpose and significance which gradually becomes clear as the confession progresses. Similarly there is nothing chaotic about the work, although at first glance it may give that impression. The fifty volumes are crammed with human figures, incidents, voyages, books read and commented upon, reveries, metaphysical speculations, and dramas in which she is enveloped, her daily work, her preoccupation with the welfare of others, in short, with a thousand and one things which go to make up her life. It is a great pageant of the times patiently and humbly delineated by one who considered herself as nothing, by one who had almost completely effaced herself in the effort to arrive at a true understanding of life. It is in this sense again that the human document rivals the work of art, or in times such as ours, *replaces* the work of art. For, in a profound sense, this *is* the work of art which never gets written—because the artist whose task it is to create it never gets born. We have here, instead of the consciously or technically finished work (which to-day seems to us more than ever empty and illusory), the unfinished symphony which achieves consummation because each line is pregnant with a soul struggle. The conflict with the world takes place within. It matters little, for the artist's purpose, whether the world be the size of a pinhead or an incommensurable universe. *But there must be a world!* And this world, whether real or imaginary, can only be created out of despair and anguish. For the artist there is no other world. Even if it be unrecognizable, this world which is created out of sorrow and deprivation is true and vital, and eventually it expropriates the 'other' world in which the ordinary mortal lives and dies. It is the world in which the artist has his being, and it is in the revelation of his undying self that art takes its stance. Once this is apprehended there can be no question of monotony or fatigue, of chaos or irrelevance. We move amid boundless horizons in a perpetual state of awe and humility. We enter, with the author, into unknown worlds, and we share with the latter all the pain, beauty, terror and illumination which exploration entails.

—Henry Miller, "Un Etre Etoilique," *Criterion* (October 1937), excerpted in *Twentieth-Century American Literature*, ed. Harold Bloom (New York: Chelsea House Publishers, 1986), 2835–38

PAUL ROSENFELD

⟨After her father's desertion, the young Anais⟩ was in love or fancied herself in love with her father, possibly because she had received little understanding from him. His brutality profoundly shocked her. To help make the desolation of life endurable she began keeping a journal. She has told us that it was a monologue or dialogue dedicated to him, inspired by the superabundance of thoughts and feelings caused by the pain of his leaving. In her own words, "little by little she shut herself up within the walls of her diary. She talked to it, addressed it by name as though it were a living person, her own self, perhaps. . . . Only in her diary could she reveal her true self, her true feelings. What she really desired was to be left alone with her diary and her dreams of her father. In solitude she was happy."

The diary grew, persisted in the process of development. It is said actually to comprise fifty-odd sections or notebooks. Fragments which have been circulated suggest that despite monotonies it belongs to literature more thoroughly than does the famous journal of Marie Bashkirtseff. Romantic posturing, narcissistic self-portraiture seem fairly absent here. One feels the effort of truth in the face of curious reticences and obscurities. The vast congeries of prose is lyrically expressive of certain feminine, in instances almost imperceptible, feelings connected with an aesthetic world mainly that of decadent Paris; expressive even more of a feminine self-consciousness strangely enamored of the very state of feeling, yet singularly perceptive of the subliminal and marvelous. The element of the irrational, germane to all lyricism, is included in the style: it is prevalently surrealistic. Audaciously it exploits the connotative power of language while presenting the unseen through wild, often far-flung analogies. Still many of these analogies are remarkably exact: that, for example, which reveals the semi-conscious rhythmic unity of feeling between two intimates—almost on the musical level—through an image of orchestral sonorities; or that shadowing forth neurotic conflicts with the symbol of the high strain and hubbub of a giant New York hotel. Taste, indeed, remains in evidence throughout: plainly in the style's refusal, for all its periodic exaltation, to violate the genius of prose, the tone of speech, and fully commit oratory or prose-poetry.

Frequently in these years, we feel, the author must have entertained an impulse to improve on her lyrical diary in the way of unification and impersonality by recasting some of its materials in narrative shape, with herself as the center of an epical event. As frequently, we guess, she must have had moments which revealed not only the growing difference between the imago who was the recipient of her confidences and her actual father but the former's steady tendency to sublimation. Both hunches are corroborated by "Winter of Artifice," the present little volume—sensuously so attractive with its shapely typography, good ink, softly toned paper, and the delicate line drawings by Ian Hugo. With the disposition of some of the material of the journal at a certain distance from her own center of gravity, it exhibits—awkwardly at times but altogether fluently and touchingly—two of these moments of revelation. The first was incidental to her seductive parent's long-looked-for reappearance in her life. In the course of an effective portrait of him we see Joaquin Nin take her to stay in the south of France and her conception of a temporary feeling that he is the person closest to herself. Shortly the disharmony which always had existed between their ways of living grows plain. She becomes aware that she has outgrown her need of him.

The second experience reaches us in the course of an ingenious account of a psychoanalysis. We grasp the event of the partial transference to the physician of the patient's discovery of her own poles of warmth and coldness under different feminine names. We see her new enjoyment of her own body and final disinclination or inability to dissolve her early fixation and completely accept normality in the orthodox sense. The final charmingly imaginative pages tragically reidentify the fixated being who imperiously and jealously holds her allegiance in torment and bliss, in living and keeping her journal. She calls it "the dream": it wears the look of her own individuality, in which as if it were a shell she hears the murmur of life. The suspicion that from the first Anais Nin was both something of an artist and a solitary, that her *"beata solitudo, sola beatitudo"* in keeping a journal made her more of both, is inevitable. Journals famously are a resource in solitude, a means of breathing in the desert. Fatally they also are its co-creators.

—Paul Rosenfeld, "Refinements on a Journal," *The Nation* (26 September 1942): 276–77

WILLIAM CARLOS WILLIAMS

When women as writers finally get over the tendency to cut their meat so fine, really "give" out of the abundance of their unique opportunity, as women, to exploit the female in the arts, Anais Nin may well be considered to have been one of the pioneers. I speak of her new book, *The Winter of Artifice*, hand printed by herself.

It's hard to praise a book of this sort. Either you say too much and overdo it or you say too little and seem to condemn. And I want to praise. To face an accusation of artiness would be its danger and nothing in a writer is more damnable. But if there is that that seems superlative, in the use of the words, in the writing, spotted like a toad though it may be or a lily's throat—then go ahead. Make the blunder. This is a woman in her own right.

In *The Winter of Artifice*, the first of these stories, from which the general title is taken, a man is carefully, lovingly placed in his living grave by a devoted daughter. In the second, *The Voice*, a woman destroys a psycho-analyst who is rather a baby—or perhaps shrewd enough, professionally, never to fall in love with a woman he knows he can get.

This doesn't sound too good: the familiar pattern common among female writers in recent years. The mantis that takes her mate in her arms, bites an eye out then consumes him to the last whisker. Transformed to a vanished packet of eggs he will be fastened anon to the thorn of some nearby rose bush. Women enjoy this sort of thing. With Anais Nin it is a means and not an end.

Women in the arts have had many special difficulties to overcome. First it was the time lag between the general ascendancy of man as against woman to intellectual distinction, particularly in the arts. This placed woman too much on the defensive in a world lacking much that she had to offer, by which an astringency was forced upon her from which she could neither gain satisfaction nor escape. Some of them get tough and want to throw it around like men. What the hell? It's only a sort of boil anyway. Others take other means of escape. But until they recover completely from this negative combative stage they will fail to realize their full opportunity.

In these two stories of Anais Nin a titanic struggle is taking place below the surface not to succumb to just that maelstrom of hidden embitterment which engulfs so many other women as writers. I feel the struggle and find myself deeply moved by it. It's the writing itself which effects this sense of doomed love striving for emergence against great odds. It is in the words, a determination toward the most complete truth of expression, clean observation, accurately drawn edges and contours—at the best. But the characters of the story, do what they may, are drawn down. Something in the writing is not drawn down, survives.

To me the leading character of Anais Nin's first story and Lilith of the second are the same person though not spoken of as though they were, in the telling. They, as a matter of fact, complement each other: if the outcome of the first story had not been what it is the second would have missed its occasion for being. The young woman of *The Winter of Artifice* not having achieved what she set out to do, repossess the father, the development found in the second story becomes all but inevitable.

It is woman trying to emerge into a desired world, a woman trying to lift herself from a minor key of tenderness and affection to a major love in which all her potentials will find employment, qualities she senses but cannot bring into play. The age and times are against her. But if I speak of discovery here I mean that the strain, the very failures of the characters in both these stories tell of something beyond ordinary desiring. Whether Anais Nin is correct in her final analysis of what that is is something else again.

It is hard to say: the effect is, from my viewpoint, of a full vigor striving to emerge through a minor perversity. Another might read it the other way. Let it not be forgot that the girl's father of *The Winter of Artifice*, on whom she lavished her love (not forgetting that without a quiver she abandons a resourceful mother who had made a home for her during her infant years) is not destroyed willingly. The girl who has lived for him, who has welcomed him a visitor in her dreams and flies to his side at the first opportunity, puts up a real fight to rescue him from his self-destroying lies. But he will not have it. He either won't or can't come clean with her until, after a tremendous effort, she gives him up and goes her way.

What might have happened had she won? What might not have come out of the association between father and daughter, for truth, for relief from a besotted world *had* the man allowed the daughter's pure and devoted love to triumph? Light was refused, he preferred his enshrouding lies. She was the true light bringer for him but he failed to receive it. She did not falter, it was he not she who was perverse.

The second story grows out of this failure. This time it is another person but the character is about the same. Lilith releases herself to her fate and who shall say whether she or The Voice is at fault at the end. She has been conditioned in the first story, or we have, and this second is the result of it. These might easily be the two first chapters of a longer novel of great promise.

Maximum vigor lies in two strong poles between which a spark shall leap to produce equilibrium in the end. When we get a piling up at one pole without the relief the feeling is transitional. A passage from the second story, *The Voice*, will show this piling up at the negative pole: "Lilith entered Djuna's room tumultuously, throwing her little serpent skin bag on the desk, her undulating scarf on the bed, her gloves on the bookshelf, and talking with fever and excitement: . . . What softness between women. The marvelous silences of twinship. To turn and watch the rivulets of shadows between the breasts, . . . the marvelous silence of woman's thoughts, the secret and the mystery of night and woman become air, sun, water, plant . . . When you press against the body of the other you feel this joy of the roots compressed, sustained, enwrapped in its brownness with only the seeds of joy stirring . . . The back of Lilith, this soft, musical wall of flesh, the being floating in the waves of silence, enclosed by the presence of what can be touched." This is the mood and the background, a stasis, an absolute arrest. Proust is one of its triumphs. But were that all, frankly, I shouldn't bother with the book though good writing will be good writing to the end of time. To me Anais Nin carries the impetus a little further; from that undertone a new melody tries to lift itself, tries and fails in what constitutes, I believe, an upturn in the writing.

For much of the confusion and all the "mysteries" concerned in a certain pseudo-psychological profundity of style well known among women comes from a failure to recognize that there is an authentic female approach to the arts. It has been submerged, true enough; men have been far too prone to point out that all the greatest masterpieces are the work of males as well as of the male viewpoint or nearly so. Women swallow this glibly, they are the worst offenders. But the fact is, without "mystery" of any sort, that an elementary opportunity to approach the arts from a female viewpoint has been badly neglected by women. More important, without a fully developed female approach neither male nor female can properly offset each other. Am I right in presuming that Anais Nin cares a fig about that or even agrees with me in my main premise?
   —William Carlos Williams, " 'Men . . . Have No Tenderness': Anaïs Nin's *Winter of Artifice*," *New Directions in Prose and Poetry* 7 (1942): 429–32

ISAAC ROSENFELD

According to what Henry Miller and William Carlos Williams have written about her, Anais Nin is a pioneer among women writers, striking out into a new area in the experience and expression of her sex. There are two reasons why "Under a Glass Bell" fails to present evidence for this claim. The first is that a truly pioneer figure, the equivalent for the feminine sex of Daniel Boone or Natty Bumpo, will never be found. And not because the will or the temperament is lacking, but because the wilderness is lacking. There are no regions of sex where a few well equipped masculine surrealists cannot penetrate, or to which, even if women be the ultimate discoverers, Freud, D. H. Lawrence and James Joyce cannot be taken as guides. I do not deny that Djuna Barnes, for example, inhabits a unique place; she does, however, have neighbors. Literary discoveries in sex, granting their indebtedness to the work that has already been done both in modern writing and psychology, no longer come as a complete surprise, but rather, as the fulfillment of our expectations. (This, I admit, is a-priori reasoning, for I have not read Anais Nin's unpublished journals on the basis of which the above claim is made.)

The second reason why "Under a Glass Bell" does not advance Anais Nin as a pathfinder has to do with the very writing of her book. It is the sort of writing which conveys more about the author, in a general sense, than it does, specifically, about itself. There are eight short stories or sketches in her book dealing with life in a house boat on the Seine, schizophrenia, the relations between the author and a servant girl, and the experience of childbirth. There is a delicacy in all these stories which resembles the lines of the semiabstract copper engravings (by Ian Hugo) which so suitably accompany this book. There is delicacy even in "Birth," the story of a woman in labor with her dead child, her prolonged, intolerable pain resulting from her unconscious refusal to part with the child. It is the delicacy of the small scope, the needle point, confining the emotion exactly to the scale Anais Nin is working in—and naturally, it is better suited to concentration than discovery. Even the fantastic overtones she strikes in her sketches of schizophrenia, such as "Je Suis le Plus Malades des Surrealistes" and the title story, suggest an approach determined more by the conscious selection of sensibility than the instinctual imagery of sex.

What the stories in "Under a Glass Bell" do convey is a sense of craftsmanship and design, a set of values rarely imposed upon writing. Most short-story writers now practising their trade in this country are content with the ready-made design which follows the conventional beginning-middle-climax-end pattern suitable to conventional dramatic narrative. While experiments in focus, scale and design are interesting for their own sake, they turn out successfully only when the writer can make them conform to the demands of his craft. This Anais Nin has done, profiting even from the occasional lapses, like a stitch gone astray in embroidery, which appear in her work with the imperfection of an intimate product.

"Under a Glass Bell" was hand set by the author—a fact well in keeping with the non-commercial intent and quality of her writing.

—Isaac Rosenfeld, "The Eternal Feminine," *The New Republic* (17 April 1944): 541

EDMUND WILSON

The unpublished diary of Anaïs Nin has long been a legend of the literary world, but a project to have it published by subscription seems never to have come to anything, and the books that she has brought out, rather fragmentary examples of a kind of autobiographical fantasy, have been a little disappointing. She has now, however, published a small volume called *Under a Glass Bell*, which gives a better impression of her talent.

The pieces in this collection belong to a peculiar genre sometimes cultivated by the late Virginia Woolf. They are half short stories, half dreams, and they mix a sometimes exquisite poetry with a homely realistic observation. They take place in a special world, a world of feminine perception and fancy, which is all the more curious and charming for being innocently international. Miss Nin is the daughter of a Spanish musician, but has spent much of her life in France and in the United States. She writes English, but mostly about Paris, though you occasionally find yourself in other countries. There are passages in her prose which may perhaps suffer a little from an hallucinatory vein of writing which the Surrealists have overdone: a mere reeling-out of images, each of which is designed to be surprising but which, strung together, simply fatigue. In Miss Nin's case, however, the imagery does convey something and is always appropriate. The spun glass is also alive: it is the abode of a secret creature. Half woman, half childlike spirit, she shops, employ servants, wears dresses, suffers the pains of childbirth, yet is likely at any moment to be volatilized into a superterrestial being who feels things that we cannot feel.

But perhaps the main thing to say is that Miss Nin is a very good artist, as perhaps none of the literary Surrealists is. "The Mouse," "Under a Glass Bell," "Rag Time," and "Birth" are really beautiful little pieces. "These stories," says Miss Nin in a foreword, "represent the moment when many like myself had found only one answer to the suffering of the world: to dream, to tell fairy tales, to elaborate and to follow the Labyrinth of fantasy. All this I see now was the passive poet's only answer to the torments he witnessed. . . . I am in the difficult position of presenting stories which are dreams and of having to say: but now, although I give you these, I am awake!" Yet this poet has no need to apologize: her dreams reflect the torment, too.

    —Edmund Wilson, "Doubts and Dreams: *Dangling Men* and *Under a Glass Bell*," *The New Yorker* (1 April 1944): 81–82

ELIZABETH HARDWICK

⟨Anaïs Nin⟩ shuns the real world as if it had a bad reputation. This elegant snobbishness seems not designed to get her on in good society, but to allow her to sneak away to the psychological underworld revealed in the following, frightening images. "I walked pinned to a spider web of fantasies spun during the night, obstinately followed during the day. This spider web was broken by a foghorn, and by the chiming of the hours. . . . I sank into a labyrinth of silence. My feet were covered with fur, my hand with leather, my legs wrapped in accordion-pleated cotton, tied with silken whips. Reindeer fur on my breast."

A few of the short pieces in *Under a Glass Bell* are quite effective, but in all of them there is too much straining for the exotic and a pathological appetite for mystification. Miss Nin likes abstractions ("The unveiling of a woman is a delicate matter. It will not happen overnight. We are all afraid of what we shall find.") and falls without warning into an ecstasy which reminds me of nothing so much as those smalltown spiritualists who spoil their productions by undramatic impatience and go into a trace before they have taken off their hats.

The subject matter of these stories is usually the eternal feminine. On the surface there is the hint that great secrets are being revealed for the first time and yet, as the atmosphere of revelation thickens, the language becomes increasingly indirect and unsuggestive. It seems to be characteristic of women writers to "unveil" by pulling out every old veil in the trunk. The more they know about themselves and their sex the more they are, unconsciously I believe, determined to keep the faith. They set out grimly to make a speech, weaken, and end by doing a pantomime with gestures, moods, and rhythms, a sort of modern dance, which gives the illusion of having opened the bedroom door without involving the performer in a recognizable scandal. It is not the discretion that is out of place, but the implication that an innocent tea party has really been a brawl. As Jung observed, men worship Circe, a clear and realistic figure, while the women set out grandly after the Flying Dutchman. This hapless journey through space soon becomes dull, in spite of the quick, nervous energy women writers put into it. Facts, drama, and temptation are replaced by the rhetoric of enormous emotion; the scenery of passion, the garden of love, are wonderfully rendered in the elaborate, elusive style for which women are famous. It is only in the end, after the clever spell is broken, that we realize Adam and Eve have been omitted. Or were they present in disguise, perhaps speaking to us as a tree and a brook?

All of these hesitations in the woman writer's treatment of love and sexual emotion are particularly important in Anaïs Nin's work, because sex is the true object of her considerable literary devotions. And she is thoroughly feminine in that this subject, certain to assure a man's income for life, has not only made her work commercially unprofitable, but almost unreadable. The contemplation of passion and the soul of a woman leads her not to the rocks, but high up in the stratosphere, so high the mind cannot follow her curious flight.

Another bedeviling aspect of Anaïs Nin's work is the problem of the fabulous diary. This diary, unpublished so far as I know, is said to be at present in its sixty-fifth volume. At least Henry Miller has read it and his opinion goes, "When given to the world it will take its place beside the revelations of St. Augustine, Petronius, Rousseau, Proust, and others." I would not mention this private, buried work if its contents were not so often necessary to the understanding of Miss Nin's fiction. One story begins, "I was eleven years old when I walked into the labyrinth of my diary," and another ends, "The little donkey—my diary burdened with my past—with small faltering steps is walking to the market. . . ." We are told nothing about the diary, but asked to feel, by some mysterious projection, its significance and power as a dominating theme. And then, in a really extraordinary way, the undivulged contents of the diary seem to contain the meaning of a long novelette, *Winter of Artifice*, reprinted in this new collection. The tone of this story is heavy, urgent, and ominous; there is not a moment of humor, not a word of relief from its underwater agony. In it you learn vaguely that a girl has loved her father too well, though in just what way is ambiguous, but she has loved him so terribly she must be psychoanalyzed. "Her father's jealousy began with the reading of her diary." No doubt the diary fully explains the relationship and gives adequate motivation for the anguish echoed here. As it is, however, *Winter of Artifice* can only be read as a Greek chorus chanting about the most miserable of women and apparently unaware that the tragedy has been withheld from the audience.

—Elizabeth Hardwick, *Partisan Review* (June 1948), excerpted in *Twentieth-Century American Literature*, ed. Harold Bloom (New York: Chelsea House Publishers, 1986), 2834–35

VIOLET LANG

Last fall Dutton published *Children of the Albatross*, by Anais Nin, without any of the usual publisher's ballyhoo—the commercial or the avant-garde variety. This winter they republished her collected short stories together with the novelette, *Winter of Artifice* (the stories have had both an English and a private edition). It may be that we have grown able, in this country, to recognize and accept this specialized and deeply private kind of experience—the kind of experience that a Surrealist painting commands and evaluates, the kind of experience found crystallized in *Winter of Artifice*—without our old reaction of scorn or of indignation at the baffling in art: the past decade has forced us into the recognition of the internal drama.

I think some part of the hostility with which Anais Nin has been dismissed by some readers may be attributed to this betrayal of objectivity; she is *embarrassing*. She has discredited the importance of environment of place and time; her streets are alike in New York or in Paris; she has returned to the natural city. Her emphasis is upon emotional interdependence, upon creation and upon destruction, upon the familial situation. Because these written lives are not lived in the language or seen from the perspective we are accustomed to assume, in the act of recognition, we are caught unawares. This is unsettling, and we are not used to it. We have not the conventions to do so. We look for a careful balance between reality and poised mentality in our novels; we look for a habit of intelligence, an intellectual capacity, which we identify readily as insight, character, typical behavior of a familiar type. Anais Nin upsets all this; she dismays the balance; the vivid discord of this painful inner reality must rise to create its own balance, demand its own perspective.

It is possible, on the other hand, to deny that the adjustment must be made, or that participation is required of the reader; it is possible to condemn the whole, discomfiting assumption of experience by unquestionable critical principles. She can be condemned for indiscretions of plot-manipulation (which have little importance to her), for repetitions and exaggerations, too rich characterizations, or even for her overwhelming use of emotional and connotative language—but this condemnation is pointless. She is not an objective writer; she is not trying to tell a good story; she is above all not attempting to manipulate social action.

What she is trying to do, and does very well, is to interpret deep personal relationships by writing of them in those circumstances which interpret them, the moments of change, the moments of revelation, the time of terrible intensity. She does this with deep sincerity, and with humility. ⟨. . .⟩

⟨. . .⟩ It is certain that her influence has already been felt, that she has affected many young writers and will continue to do so—and that the infusion, amidst the current dried-out imitations of Faulkner and Hemingway, enriches contemporary writing here and abroad.

She is a courageous writer, never leaning on the props of humor or colloquial speech, never having to reinforce the written situation with direct allusions to place or contemporary, physical detail. Indeed, one occasionally suspects that she has no sense of humor, and wonders where she has written or lived, in what time and in what place. And bound by her sincerity as she is to the real feeling, the essential situation, she must wander by night through the dark wood of neurosis, obeying that obligation of distortion and bedevilment, approaching the moment of dread, or the moment of realization.

So it is that she has this faculty for embarrassment. With other writers, in the portrayal of the personal drama, there is the indication on the writer's part of his authority, the convention of objectivity; there is a formal affiliation possible, between the author and the reader, in the examination of the text. With Anaïs Nin this is not possible. There is no longer the framework of author, reader, people-in-a-book. The children of the albatross are living—threatening. There is no definable distance between them, the writer and the reader. These are marine characters of perilous delicacy, but they are real. Their reality exists outside of language, outside of description, dependent on the synthesis of these intense moments for the revelation of who they are.

Recognition is slow at first; then the first, familiar undertones of personality begin to merge into a whole, the whole of dream and consciousness, of spoken word and myth, of symbol and action. When it touches and at last affects, this recognition is a little frightening.

—Violet Lang, [Review of *Under a Glass Bell*], *Chicago Review* 2.4 (Spring 1948): 162–63

NANCY SCHOLAR

Anaïs Nin's greatest achievement was her multi-faceted self-portrait, contained in both her Diary and her experimental fiction. The Diary is by far her more successful literary accomplishment, especially the first two volumes which are Nin's finest works of art. Throughout the Paris Diaries, there are passages of extraordinary brilliance and perception, descriptions of psychic states of confusion and duality, dramatic scenes which captivate and delight us with their candor and charm. The spectacle of Nin's continually changing masks and roles fascinates us, as does the subtle mating dance between Nin, June, and Henry Miller. In June Miller, Nin discovers her greatest subject, her most compelling alter ego, which she also makes the basis of her most effective work of fiction, *House of Incest*.

As the pages accumulate, however, the narcissism evident in Nin's Diary from the start becomes more problematic as the author grows increasingly preoccupied with convincing herself and her readers that she is worthy of such immense attention. ⟨. . .⟩

In treading the path of her inner labyrinth, her "Inside World," Nin participated in a quest for identity and meaning which brought her into connection with the "Outside World," as she called it in adolescence. She turned herself into the modern heroine who enters the labyrinth of her life-book, as Theseus entered the Cretan labyrinth of old, prepared to struggle with the minotaur of her neurosis, of her own dark fears and desires. The monster of her own self-doubts—her right to write—was perhaps the most formidable. Nonetheless, she persisted on her circular journey despite the imposing obstacles. Her courage was not of course sustained; at times she utilized her "paper womb" as a "protective cave" in which to hide, rather than a method of self-confrontation. But her need for withdrawal and protection humanized her quest, as her interior cave brought her into relation with others, particularly her gender, so long associated with private spheres.

Many of the themes and images which haunted Nin have resonance for countless others, particularly women. Her search for identity through the looking glass and through her changing masks, her sensations of self-division, fragmentation and multiplicity are all widely shared. Perhaps most important, her conflicts and her effort to define herself as a woman artist are part of a female literary tradition. Nin's "anxiety of authorship" is almost universally shared by women writers past if not present. Her struggle between love and creation, duty and self-fulfillment, her guilt for creating and association of writing with masculinity and aggression have been widely reported. The silences which mar her work—the omission of husband and lovers from her Diary—are comprehensible in light of this tradition. Nin was born at the end of the Victorian era, subject to the same repressive forces which stifled Woolf and many more.

The defects in Nin's work cannot all, however, be eradicated from this viewpoint. Her difficulty in seeing others as well as herself without distortion or a romantic patina is an individual matter. Nin was reluctant to come to grips with the painful side of reality, with unattractive aspects of human nature, especially her own. This human enough deficiency can be fatal to an autobiographer, as can the tendency to self-idealization also apparent in the Diary. Like her father, Nin was too dazzled by her own reflection, and not fascinated enough by the infinite variety of humanity, except in the form of worthy artistic subjects to be won over, captured in her book. She tended to discount the importance of aesthetic matters in part because of her agreement with the surrealist and psychoanalytic emphasis on free association and spontaneity. As a result, her style is noticeably uneven, with passages of precision and beauty, especially in her early writing, but others that are stockpiled with nouns and adjectives which do not yield the results Nin intended. Repetitions abound in the Diary; many of the same incidents and phrases appear in the sixth Diary as in the fifth, and the same is true in *Cities of the Interior*. Nin's carelessness about syntax also undermines the integrity of her work, especially in the middle journals and the fiction.

Journal-keeping all those years may well have discouraged the full development of Nin's writing ability, as well as encouraged a satisfaction with first impressions rather than carefully crafted and reworked forms. Editing for Nin, according to her account, consisted "mostly of cutting"; the "act of rewriting" meant for her "tampering with the freshness and aliveness." Yet Nin cuts so much of the human and social context from her writing that at times it barely breathes at all. At the core of the problem is Nin's deep ambivalence about the autobiographical form. She was compelled to write from her own experience, had difficulty imagining other characters and worlds, yet she had a horror of revelations, of exposure to derision and abuse, as she imagined the consequences of such exposure to be. She hoped she would be "safe behind paper and ink and words," but the protective cloak of her writing proved all too transparent.

Nin's fiction is best appreciated in tandem with her Diary, since it is a variation on the autobiographical themes first set out in the journal. *House of Incest* is least in need of the Diary for support; it easily stands on its own as a fascinating surrealist descent into a woman's inner hell. The same is true for a handful of the stories in *Under a Glass Bell*, such as "The Labyrinth," "Birth," and "Hejda," which although derived from the Diary, have a highly wrought intensity and poetic condensation which are most effective. The first section of "Stella" is also extraordinarily compact and emotionally charged, but this novella does not fulfill the promise of the opening movement. The remainder of Nin's fiction subsequent to this point also disappoints as a whole. *Cities of the Interior* is an interesting experiment, but not a great work of art. Although it contains passages of subtlety and emotional power, overall the stylistic and

structural problems detract significantly from the effectiveness of the work. Having removed the recognizable signposts from the outer world, clearly differentiated characters or fully elaborated metaphors or themes, Nin fails to substitute a stylistic perfection which might compensate for the unsubstantiality of her text. As a stylist, Nin is undeniably flawed, but as the author of a complex, enigmatic self-portrait of great richness and charm, Nin will continue to captivate readers of the future.
—Nancy Scholar, *Anaïs Nin* (Boston: Twayne Publishers, 1984), 131–33

BIBLIOGRAPHY

D. H. Lawrence: An Unprofessional Study. 1932.
House of Incest. 1936.
Winter of Artifice. 1939.
Under a Glass Bell. 1942.
This Hunger. 1945.
Ladders to Fire. 1946.
Realism and Reality. 1946.
Children of the Albatross. 1947.
On Writing. 1947.
The Four-Chambered Heart. 1950.
A Spy in the House of Love. 1954.
Solar Barque. 1958.
Cities of the Interior. 1959.
Seduction of the Minotaur. 1961.
Collages. 1964.
The Diary of Anaïs Nin. 1966–1980.
The Novel of the Future. 1968.
A Woman Speaks: The Lectures, Seminars, and Interviews of Anaïs Nin. 1975.
In Favor of the Sensitive Man, and Other Essays. 1976.
Delta of Venus: Erotica. 1977.
Waste of Timelessness and Other Early Stories. 1977.
Linotte: The Early Diary of Anaïs Nin. 1978.
Little Birds: Erotica. 1979.
The Early Diary of Anaïs Nin. 1982–1985.
The White Blackbird and Other Writings. 1985.
Henry and June: From the Unexpurgated Diary of Anaïs Nin. 1986.
A Literate Passion: Letters of Anaïs Nin and Henry Miller. 1987.

FLANNERY O'CONNOR

1925-1964

MARY FLANNERY O'CONNOR was born on March 25, 1925, in Savannah, Georgia, the only child of Edward F. and Regina Cline O'Connor. She attended St. Vincent's Grammar School and Sacred Heart Parochial School until the family moved to Atlanta in 1938. That same year Flannery and her mother moved to Milledgeville, Georgia, where she attended Peabody High School. Her father remained in Atlanta until 1940, when he retired to Milledgeville until his death, from complications of lupus, in 1941.

After graduating from Georgia State College for Women in 1945, O'Connor attended the Writers' Workshop at the University of Iowa, receiving an M.F.A. in 1947. Her first published work, a short story titled "The Geranium," appeared in *Accent* in 1946. In 1949, O'Connor studied writing in New York City, and chapters from her first novel, *Wise Blood*, were published in *Partisan Review*. O'Connor suffered her first attack of lupus in December 1950; although the progress of the disease was slowed by the use of drugs, it would eventually kill her. In 1951, she returned to Milledgeville to a farm her mother inherited called Andalusia. She would remain there with her mother the rest of her life, living modestly, raising peafowl.

Wise Blood was published in 1952, a novel that, in O'Connor's words, examines "the religious consciousness without a religion." With the publication of *A Good Man Is Hard to Find and Other Stories* (1955) O'Connor was recognized as a master of a peculiar category of litera-ture. Her grotesque and violent stories, written "from the standpoint of Christian orthodoxy," reflect both an inclination to the absurd and what has been called "a caustic religious imagination." Her articles and book reviews, published in various academic, religious, and literary journals, reflect her broad philosophical interests.

O'Connor's last novel, *The Violent Bear It Away*, was published in 1960. Published posthumously were a collection of stories, *Everything That Rises Must Converge* (1965), and *Mystery and Manners* (1969), occa-sional prose edited by Sally and Robert Fitzgerald. A collection that includes several previously unpublished stories, *The Complete Stories of Flannery O'Connor* (1971), won the National Book Award in 1971. *The Habit of Being* (1979), a volume of O'Connor's collected letters, won the Board Award of the National Critic's Circle in 1980. Among her many other prizes, O'Connor received a Kenyon Review Fellowship for fiction in 1953; an O. Henry award second prize for her short story "The Life You Save May Be Your Own" in 1954 and another in 1955 for "A Circle of Fire"; a grant from the National Institute of Arts and Letters in 1957; first prize O. Henry awards for "Greenleaf" in 1957, for "Everything That Rises Must Converge" in 1963, and for "Revelation" in 1965; and a Ford Foundation grant in 1959.

Suffering from the debilitations of lupus, Flannery O'Connor died in Milledgeville Hospital on August 3, 1964.

CRITICAL EXTRACTS

LEWIS A. LAWSON

If the content of *Wise Blood* seems bizarre and ludicrous, the rhetoric only reinforces that appearance. Extremely incongruous images, oxymorons, and synesthesia convince us that here indeed is a strange new world. Objects are like humans and animals, human beings are like animals and insects, and animals are like human beings. But the unconventional rhetoric is not an embellishment pasted upon a basically conventional view of the world. It is indeed a warped world, one which has been likened to a Chagall painting, and the comparison of the novel to the modern painting seems especially apt for Miss O'Connor often appears to share modern painting's preoccupations. Her world frequently is that of a dream (in keeping with her topsy-turvey aesthetic, dreams are perhaps the most lucid and conventional parts of the book), with characters who transpose themselves, with aimless action endlessly performed, with bizarre mixtures of the known and the unfamiliar. Surrealistically, soda fountain chairs are "brown toad stools," trees look "as if they had on ankle-socks," and a cloud has "curls and a beard" before it becomes a bird. The physical world partakes of the strangeness which colors character and action: the sky leaks and growls, the wind slashes around the house, "making a sound like sharp knives swirling in the air," and "the sky was like a piece of thin polished silver with a dark sour-looking sun in one corner of it."

Miss O'Connor believed that it was her Catholicism which prompted her to describe the world as a bizarre and sinister dream: "My own feeling is that writers who see by the light of their Christian faith will have, in these times, the sharpest eyes for the grotesque, for the perverse, and for the unacceptable." She further thought that such a specific vantage point suggested the themes with which she worked: "I will admit to certain preoccupations that I get, I suppose, because I'm a Catholic; preoccupations with belief and with death and grace and the devil." But while belief and grace offered spiritual incentive to her writing, death and the devil offered the human terrors which make fiction remarkable. "I'm born Catholic," she said, "and death has always been brother to my imagination. I can't imagine a story that doesn't properly end in it or in its foreshadowings." Her statement is borne out by the fact that *Wise Blood* begins and ends with a memento mori: "The outline of a skull under his skin was plain and insistent" and "The outline of a skull was plain under his skin and the deep burned eye sockets seem to lead into the dark tunnel where he had disappeared."

But, for all that has been said, there may linger a suspicion that content and form are not joined in *Wise Blood*. Nearly everyone who has commented on the novel has noticed the malformed characterizations, the complete absurdity of action and event, and other features which depart from convention. Is it not, then, a farfetched story, which the author has attempted to dignify by grafting on a highly unconventional rhetoric? I think not. Given the author's many statements of her intentions, we must assume that she would have expected her work to be judged by its communicability, and would not have departed from the conventional structure and treatment of the novel, if she had thought innovations in style or absurdities in content would detract from her vision. ⟨. . .⟩

Miss O'Connor was fully conscious that her work lay within a "school of the grotesque." She made several remarks about the presence of the grotesque in her art. Though she felt that modern life has made grotesques of us all, still, she thought that too often her work was termed "grotesque" when she had no intention of achieving that response. She justified her use of it as the only mode of illusion through which she could reach her audience. I doubt that she would have attempted a rigid definition for "grotesque"; she had used the term in too many contexts. I do believe, however, that her purpose in using it can be safely stated: the grotesque for her was a form of religious hyperbole. There is always the danger than an audience not attuned to the form will misunderstand such hyperbole. That is the chance that Miss O'Connor must have felt she had to take. Certainly she was deadly serious when she used the grotesque, and its use was not merely gratuitous. Just as certainly she was not merely celebrating southern degeneracy.

Flannery O'Connor was, on the contrary, perhaps the writer of the modern Southern school most conscious of the chaotic world caused by the declining belief in older religious institutions. Thus her satire was the most desperate, for to her it was most obvious that the old order was crumbling. But she saw that the old order in religion remained a husk; therefore she had to attack those people who play out their lives within the old form without giving allegiance to it and those people who have gone over more obviously to some other allegiance. There was no place in her world for any norms; from her vantage point the entire world did look grotesque, since her audience did not recognize the normative value of faith.

> —Lewis A. Lawson, "The Perfect Deformity: *Wise Blood*," *Renascence: Essays on Values in Literature* 17, no. 2 (Spring 1965), originally entitled "Flannery O'Connor and the Grotesque: *Wise Blood*" (Catholic Renascence Society, Inc., 1964), reprinted in *Flannery O'Connor*, ed. Harold Bloom (New York: Chelsea House Publishers, 1986), 37–38

BARNABAS DAVIS

Flannery O'Connor was firmly convinced that the fiction writer with Christian concerns finds deformities in modern life which are grossly repugnant to the believer. When these incongruities are in actual fact moral aberrations, then, she believed, they should appear as such to any audience used to accepting them as commonplace. If the literary artist and his readership hold the same attitudes toward ethical values, she argued, the artist will have little trouble communicating; he may then employ a normal tone of voice, so to speak. Obviously, contemporary America did not share Miss O'Connor's vibrant faith in Christ: in this estrangement situation, she felt a different tack required. It was from this perspective that her technique evolved; she reasoned that "you have to make your vision apparent by shock, and for the almost blind you draw large and startling pictures." ⟨. . .⟩

It is really not so surprising that Miss O'Connor grasped the intrinsic connection between Christ and man's perversion through sin. What tends to startle us is that she was able to express this relationship in artistically valid terms while still quite young; no doubt it was this accomplishment that won her Mr. ⟨Evelyn⟩ Waugh's measured admiration. Man is viewed in her work at the extreme limits of his condition, in a predicament where he is fallen in nature but redeemed through grace by Christ—if he will only accept that Christ-life when proffered him.

As in Miss O'Connor's first novel, *Wise Blood*, the portrayal of this struggle is usually carried out in rural Protestant America by characters such as Hazel Motes. Although a deeply sincere individual, Motes loses his faith in Jesus as Saviour during military service; now he preaches a new redemption with his own Church of Christ without Christ. His salvation has come through technology; he preaches a redemption to be found in the good life of modern convenience from the car he uses as a pulpit. Motes is modern man exposed in full absurdity as he seeks a brand of Christianity which will not involve commitment. If he is an uncomfortable refraction from the prism of our age, it is not one of complete tragedy. Miss O'Connor was an artist rather than a cartoonist and she sketches into Motes's character the very real generosity and potential of his non-fiction counterpart. When he eventually loses his "pulpit,"

Hazel realizes God does not wish to speak to man through this kind of Christ-less Christianity. With Old Testament severity, Motes impulsively blinds himself with quicklime in a gesture of self-punishment.

Wise Blood does not contrive a plot to "get across" a religious message; even without the supernatural dimension the story is an integral piece of fictional art. And yet the higher meaning is almost unavoidable: sin is the real cause of Motes's blindness, a self-inflicted punishment for his enormous crime of substituting for Christ. Ultimately all the moral and physical deformities of Miss O'Connor's characters dramatize this theme of sin for sin.

—Barnabas Davis, "Flannery O'Connor: Christian Belief in Recent Fiction," *Listening* (August 1965), excerpted in *Twentieth-Century American Literature*, ed. Harold Bloom (New York: Chelsea House Publishers, 1987), 2866–67

WALTER SULLIVAN

The stories in *Everything That Rises Must Converge* are the last fruits of Flannery O'Connor's particular genius; and though one or two of them display an uncertainty that must have been the result of her deteriorating health, they are for the most part successful extensions of her earlier fiction. Godridden and violent—six of the nine end in something like mayhem—they work their own small counter reformation in a faithless world. Flannery O'Connor's limitations were numerous and her range was narrow: she repeated herself frequently and she ignored an impressively large spectrum of human experience. But what she did well, she did with exquisite competence: her ear for dialogue, her eye for human gestures was as good as anybody's ever were: and her vision was as clear and direct and as annoyingly precious as that of an Old Testament prophet or one of the more irascible Christian saints.

Her concern was solely with the vulgarities of this world and the perfections of the other—perfections that had to be taken on faith, for the postulations and descriptions of them in her work are at best somewhat tawdry. She wrote of man separated from the true source of his being, lost, he thinks and often hopes, to God; and of a God whose habits are strange beyond knowing, but Who gets His way in the end. That she was a Southerner and wrote about the South may have been a fortunate coincidence. The South furnished her the kind of flagrant images her theme and her style demanded, and Southern dialogue augmented and perhaps even sharpened her wit. But the South as locale and source was quite peripheral. She once wrote Robert Fitzgerald, "I would like to go to California for about two minutes to further these researches [into the ways of the vulgar]. . . . Did you see that picture of Roy Rogers' horse attending a church service in Pasadena?" Had she been born in Brooklyn or Los Angeles, the surface agonies of her work would have been

altered: perhaps they would have been weakened: but the essential delin-
eations of her fiction, the mythic impulse itself would, I believe, have been
essentially unchanged. ⟨. . .⟩

In "A Good Man Is Hard to Find," the Misfit represents the plight of man
from the beginning of Christian history to the modern age, and he sets forth
the dilemma with such blunt clarity that it cannot be misread. Jesus was truly
God or he was not: between being God and not being God there is no middle ground. If He were, then He must be followed. If He were not, then all
men are free to work out their own destinies and the terms of their own happiness for themselves. The Misfit is aware of his own helplessness. Life is a
mystery to him: the ways of fate are inscrutable: he denies flatly that he is a
good man, and he expects neither human charity nor the mercy of God. He
knows only that he does not know, and his awareness is the beginning of all
wisdom, the first step toward faith.

It is an awareness that the grandmother and the other characters in the
story do not share. "You're a good man!" she says to Red Sammy Butts, owner
of the roadside restaurant, and he readily agrees. But he is not: nor is she a
good woman: nor are Bailey or his wife or his children good. Their belief in
their own virtue is a sign of their moral blindness. In pride they have separated
themselves from God, putting their trust in modern technology: in paved
roads and automobiles (Red Sammy gave two men credit because they were
driving a Chrysler); in advertising messages along the highway and tap-danc-
ing lessons for children and in motels and pampered cats. "A Good Man Is
Hard to Find" makes clear—as does *Wise Blood*—that the characters in Flannery
O'Connor's work may not be distinguished as good or bad, or as guilty or
innocent. All are guilty; all are evil. The distinctions are between those who
know of God's mercy and those who do not, between those who think they can
save themselves, either for this life or for the next, and those who are driven,
in spite of their own failings, to do God's purpose. In the general retreat from
piety, man and the conditions under which he lives have been perverted.

It was Flannery O'Connor's contention that the strange characters who
populate her world are essentially no different from you and me. That they are
drawn more extravagantly, she would admit, but she claimed that this was
necessary because of our depravity: for the morally blind, the message of
redemption must be writ large. This is not to say that she conceived of her art
as a didactic enterprise: but rather that like all writers of all persuasions, she
wrote out of her own ontological view which remained orthodox and
Catholic, while the society in which she lived and for which she wrote became
more profane and more heretical every day. She could no sooner have stopped
writing about God than Camus could have ceased being an existentialist. She
was committed and she had to shout to be heard.

But in writing, as in all other human endeavors, one pays his money and makes his choice. He gives up something to get something, and to get the outrageously drawn, spiritually tormented character, it is necessary to sacrifice the subtlety that long fiction demands. Complex characterization is the *sine qua non* of the novel: the characters must not only have epiphanies: they must change and develop in terms of what they have done and seen. It was the nature of Flannery O'Connor's fictional vision that discovery on the part of her people was all. When one has witnessed the flaming bush or the tongues of fire or the descending dove, the change is final and absolute and whatever happens thereafter is anticlimax. This is why the characters in O'Connor's novels fade and become static and often bore us with their sameness before we are done with the book. But fulfilling their proper roles—that is of revelation, discovery—in the short stories, they are not boring and they do what they were conceived to do.

— Walter Sullivan, "Flannery O'Connor, Sin, and Grace: *Everything That Rises Must Converge*," *Hollins Critic* (September 1965), excerpted in *Twentieth-Century American Literature*, ed. Harold Bloom (New York: Chelsea House Publishers, 1987), 2871–72

JOYCE CAROL OATES

Paradoxically, the way into O'Connor's vision that is least ambiguous is through a story that has not received much attention, "The Lame Shall Enter First." This fifty-seven-page story is a reworking of the nuclear fable of *The Violent Bear It Away* and, since O'Connor explored the tensions between the personalities of the Rationalist-Liberal and the object of his charity at such length in the novel, she is free to move swiftly and bluntly here. "We are accustomed to consider," says Teilhard ⟨de Chardin⟩ in a discussion of the energies of love "Beyond the Collective," "only the sentimental face of love. . . ." In "The Lame Shall Enter First" it is this sentimental love that brings disaster to the would-be Savior, Sheppard. He is a young, white-haired City Recreational Director who, on Saturdays, works as a counselor at a boys' reformatory; since his wife's death he has moved out of their bedroom and lives an ascetic, repressed life, refusing even to fully acknowledge his love for his son. Befriending the crippled, exasperating Rufus Johnson, Sheppard further neglects his own son, Norton, and is forced to realize that his entire conception of himself has been hypocritical. O'Connor undergoes the religious nature of his experience by calling it a *revelation:* Sheppard hears his own voice "as if it were the voice of his accuser." Though he closes his eyes against the revelation, he cannot elude it:

> His heart contracted with a repulsion for himself so clear and so
> intense that he gasped for breath. He had stuffed his own emptiness

> with good works like a glutton. He had ignored his own child to feed
> his vision of himself. He saw the clear-eyed Devil, the sounder of
> hearts, leering at him. . . . His image of himself shrivelled until every-
> thing was black before him. He sat there paralyzed, aghast.

Sheppard then wakes from his trance and runs to his son, but, even as he hurries to the boy, he imagines Norton's face "transformed; the image of his salvation; all light," and the reader sees that even at this dramatic point Sheppard is deluded. It is still *his* salvation he desires, *his* experience of the transformation of his son's misery into joy. Therefore it is poetically just that his change of heart leads to nothing, to no joyous reconciliation. He rushes up to the boy's room and discovers that Norton has hanged himself.

The boy's soul has been "launched . . . into space"; like Bishop of *The Violent Bear It Away* he is a victim of the tensions between two ways of life, two warring visions. In the image of Christ there is something "mad" and "stinking" and catastrophic, at least in a secularized civilization; in the liberal, manipulative humanitarianism of the modern world there is that "clear-eyed Devil" that cuts through all bonds, all mystery, all "psychical convergence" that cannot be reduced to simplistic sociological formulas. It is innocence that is destroyed. The well-intentioned Savior, Sheppard, has acted only to fill his own vacuity; his failure as a true father results in his son's suicide.

He had stuffed his own emptiness with good works like a glutton.

Perhaps this is O'Connor's judgment, blunt and final, upon our civilization. ⟨. . .⟩ What is difficult, perhaps, is to see how the humanitarian impulse—when it is not spiritual—is an egoistic activity. O'Connor's imagination is like Dostoevsky's: politically reactionary, but spiritually fierce, combative, revolutionary. If the liberal, atheistic, man-centered society of modern times is dedicated to manipulating others in order to "save" them, to transform them into flattering images of their own egos, then there is no love involved—there is no true merging of selves, but only a manipulative aggression. This kind of love is deadly, because it believes itself to be selfless; it is the sudden joy of the intellectual Julian, in the story "Everything That Rises Must Converge," when he sees that his mother is about to be humiliated by a black woman who is wearing the same outrageously ugly hat his mother has bought—"His grin hardened until it said to her as plainly as if he were saying aloud: Your punishment exactly fits your pettiness. This should teach you a permanent lesson." The lesson his mother gets, however, is fatal: the permanence of death.

"He thinks he's Jesus Christ!" the club-footed juvenile delinquent, Rufus Johnson, exclaims of Sheppard. He thinks he is divine, when in fact he is empty; he tries to stuff himself with what he believes to be good works, in order to disguise the terrifying face of his own emptiness. For O'Connor *this* is the gravest sin. Her madmen, thieves, misfits, and murderers commit crimes of a secular nature, against other men; they are not so sinful as the criminals who attempt to usurp the role of the divine. In Kafka's words, "they . . . attempted to realize the happiness of mankind without the aid of grace." It is an erecting of the Tower of Babel upon the finite, earthly Wall of China: a ludicrous act of folly.

> —Joyce Carol Oates, "The Visionary Art of Flannery O'Connor," *Southern Humanities Review* 7, no. 3 (Summer 1973), reprinted in *Flannery O'Connor*, ed. Harold Bloom (New York: Chelsea House Publishers, 1986), 44–46

REBECCA R. BUTLER

When Flannery O'Connor was asked why the story about the grisly family murder, "A Good Man Is Hard to Find," appeared to be her favorite, she corrected that impression: She chose that story for her public reading engagements, she explained, not because of a special preference for it, but because, she said, it was the only one she could get through out loud without laughing.

Now, if any of you have ever studied or taught that particular O'Connor short story, you may agree with the author that it is entirely possible to read right through it without once being incapacitated by laughter. I know myself that I can keep a perfectly straight face as I read of the children and their mother being marched off into the woods at gunpoint, followed by the sounds of shots. And when the grandmother calls out to the Misfit, "'You're one of my own children!'" and he shoots her three times in the chest, I don't even smile. On the other hand, I think it would take some practice for me to maintain a deadpan throughout the grandmother's story of her youthful suitor, Mr. Edgar Atkins Teagarden from Jasper, Georgia, whose love-token, a watermelon carved with his initials, E. A. T., and left on the front porch, was eaten by an evidently literate "nigger boy." Similarly, the repartee between the grandmother and her saucy granddaughter, June Star, and the entire episode at Red Sammy Butts' barbecue house do give rise to laughter. To explain just how and why this story, which ends with the grandmother dead in a pool of her own blood, can be called comic is risky. E. B. White gives this warning to would-be analysts of comedy: "Humor can be dissected," he wrote, "as a frog can, but the thing dies in the process and the innards are discouraging to any but the pure scientific mind." O'Connor herself used the same image in voicing a similar complaint about the fate of her stories: "Every time a story of mine appears in a freshman anthology," she said, "I have a vision of it, with its little organs laid open, like a frog in a bottle." So it seems that, as an investigator of the comic, I face two alternatives: to step aside now or to proceed with caution. I will take the second route, using as my guide Louis Rubin, himself a masterful analyst of the American comic tradition who, in his Preface to *The Comic Imagination in American Literature*, acknowledged that "writing *about* humor and humorists" is necessarily "an awkward business" which always risks making the analyst look ridiculous. But he went right ahead and wrote, adhering to the principle that understanding heightens enjoyment.

Despite O'Connor's implication that many of her stories were too funny for her to read before an audience, some critics have failed to see the humor in the O'Connor canon. ⟨. . .⟩

It is not unusual to be tone-deaf when encountering a new style. My own students, I know, are sometimes unable to see anything comic in Manley Pointer's theft and desertion of Joy-Hulga in "Good Country People," nor do they always laugh at Mrs. Crater's sly campaign to marry her not-entirely-eligible only daughter, Lucynell, to Mr. Shiftlet. For critics to be so unappreciative, however, is disappointing. The students, after all, know little of the stylistics of comedy, and they are only beginning to develop their imaginative "ears." For the benefit of the student or any reader new to O'Connor's fiction, a relatively brief tuning-up period is in order. First on the checklist are titles: occasionally the title will sound a bit peculiar or zany itself, like "The Artificial Nigger" or "You Can't Be Any Poorer Than Dead." More often the title gains comic momentum as it recurs in the story, the way "A Good Man Is Hard to Find," a familiar song title, does as it reappears as a hackneyed expression in Red Sammy Butt's conversation, and is repeated with a twist by the Misfit who, by his own admission is not a good man, but would like to be able to verify the reported goodness of Jesus. "The Life You Save May Be Your Own" was actually the winning slogan in a contest sponsored by the Department of Public Safety during the early 1950's when highway deaths were on the rise. The phrase is particularly appropriate for Mr. Shiftlet, being, as it is, a direct descendant of Simon Suggs' motto: "It is good to be shifty in a new country." The second benchmark, applicable in any comic work, is the name of any character or place. Why name a con artist Manley Pointer, or Hoover Shoats for that matter, if your aim is a primarily sober one? And we have already mentioned Red Sammy Butts, an ideal name for a buffoon-host. Although all of O'Connor's names are actually well-known in certain Southern regions, usually they are uncommon; they seem to be chosen for their suggestiveness or their sound effect: Hooten, Parrum, Turpin, Cheatham, Godhigh, Farebrother, Ham, Block, Fox, Pitts. Place names work in a similar fashion: Taulkinham, Eastrod, Toombsboro, Timberboro, Partridge. And there are the ladies with three names, for some reason always good for a laugh: Sally Poker Sash, Lucynell Crater, Sarah Ruth Cates. In "The Displaced Person," Mrs. McIntyre's litany of worthless tenants suggests a recital of the plagues of Egypt: there were the Shortleys, Ringfields, Collinses, Garrits, Jarrells, Perkinses, Pinkins, and Herrins. From the same story, the unpronounceable Guizac is rendered "Gobblehook" by Mrs. Shortley, who also says that she'd as soon call a child Bollweevil as Sledgewig. Such films as "The Displaced Person," televised by the Public Broadcasting System as part of its American Short Story series, demonstrate a third way to overcome quickly the handicap of "wooden ear" which can strike any of us upon encountering a new writer. Because a dramatization allows us to see and hear the characters in action, the imaginative ear does not have to bear the burden of interpretation alone. Furthermore, I have seen illuminating dramatizations of "A Good Man Is Hard to Find," "A View of the Woods," and "Revelation." The rhythm and lilt of O'Connor's dialogue, for instance, can enter through the ear rather than be interpreted on the silent page. This can be especially important to a reader who is not native to the South. Perhaps you remember this little speech by Mr. Shortley, the dairyman whose position is threatened by a new tenant, a refugee from Poland, Mr. Guizac:

> "All men was created free and equal," he said to Mrs. McIntyre, "and I risked my life and limb to prove it. Gone over there and fought and bled and died and come back over here and find out who's got my job—just exactly who I been fighting. It was a hand-grenade come that near to killing me and I seen who throwed it—little man with eye-glasses just like his. Might have bought them at the same store. Small world," and he gave a bitter little laugh. He had the power of making other people see his logic. He talked a good deal to the Negroes.

Comic dialogue is, of course, O'Connor's specialty ⟨. . . .⟩

Now there's one other element of O'Connor's fiction that perhaps cannot be analyzed and explained as readily as the first three items on our checklist, but it cannot be ignored, and that is the sense of threat, of danger, of violence that, in some form, permeates all of her stories. It is a commonplace, of course, that all accomplished comedy contains or rests upon some deeply serious or horrifyingly repugnant reality. While the underlying seriousness of O'Connor's humour is relatively obvious, a simple definition will not do it justice. I am not convinced that this Southern woman, for example, was evangelizing through her fiction. I have found a comment by E. B. White on this topic that sounds so much like something she would have written that I will let it serve. White does not agree with those who say that the humorist is fundamentally a very sad person. ". . . [I]t would be more accurate, I think," he writes, "to say that there is a deep vein of melancholy running through everyone's life and that the humorist, more sensible of it than some others, compensates for it actively and positively. Humorists fatten on trouble. They have always made trouble pay.

They struggle along with a good will and endure pain cheerfully, knowing how well it will serve them in the sweet by and by." And serve it does! It serves as an antidote to that mind-dulling sentimentality O'Connor attacked at every opportunity. Again and again in her occasional prose we find this word, *sentimentality*, used as a scourge against mindless Catholic readers, mindless critics, mindless writers. A similar favorite phrase was "hazy compassion," and she described one of her reader's affection for the Misfit as "sentimental." In her resistance to heart-warming and uplifting characterization, O'Connor is adhering to one of Comedy's oldest purposes—that of dispelling illusion. Sentimentality, as represented by the Grandmother and quite a number of upright matrons, is a self-deceit that O'Connor shock tactics are designed to expose. A sentimental comedy, of course, would contain no murders, no abandonments, no strokes, no handicaps nor illnesses of a disfiguring nature. No wooden legs, no coffins too small for the body, no cans of peanut brittle filled with teeth-fracturing springs, no women pregnant in iron lungs, no wheel chair veterans left in the sun beside the Coke machine. The "paraphernalia of suffering," as Nathanael West called it, serves as unlikely fodder for this "realist of distances," as O'Connor called herself.

—Rebecca R. Butler, "What's So Funny about Flannery O'Connor?" (1979), *Flannery O'Connor Bulletin* (Autumn 1980), excerpted in *Twentieth-Century American Literature*, ed. Harold Bloom (New York: Chelsea House Publishers, 1987), 2876–77

ANDRÉ BLEIKASTEN

What is it that startles and shocks us in reading a story like "Parker's Back"? Obviously, its most arresting feature, the one most likely to disturb a modern reader, is Parker's *tattooing*. The more surprising it is that in most discussions of the story it should have been given so little consideration. To be sure, all commentators refer to it, vaguely puzzled and perhaps even a bit disgusted (tattooing, in our "civilized" countries, has come to be considered an "unnatural" practice, associated with either savagery or deviant behavior), yet, in their eagerness to convert it at once into a secular metaphor for Parker's supposed spiritual quest, they tend to overlook its complex and shifting implications in the story of his development.

Parker's obsession with tattoos, we are told, begins when he is fourteen (in many cultures the canonical age for initiation) and sees a circus performer tattooed from head to foot, "flexing his muscles so that the arabesque of men and beasts and flowers on his skin appeared to have a subtle motion of its own." The youth is at once fascinated by the spectacle and undergoes a kind of illumination, after which the course of his existence will take a radically different turn:

> Parker had never before felt the least motion of wonder in himself. Until he saw the man at the fair, it did not enter his head that there was anything out of the ordinary about the fact that he existed. Even then it did not enter his head, but a peculiar unease settled in him. It was as if a blind boy had been turned so gently in a different direction that he did not know his destination had been changed. (513)

O'Connor here emphasizes—rather heavily, as she is often prone to do—the turning-point the experience at the country fair represents in Parker's destiny, and the reader is clearly "programmed" to see it not only as the beginning of a new life of "unease" and unrest, but also as a prefiguration of Parker's later conversion. One might see it too, however, less spiritually and more psychologically, as the beginning of an "identity crisis," a period of psychic disturbance taking Parker to the verge of madness. And what seems to be at stake in this crisis is above all his *body*.

No sooner has Parker seen the tattooed man than he identifies with him. Yet, strictly speaking, there is no identification with a person (the man is watched from a distance, and will never be more to him than a remembered object of vision). What enthralls Parker is a body or, more precisely, a body *image*, the seductive spectacle of a pattern engraved on a human skin. The word "pattern" could not be more apropos, referring as it does to either an ornamental design or a model worthy of imitation. To Parker it is clearly both. Henceforth he will not rest until he has equalled his model, driven on by the compulsion to collect tattoos on his own body, to have his whole skin covered with them, to become in turn a pattern made flesh. Each new tattoo, however, only leads to further frustration:

> Parker would be satisfied with each tattoo about a month, then something about it that had attracted him would wear off. Whenever a decent-sized mirror was available, he would get in front of it and study his overall look. The effect was not of one intricate arabesque of colors but of something haphazard and botched. (514)

At this point, anyone familiar with Jacques Lacan's writings will be reminded of that decisive moment in the constitution of the ego which he designates by the name of "mirror stage" (*stade du miroir*). According to Lacan, that moment normally occurs between six and eighteen months, when the child comes to recognize his or her own image in the mirror, and thereby anticipates his future acquisition and mastery of the bodily integrity which he still lacks. What Parker goes through during his encounter with the tattooed man is like a replay of that infantile experience: it is the unexpected meeting of a mirror self, the discovery of an ideal double. The man, as Parker sees him, is "one intricate arabesque of colors"; he has managed, that is, to achieve unity, integrity, and harmony, by making his body into an artifact, a work of art, and so comes quite naturally to serve as paradigm to Parker's own imaginarily anticipated metamorphosis. A boy, up to then, "whose mouth habitually hung open" (513), he could hardly be credited with a self of his own. The sight of the tattooed man startles him out of his drooling stupor into awareness of a body not yet totally his, a body to be appropriated and made whole and beautiful. An "awakening" has indeed occurred, but not in any spiritual sense, as Parker's exclusive concern, once he has had his "revelation," is the individuation of his body through systematic adornment of his skin. His enthrallment with the tattooed man points to nothing else but his late awakening to the exorbitant demands of narcissism. ⟨. . .⟩

The half-comic, half-pathetic ending of "Parker's Back" may well leave the reader puzzling whether, after all, he has not been treated to a stark and savage travesty à la Nathanael West, rather than to an edifying religious fable. For all overt symbols and authorial intrusions, ambiguity doggedly persists to the story's very end, and the contradictions and tensions that give it life are not dissolved. Perhaps they also remained unresolved in the author, and it is indeed tempting to read O'Connor's text as well as an almost autobiographical parable, in which are raised in analogical fashion some of the questions she had herself to face as artist and believer. Was the image, the representation of the sacred not also *her* problem? The writer deals in words, not in images, yet good writers have always been credited with "imagination," and whoever writes fiction attempts to make words into images, to move from the abstract mediacy of language to the vivid immediacy of the actual, and to render, as Joseph Conrad put it, "the highest kind of justice to the visible universe." As to O'Connor, she wanted moreover to render the highest kind of justice to the invisible universe, to reconcile, as the Byzantine artists had done, the aesthetic with the religious. Yet, alert as she was to all manifestations of evil, she must have sensed from the outset that artistic activity is never quite innocent, that it is always potentially guilty, especially when it takes over and turns into an exclusive passion. Art springs from a refusal of life *as given*. And so does tattooing, which is perhaps one of the most elementary and most archaic forms taken by the aesthetic impulse. The urge to adorn one's body reflects dissatisfaction with one's body in its natural state, as a mere given, a random and transient fragment of the world. As we have pointed out, Parker's tattooing rage, at least in its early phase, has no other source: he rejects his given body, even as he rejects his given name, because he wishes to become the sovereign shaper of his own gorgeous self. This wish is surely also the artist's, the writer's, and Parker, therefore, should be seen, not only as one of O'Connor's preacher figures, but also as an artist figure, and probably even as a comically distorted projection of the writer. Which is to say that tattooing in "Parker's Back" is as well a metaphor of writing, a metaphor the more relevant as its tenor and vehicle are indeed homologous: as tattooing is to the flesh, writing is to the blank page, to the ground of writing, and in both cases the move is from blankness to inscription, from undifferentiated and senseless matter to an "arabesque" of signs expanding into a unique individual blazon, a signature that cannot be mistaken for any other. Writing, in the last resort, is perhaps little more than an elaborate and displaced form of tattooing, a sublimation of the tattooed body into the *corpus*, tomb and temple of the written self.

This it certainly also was for Flannery O'Connor. As any true writer, she did her best to recover through her writing a unity and permanence of being she was unable to achieve in life. Hers was, as we know, a short one, soon ravaged by disease and overshadowed by the certainty of an untimely death. At twenty-five she knew that she would not live long, but long enough to suffer, long enough to witness her physical deterioration and watch the progress of her illness to its fatal end. How bravely she put up with her fate is evidenced by her letters, none of which shows the slightest trace of self-pity. What her letters also attest to is that her courage was sustained throughout by her faith and her work. To wonder which was the more important to her would be idle speculation, yet the extraordinary energy and stubbornness with which she clung to writing, and did so to the very last, leave no doubt about the impassioned intensity of her devotion to art. Writing was her "no" to despair, her "no" to death, the erasure of her diseased, disfigured and slowly dying body and the production, in its stead, of a "well-wrought urn" that would endure. Or, to reuse the central metaphor of "Parker's Back," she added tattoo after tattoo, hoping that in the end they would cohere into a beautiful design. And where Parker, her ultimate fictional double, her brother in suffering, failed, she did indeed succeed. Her grotesques and arabesques have not paled. They are as fresh, as mysterious, and as compelling as ever, and insofar as the reader is *impressed*, he becomes in turn the writer's posthumous second skin.

—André Bleikasten, "Writing on the Flesh: Tattoos and Taboos in 'Parker's Back,'" *Southern Literary Journal* (Spring 1982), excerpted in *Twentieth-Century American Literature*, ed. Harold Bloom (New York: Chelsea House Publishers, 1987), 2884, 2886

FREDERICK ASALS

⟨"A View of the Woods" is⟩ perhaps, of all O'Connor's stories, the one that most overtly makes use of the double motif. In her own terse words, "Mary Fortune and the old man [are] images of each other but opposite in the end" (*The Habit of Being*). For this metamorphosis of an apparent replica into a genuine alter ego, the pivot on which the action turns is the process of denial. Like a number of her other protagonists, seventy-nine-year-old Mark Fortune tries to reject the finality of his own death, in this case by "insur[ing] the future." Aware that the family over which he exercises an absolute despotism is "waiting impatiently for the day when they could put him in a hole eight feet deep and cover him up with dirt," he has attempted to perpetuate himself indefinitely in two ways. First, he has so dedicated himself to material progress that he expects the town being built mostly on his former property to be called Fortune, Georgia (his present project, in which a machine digs a hole out of the soft clay, is his symbolic resistance to that other and final hole). Second, he has trained his favorite granddaughter and heiress, Mary Fortune, to be in every way another edition of him. "A View of the Woods" presents what happens when these two schemes for self-perpetuation suddenly come into conflict.

The opening pages of the story repeatedly stress Mr. Fortune's awareness of the remarkable resemblance his granddaughter bears to him. Not only is she physically "a small replica of the old man," but "she was like him on the inside too. She had, to a singular degree, his intelligence, his strong will, and his push and drive." Despite the difference in their ages, "the spiritual distance between them was slight." All of this is a source of great satisfaction to the old man, who politely ignores the fact that Mary Fortune bears the family name Pitts and habitually speaks of the Pittses as if they are some tribe foreign to the two of them. "He liked to think of her," O'Connor writes, "as being thoroughly of his clay," made, presumably, of the same stuff as the rest of his property. And insofar as clay suggests his earth-bound vision, he seems to be right. Bearing "his unmistakable likeness," the child at first appears a precise copy of her grandfather, a clone that has unaccountably skipped a generation.

But it emerges that Mr. Fortune detects in her "one failure of character," which to him means "one point in which she did not resemble him." When her father summons Mary Fortune outside for a whipping, Mr. Fortune sees on her face a look "foreign" to it—a look, that is, that he cannot recognize as one he would be capable of—"part terror and part respect and part something else, something very like cooperation." When he berates the child for her submission, he cannot understand her ritualistic denial, "nobody's ever beaten me in my life and if anybody did, I'd kill him," although he dimly sees that these episodes are "Pitts's revenge on him," Pitts's indirect retaliation for the cruel power the old man holds over him. Nonetheless, this one flaw in an otherwise perfect child—perfect, of course, in her resemblance to him—remains for Mr. Fortune "an ugly mystery."

That flaw becomes the fissure that widens between them when Mary Fortune unexpectedly opposes his scheme to sell off the field in front of their house, a growing division in which the use of names, and thus of identity, is the central weapon. 〈. . . As〉 she stubbornly sets herself against the projected sale, he finds himself telling her, "You act more like a Pitts than a Fortune," his lowest insult and one he immediately regrets. Nevertheless, she perseveres in her resistance until he is driven to confront her:

> "Are you a Fortune," he said, "or are you a Pitts? Make up your mind."
> Her voice was loud and positive and belligerent.
> "I'm Mary—Fortune—Pitts," she said.
> "Well I," he shouted, "am PURE Fortune!"

The trumping of her claim to mixed identity is a challenge that she answers with physical violence, and when she momentarily bests him in their fight, as "pale identical eye looked into pale identical eye," she informs him, "You been whipped . . . by me . . . and I'm PURE Pitts." Enraged that "the face that was his own . . . had dared to call itself Pitts," with a surge of fury the old man crushes her head against a rock, saying, "There's not an ounce of Pitts in me."

It is an idle and self-defeating boast. Beneath the varieties of pride and family loyalty conveyed in the manipulations of these names, the very words themselves suggest irreconcilable values. *Fortune* proclaims the Faustian self— an identity dramatized in the old man's pact with the snakelike Tillman—the assertion of the egoistic seeker of power, self-inflating and self-aggrandizing, devotee of the ancient bitch-goddess of this world, projecting himself infinitely through time, "gorging" himself on earthly "clay." *Pitts*, however, expresses a knowledge that is biblical rather than Faustian: the Psalmist's pit of powerlessness and suffering, of pain, loss, and worldly defeat, from which opens an appalling glimpse of the bottomless pit and the inescapable awareness of that earthly pit to which we all go. Thus when Mary Fortune confronts her grandfather with his own image and labels it Pitts, the old man finds this alter ego intolerable precisely because 〈. . .〉 it is true. It is Mr. Fortune, after all, who has had the momentary vision of the woods full of blood, wounds, and "hellish red trunks"; it is Mr. Fortune who has been so challenged by the child's opposition that he has repeatedly had to marshal his "principles" to carry on with the sale; it is Mr. Fortune whose unacknowledged terror of his own obliteration lies behind both his many property deals and his attempts to view the child as merely another edition of himself. And Mary Fortune has just given him a taste of the Pitts condition, attacking him "like a pack of small demons" until he "began to roll like a man on fire." No wonder "he seemed to see his own face coming to bite him," for the child here enacts not the replica of the worldly successful Fortune but the revolt of the buried self, the despised Pitts.

Paradoxically, at the moment she defeats him and identifies herself as "PURE Pitts," she has never been more Fortune-like in her position of power, while he has been forced into the subjugated posture of the humbled Pittses. But so unyielding is the old man's refusal to accept the Pitts within that he *must* reverse their roles, even at the expense of her life. "There's not an ounce of Pitts in me" is only the last of his many denials, the final rejection of a dimension of himself and of existence that his ravenous ego will not acknowledge. The battle has a wryly ironic upshot, for in his frenzy to erase the Pitts from his own identity, Mr. Fortune has not insured the future but destroyed it, thereby presumably delivering into the hands of the despised Pittses all his worldly clay. In devoting himself to the material kingdoms of the world—"the Whore of Babylon," Mary Fortune has humorously but pertinently called him—he has lost them all except the one impossible to escape, the pit where there squats his genuine replica, the mechanical "monster . . . as stationary as he was, gorging itself on clay."

—Frederick Asals, "The Double," *Flannery O'Connor: The Imagination of Extremity* (University of Georgia Press, 1982), reprinted in *Flannery O'Connor*, ed. Harold Bloom (New York: Chelsea House Publishers, 1986), 96–99

RONALD SCHLEIFER

"The problem of the novelist who wishes to write about a man's encounter with this God," O'Connor has written, "is how he shall make the experience—which is both natural and supernatural—understandable, and credible, to his reader." This is O'Connor's literary problem, to make the Sacred literal in a world in which it seems at best metaphorical, originating in a mode of perception rather than in the created world. Her problem, then, is the problem of the Gothic. Perhaps the best place to see her struggling with the problem is in one of her less successful stories, one that comes close to parodying the more powerful expressions of her repeated theme and plot, "An Enduring Chill." This story relates the return to rural Georgia from New York of Asbury Fox. Asbury, a twenty-five-year-old man, had gone to New York to become a literary artist, but now he is returning home to his mother without having written anything because he finds himself dying. Asbury is one of the characters in O'Connor's work—Hulga in "Good Country People," Julien in "Everything That Rises," Calhoun in "The Partridge Festival" are others—who has come to believe in nothing but himself and his own powers of perception. He, like the others, wants to teach his mother a lesson before he dies, to teach her of a realm beyond what he calls "her literal mind" of larger, sophisticated, metaphorical values. Thus on earlier visits home he had smoked and drunk warm milk with the Negro workers in his mother's dairy farm in order to shock her out of her complacencies. His mother, like so many other characters in O'Connor, lives in a self-satisfied, cliché-ridden world, a world where the metaphors of cliché are never examined at all. Asbury, like Hulga and Julien, participates in the egocentric life of his mother even while he is unaware of it: his mode of shocking her is to face her with the reality of his own dying, to counter her mindless optimism with his own brand of mindless, melodramatic pessimism. He wants her to understand the meaning—the metaphorical significance—of his death. To open her eyes he has left her a letter to be opened after his approaching death:

> If reading it would be painful to her, writing it had sometimes been unbearable to him—for in order to face her, he had had to face himself. "I came here to escape the slave's atmosphere of home," he had written, "to find freedom, to liberate my imagination, to take it like a hawk from its cage and set it 'whirling off into the widening gyre' (Yeats) and what did I find? It was incapable of flight. It was some bird you had domesticated, sitting huffy in its pen, refusing to come out!" The next words were underscored twice. "I have no imagination. I have no talent. I can't create. I have nothing but the desire for these things. Why didn't you kill that too? Woman, why did you pinion me?"

Asbury's language, with its incessant "I's," is as egocentric as that of any character in O'Connor's stories. He fails to "face himself" in his letter because he himself is simply a cliché—of a writer and a son. He can only speak of himself in the tired metaphors of "freedom" and "birds," and his "desires" are projections of himself rather than desires for things in the world. He even misquotes Yeats in order to humanize Yeats's metaphor for the presence of inhuman powers and to make it the narrated description of his own imagination.

Nevertheless, the act of "facing oneself" is the recurrent action of O'Connor's stories, the action of Gothic romance. Perhaps the most striking example of this is that of O. E. Parker in "Parker's Back," who literally "faces" his own back with a giant tattoo of Jesus, the eyes of which "continued to look at him—still, straight, all-demanding, enclosed in silence." This is a representative Gothic gesture: to make the metaphorical literal. Gothic romance does this, as Todorov and others have shown, by narrating dream and nightmare as reality and projecting our deepest impulses and fears onto the landscape. The face on Parker's back—its "all-demanding" eyes—made Parker feel "that his dissatisfaction was gone, but he felt not quite like himself. It was as if he were himself but a stranger to himself, driving into a new country though everything he saw was familiar to him, even the night." Such a feeling—a feeling that the reader is never sure Asbury achieves or not, hence the relative failure of "An Enduring Chill"—is what Freud calls the "uncanny," "that class of terrifying which leads back to something long known to us, once very familiar"; "the uncanny," Freud says, "would always be that in which one does not know where one is, as it were." The uncanny is familiar and strange, just as Parker is both familiar and strange to himself with God's constant eyes literally *upon* him, and he is in a country in which he is both native and alien.

> —Ronald Schleifer, "Rural Gothic," *Modern Fiction Studies* 28, no. 3 (Autumn 1982), originally entitled "Rural Gothic: The Stories of Flannery O'Connor" (West Lafayette, IN: Purdue Research Foundation, 1982), reprinted in *Flannery O'Connor*, ed. Harold Bloom (New York: Chelsea House Publishers, 1986), 85–86

MADISON JONES

Flannery O'Connor's "A Good Man Is Hard to Find" has been for the past decade or more a subject of virtually countless critical readings. Any brilliant work of fiction resists a single interpretation acceptable to everyone, but judging by the variousness and irreconcilability of so many readings of "A Good Man" one might conclude, as R. V. Cassill does, that like the work of Kafka the story "may not be susceptible to exhaustive rational analysis." The suggestion, I believe, would be quite apt if applied to a good many O'Connor stories. Not this one, however. ⟨. . .⟩

The Misfit is introduced at the very beginning of the story by the grandmother who is using the threat of him, an escaped convict and killer, as a means of getting her own way with her son Bailey. After this the Misfit waits unmentioned in the wings until the portrait of this representative family is complete. His physical entrance into the story, a hardly acceptable coincidence in terms of purely realistic fiction, is in O'Connor's spiritual economy—which determines her technique—like a step in a train of logic. Inert until now, he is nevertheless the conclusion always implicit in the life of the family. Now events produce him in all his terror.

The Misfit comes on the scene of the family's accident in a car that looks like a hearse. The description of his person, generally that of the sinister redneck of folklore, focuses on a single feature: the silver-rimmed spectacles that give him a scholarly look. This is a clue and a rather pointed one. A scholar is someone who seeks to know the nature of reality and a scholar is what the Misfit was born to be. As the Misfit tells the grandmother:

> "My daddy said I was a different breed of dog from my brothers and sisters. 'You know,' Daddy said, 'it's some can live their whole life without asking about it and it's others has to know why it is, and this boy is one of the latters. He's going to be into everything!'"

And in the course of his life he has been into everything:

> "I was a gospel singer for a while," the Misfit said. "I been most every-
> thing. Been in the arm service, both land and sea, at home and
> abroad, been twict married, been an undertaker, been with the rail-
> roads, plowed Mother Earth, been in a tornado, seen a man burnt
> alive oncet," . . . "I even seen a woman flogged," he said.

Life and death, land and sea, war and peace, he has seen it all. And his conclusion, based on his exhaustive experience of the world, is that we are indeed
in the "terrible predicament" against which Bailey, who is about to be mur-
dered for no cause, hysterically cries out. "Nobody realizes what this is," Bailey
says, but he is wrong. The Misfit knows what it is: a universal condition of
meaningless suffering, of punishment that has no intelligible relationship to
wrongs done by the victim. ⟨. . .⟩

What has driven the Misfit to his homicidal condition is his powerful but
frustrated instinct for meaning and justice. It may be inferred that this same
instinct is what has produced his tormenting thoughts about Christ raising the
dead, making justice where there is none. If only he could have been there
when it happened, then he could have believed.

> "I wisht I could have been there," he said, hitting the ground with his
> fist. "It ain't right I wasn't there because if I had of been there I would
> of known. Listen lady," he said in a high voice, "if I had of been there
> I would have known and I wouldn't be like I am now."

It is torment to think of what might have been, that under other circumstances
he would have been able to believe and so escape from the self he has become.
In light of this it is possible to read the Misfit's obscure statement that Jesus
"throwed everything off balance," as meaning this: that it would have been
better, for the world's peace and his own, if no haunting doubt about the awful
inevitability of man's condition ever had been introduced. In any case it could
only be that doubt has made its contribution to the blighting of the Misfit's
soul.

But doubts like this are not enough to alter the Misfit's vision. In the modern manner he believes what he can see with his eyes only, and his eyes have
a terrible rigor. It is this rigor that puts him at such a distance from the grandmother who is one of the multitude "that can live their whole life without ask-
ing about it," that spend their lives immersed in a world of platitudes which
they have never once stopped to scrutinize. This, his distinction from the vulgarians whom the grandmother represents, his honesty, is the source of the
Misfit's pride. It is why, when the grandmother calls him a "good" man, he
answers: "Nome, I ain't a good man," . . . "but I ain't the worst in the world neither." And it is sufficient reason for the violent response that causes him so

suddenly and unexpectedly to shoot the grandmother. Here is what happens, beginning with the grandmother's murmured words to the Misfit:

> "Why, you're one of my babies. You're one of my own children." She reached out and touched him on the shoulder. The Misfit sprang back as if a snake had bitten him and shot her three times through the chest.

Given the Misfit's image of himself, her words and her touching, blessing him, amount to intolerable insult, for hereby she includes him among the world's family of vulgarians. One of her children, her kind, indeed!

This reason for the Misfit's action is, I believe, quite sufficient to explain it, even though Flannery O'Connor, discussing the story in *Mystery and Manners*, implies a different explanation. The grandmother's words to the Misfit and her touching him, O'Connor says, are a gesture representing the intrusion of a moment of grace. So moved, the grandmother recognizes her responsibility for this man and the deep kinship between them. O'Connor goes on to say that perhaps in time to come the Misfit's memory of the grandmother's gesture will become painful enough to turn him into the prophet he was meant to be. Seen this way, through the author's eyes, we must infer an explanation other than my own for the Misfit's action. This explanation would envision the Misfit's sudden violence as caused by his dismayed recognition of the presence in the grandmother of a phenomenon impossible to reconcile with his own view of what is real. Thus the Misfit's act can be seen as a striking out in defense of a version of reality to whose logic he has so appallingly committed himself.

Faced with mutually exclusive interpretations of a fictional event, a reader must accept the evidence of the text in preference to the testimonial of the author. And where the text offers a realistic explanation as opposed to one based on the supernatural, a reader must find the former the more persuasive. If the two are in fact mutually exclusive. And if, of course, it is true that the acceptability of the author's explanation does in fact depend upon the reader's belief in the supernatural. As to this second condition, it is a measure of O'Connor's great gift that the story offers a collateral basis for understanding grace that is naturalistic in character. This grace may be spelled in lower case letters but the fictional consequence is the same. For sudden insight is quite within the purview of rationalistic psychology, provided only that there are intelligible grounds for it. And such grounds are present in the story. They are implicit in the logic that connects the grandmother and the Misfit, that makes of the Misfit "one of my own children." In the hysteria caused by the imminence of her death, which strips her of those banalities by which she has lived, the grandmother quite believably discovers this connection. And so with the terms of the Misfit's sudden violence. His own tormenting doubt, figured in those preceding moments when he cries out and hits the ground, has prepared him. Supernatural grace or not, the Misfit in this moment sees it as such, and strikes.

These two, the author's and my own, are quite different explanations of the Misfit's sudden violence. Either, I believe, is reasonable, though surely the nod should go to the one that more enriches the story's theme. *If* the two are mutually exclusive. I believe, however, that they are not. Such a mixture of motives, in which self-doubt and offended pride both participate, should put no strain on the reader's imagination. And seen together each one may give additional dimension to the story.

—Madison Jones, "A Good Man's Predicament," *Southern Review* (October 1984), excerpted in *Twentieth-Century American Literature*, ed. Harold Bloom (New York: Chelsea House Publishers, 1987), 2887–88

BIBLIOGRAPHY

Wise Blood. 1952.
A Good Man Is Hard to Find and Other Stories. 1955.
The Violent Bear It Away. 1960.
Everything That Rises Must Converge. Eds. Sally and Robert Fitzgerald. 1965.
Mystery and Manners: Occasional Prose. Eds. Sally and Robert Fitzgerald. 1969.
The Complete Stories of Flannery O'Connor. 1971.
The Habit of Being: Letters of Flannery O'Connor. 1979.

DOROTHY PARKER

1893-1967

DOROTHY ROTHSCHILD was born August 22, 1893, in West End, New Jersey. Her father, J. Henry Rothschild, was a prosperous New York haberdasher; her mother, Eliza A. Marston Rothschild, a Scottish Presbyterian, died shortly after Dorothy's birth. Dorothy attended Catholic and mostly Protestant schools but largely educated herself. In 1913, she joined the staff of *Vogue*, writing captions for fashion illustrations, but by 1915 she had moved to the more sophisticated and satirical *Vanity Fair*, which published her first prose work, "Why I Haven't Married," as well as captions for drawings, several essays, and free verse she called "Hate Songs." Dorothy did in fact marry (Edwin Pond Parker in 1917); but she would divorce him in 1928.

Increasingly famous for her wit, acerbic criticism, and seemingly glib poems of suicide, Parker was fired from *Vanity Fair* in 1920. She joined *Ainslee's* as drama critic and, during the next three years, published poems, literary criticism, and essays in *Life*, *Saturday Evening Post*, and *Ladies' Home Journal*. Her first published story, "Such a Pretty Little Picture," an interior monologue, appeared in *Smart Set* in 1922. One of Parker's best short stories, "Mr. Durant," about an abortion, appeared in *American Mercury* two years later, and at the same time a chapter from her novel *Bobbed Hair* was published in *Collier's*. She then turned to film, completing *Business Is Business* with George S. Kaufman. She was as an editor of the first issue of *The New Yorker* in 1925 and later, as the magazine's book editor, became famous for her column "Constant Reader."

Very much part of the literary scene and a member of a set of social literati called the Algonquin Round Table, Parker met Ernest Hemingway in 1926 and accompanied him and others to France. There she was introduced to the expatriate world, meeting Archibald MacLeish, Gilbert Seldes, and Scott and Zelda Fitzgerald. A volume of her poems, *Enough Rope*, was published the same year. In 1929, Parker won an O. Henry Memorial Prize for "Big Blonde," a powerful and well-crafted story that was in many ways autobiographical. She continued publishing prolifically: a collection of short stories, *Laments for the Living* (1930); a collection of poems, *Death and Taxes* (1931); another story collection, *After Such Pleasures* (1933); and articles and stories in *Harper's Bazaar*, *The New Yorker*, *Vanity Fair*, and *Cosmopolitan*.

Parker married actor Alan Campbell in 1933 and collaborated with him on dialogue and screenplays, but she disliked writing for films. She began drinking heavily and made several attempts at suicide. She returned to New York in 1936 and published *Not So Deep as a Well*, a collection of poems that went through five printings. Parker and Campbell continued to work as a team, and in 1937 their screenplay for *A Star Is Born* was nominated for an Academy Award. They completed *The Little Foxes* in 1941, and in 1942 Parker collaborated on the original screenplay for Alfred Hitchcock's *Saboteur*. Other work includes *Smash-Up—The Story of a Woman* (1947); *The Fan* (1949); a play, *The Coast of Illyria* (1949); and her last drama, *The Ladies of the Corridor* (1953), in collaboration with Arnaud D'Usseau.

As early as 1927, Parker began devoting time to radical causes. She protested against the execution of Sacco and Vanzetti, supported an Actors' Equity strike, and, as "Constant Reader," criticized Mussolini and Fascism. She declared herself a Communist in 1934 and, with Dashiell Hammett and Lillian Hellman, helped organize the powerful Screen Writers Guild. Parker was a founder of the Anti-Nazi League in 1936, organized to bring writers out of Germany and to alert Americans to the threat of Hitler. In 1937, she reported on the Loyalist cause from Spain for *The New Masses* and wrote "Soldiers of the Republic" for *The New Yorker*.

Parker won the Marjorie Peabody Waite Award for fiction and poetry in 1958 and was inducted into the American Academy of Arts and Letters. She was found dead of a heart attack in her New York apartment on June 7, 1967.

CRITICAL EXTRACTS

ALEXANDER WOOLLCOTT

Mrs. Parker's published work does not bulk large. But most of it has been pure gold and the five winnowed volumes on her shelf—three of poetry, two of prose—are so potent a distillation of nectar and wormwood, of ambrosia and deadly nightshade, as might suggest to the rest of us that we all write far too much. 〈. . .〉

〈. . . For〉 the most part, Mrs. Parker writes only when she feels like it or, rather, when she cannot think up a reason not to. Thus once I found her in hospital typing away lugubriously. She had given her address as Bed-pan Alley, and represented herself as writing her way out. There was the hospital bill to pay before she dared get well, and downtown an unpaid hotel bill was malignantly lying in wait for her. Indeed, at the preceding Yuletide, while the rest of us were all hanging up our stockings, she had contented herself with hanging up the hotel.

Tiptoeing now down the hospital corridor, I found her hard at work. Because of posterity and her creditors, I was loath to intrude, but she, being entranced at any interruption, greeted me from her cot of pain, waved me to a chair, offered me a cigarette, and rang a bell. I wondered if this could possibly be for drinks. "No," she said sadly, "it is supposed to fetch the night nurse, so I ring it whenever I want an hour of uninterrupted privacy."

Thus, by the pinch of want, are extracted from her the poems, the stories, and criticisms which have delighted everyone except those about whom they were written. There was, at one time, much talk of a novel to be called, I think, *The Events Leading Up to the Tragedy*, and indeed her publisher, having made a visit of investigation to the villa where she was staying at Antibes, reported happily that she had a great stack of manuscript already finished. He did say she was shy about letting him see it. This was because that stack of alleged manuscript consisted largely of undestroyed carbons of old articles of hers, padded out with letters from her many friends.

Then she once wrote a play with Elmer Rice. It was called *Close Harmony*, and thanks to a number of circumstances over most of which she had no control, it ran only four weeks. On the fourth Wednesday she wired Benchley: "CLOSE HARMONY DID A COOL NINETY DOLLARS AT THE MATINEE STOP ASK THE BOYS IN THE BACK ROOM WHAT THEY WILL HAVE."

The outward social manner of Dorothy Parker is one calculated to confuse the unwary and unnerve even those most addicted to the incomparable boon of her company. You see, she is so odd a blend of Little Nell and Lady Macbeth. It is not so much the familiar phenomenon of a hand of steel in a velvet glove as a lacy sleeve with a bottle of vitriol concealed in its folds. She has the gentlest, most disarming demeanor of anyone I know. Don't you remember sweet Alice, Ben Bolt? Sweet Alice wept with delight, as I recall, when you gave her a smile, and if memory serves, trembled with fear at your frown. Well, compared with Dorothy Parker, Sweet Alice was a roughshod bully, trampling down all opposition. But Mrs. Parker carries—as everyone is uneasily aware—a dirk which knows no brother and mighty few sisters. "I was so terribly glad to see you," she murmurs to a departing guest. "Do let me call you up sometime, won't you, please?" And adds, when this dear chum is out of hearing, "That woman speaks eighteen languages, and can't say No in any of them." Then I remember her comment on one friend who had lamed herself while in London. It was Mrs. Parker who voiced the suspicion that this poor lady had injured herself while sliding down a barrister. And there was that wholesale libel on a Yale prom. If all the girls attending it were laid end to end, Mrs. Parker said, she wouldn't be at all surprised.

Mostly, as I now recall these cases of simple assault, they have been mut-
tered out of the corner of her mouth while, to the onlooker out of hearing, she
seemed all smiles and loving-kindness. For as she herself has said (when not
quite up to par), a girl's best friend is her mutter. ⟨. . .⟩

It should be added that that inveterate dislike of her fellow creatures
which characterizes so many of Mrs. Parker's utterances is confined to the
human race. All other animals have her enthusiastic support. It is only fair to
her eventual biographer to tip him off that there is also a strong tinge of autobiography in that sketch of hers about a lady growing tearful in a speak-easy
because her elevator man would be stuffy if she should pick up a stray horse
and try to bring him to her apartment.

⟨. . .⟩ Woodrow Wilson was, I think, the name of the dog at the end of her
leash when I first knew her. This poor creature had a distressing malady. Mrs.
Parker issued bulletins about his health—confidential bulletins, tinged with
skepticism. He *said* he got it from a lamp post.

Of her birds, I remember only an untidy canary whom she named Onan
for reasons which will not escape those who know their Scriptures. And then
there were the two alligators which she found in her taxi, where someone had
been shrewd enough to abandon them. Mrs. Parker brought them home and
thoughtfully lodged them in the bathtub. When she returned to her flat that
night, she found that her dusky handmaiden had quit, leaving a note on the
table which read as follows: "I will not be back. I cannot work in a house where
there are alligators. I would have told you this before, but I didn't suppose the
question would ever come up."

Well, I had thought here to attempt, if not a portrait, then at least a dirty
thumb-nail sketch, but I find I have done little more than run around in circles
quoting Mrs. Parker. I know a good many circles where, by doing just that,
one can gain quite a reputation as a wit. *One* can? Several can. Indeed, several
I know do.

—Alexander Woollcott, "Our Mrs. Parker" (1933), *While Rome Burns* (1934), excerpted in
Twentieth-Century American Literature, ed. Harold Bloom (New York: Chelsea House Publishers,
1987), 3037–38

EDMUND WILSON

Rereading Dorothy Parker ⟨. . .⟩ has affected me, rather unexpectedly, with an
attack of nostalgia. Her poems do seem a little dated. At their best, they are
witty light verse, but when they try to be something more serious, they tend
to become a kind of dilution of A. E. Housman and Edna Millay. Her prose,
however, is still alive. It seems to me as sharp and funny as in the years when
it was first coming out. If Ring Lardner outlasts our day, as I do not doubt he
will, it is possible that Dorothy Parker will, too.

But the thing that I have particularly felt is the difference between the general tone, the psychological and literary atmosphere of the period—the twenties and the earlier thirties—when most of these pieces of Mrs. Parker's were written, and the atmosphere of the present time. It was suddenly brought home to me how much freer people were—in their emotion, in their ideas and in expressing themselves. ⟨. . .⟩

It is a relief and a reassurance, in reading her soliloquies and dialogues—her straight short stories, which are sometimes sentimental, do not always wear quite so well—to realize how recklessly clever it used to be possible for people to be, and how personal and how direct. All her books had funereal titles, but the eye was always wide open and the tongue always quick to retort. Even those titles were sardonic exclamations on the part of an individual at the idea of her own demise. The idea of the death of a society had not yet begun working on people to paralyze their response to experience.

⟨. . .⟩ It seems to me, though I shall name no names, that it has been one of the features of this later time that it produces imitation books. There are things of which one cannot really say that they are either good books or bad books; they are really not books at all. When one has bought them, one has only got paper and print. When one has bought Dorothy Parker, however, one has really got a book. She is not Emily Brontë or Jane Austen, but she has been at some pains to write well, and she has put into what she has written a voice, a state of mind, an era, a few moments of human experience that nobody else has conveyed.

—Edmund Wilson, "A Toast and a Tear for Dorothy Parker" (1944), *Classics and Commercials* (1950), excerpted in *Twentieth-Century American Literature*, ed. Harold Bloom (New York: Chelsea House Publishers, 1987), 3035–36

JAMES GRAY

It is a little startling to realize that Dorothy Parker, even while she lives and continues to write (now and then), has achieved the kind of celebrity that belongs only to a few very great writers, like the contributors to the Bible, Shakespeare, and Alexander Pope. That is to say, Mrs. Parker is the sort of person who is always suspected of being the author of a famous, but elusive, quotation.

Whenever one is asked to identify a ringing line notable for its frightening sagacity, one automatically risks the guess that it must be from the Bible. When such a quotation bowls along competently in iambic pentameter, the ear whispers to the mind that surely this must be Shakespeare. If the point of a saying tinkles out its passage in a rhyming couplet, one draws a deep breath of relief and says, Alexander Pope. But if wisdom puts on a wry-lipped smile and expresses itself with a startling aptitude that rocks the mind momentarily out of its usual mood of somnolent acceptance, one blinks and says, Dorothy Parker.

There cannot be much doubt about it now. Dorothy Parker is one of the few writers of our time who is destined for immortality. It is nice for us who have always cherished her gift to know that in centuries to come she will represent the sad, cocky, impudent mood of our tragic era. Waking from our graves five hundred years from now, we shall be pleased to see Dorothy Parker strolling Olympus, perhaps in the company of Marguerite of Navarre and Madame de Sévigné. Proudly we shall say, "We knew her when she was just a quick-witted girl who kidded around with Robert Benchley and wrote pieces for the *New Yorker*."

—James Gray, "A Dream of Unfair Women," *On Second Thought* (1946), excerpted in *Twentieth-Century American Literature*, ed. Harold Bloom (New York: Chelsea House Publishers, 1987), 3036

BRENDAN GILL

Readers coming to Mrs. Parker for the first time may find it as hard to understand the high place she held in the literary world of forty or fifty years ago as to understand the critical disregard into which she subsequently fell. The first precaution for such readers is to bear in mind the fact that the so-called world that gave her her reputation was really only a province, and, like all provinces, it considered itself much bigger and more important than it was. Its arbiters did well to praise Mrs. Parker, but she was a better writer than they took her for, and the difference between who she was and who they supposed she was held considerable risks for her. Not the least of these risks was the likelihood that when her champions came to be swept away into the dustbin, she, too, would be swept away. The small literary set that centered on New York in the twenties and thirties and that hailed Mrs. Parker as one of its leading lights was made up largely of second- and third-raters. Mrs. Parker perceived this in her middle years and passed judgment on her old colleagues with the acerbity of one who has been overpraised by people unfit to offer either praise or blame. She *was* one of their leading lights; to be that, she might have said, it would have sufficed to be a glowworm. She pointed out that the major American writers of the period had not been members of any set ⟨. . . .⟩ Hemingway, Faulkner, Lardner, Fitzgerald, Dos Passos, Cather, Crane, and O'Neill were not to be found cracking jokes and singing each other's praises or waspishly stinging each other into tantrums on West 44th Street. ⟨. . .⟩

Mrs. Parker's reputation suffered from the literary company she kept; it suffered also from the fact that the milieu that was her natural subject matter—the narrow sector of American society that could be summed up as Eastern, urban, intellectual, and middle class—underwent a sudden and overwhelming change during the Depression. The people Mrs. Parker had kept under close scrutiny and about whom she had written with authority seemed so remote from the realities of the post-Depression period as to be stamped, for a time, with a kind of retroactive invalidity. In the forties and fifties they simply did not matter any more, and the reading public was tempted to conclude, mistakenly, that they ought never to have mattered. Little by little over the years, the period and the people who gave it its character have recovered importance. By now we find it worth while to make an effort to apprehend them fairly, according to the tone and temper of their day, and in order to do so we turn with relish to Mrs. Parker.

No doubt it will strike young readers as odd, but the twenties in which Mrs. Parker began work were considered an era of extreme and perhaps dangerous permissiveness, especially in regard to the social experiments being carried out by women. Drinking, smoking, sniffing cocaine, bobbing one's hair, dancing the Charleston, necking, getting "caught"—it was hard to imagine that things could go much farther before civilization itself broke down. The young women who set the pace were called sophisticated, though few of them were; their shocking motto was "Anything goes," and they meant it. New York was their noisy Sodom, and Mrs. Parker's verse gave glimpses of the license to be met with there and its heavy cost in terms of one's emotions. These verses, which became something of a national rage, were thought to be strong stuff: brusque, bitter, and unwomanly in their presumed cynicism. They gave the average reader an impression of going recklessly far in asserting a woman's equal rights inside a sexual relationship, including the right of infidelity. The verses do not seem brusque, bitter, and unwomanly today; moreover, the verses that at the time of their first publication appealed to readers as the real thing, full of a pain of loss splendidly borne, are the ones likeliest now to set our teeth on edge, as being tainted with a glib gallantry every bit as false as the revolting cuddly high spirits of Mrs. Parker's literary mortal enemy, A. A. Milne. ⟨. . .⟩

⟨. . .⟩ In 1944, in the course of reviewing the first edition of this book ⟨The Portable Dorothy Parker⟩, ⟨Edmund⟩ Wilson wrote in The New Yorker that, while he found Mrs. Parker's poems a little dated, her prose seemed to him as sharp and funny as in the years when it was first coming out. Again, a sensible judgment, worth quoting after almost thirty years. If it is easier to visit the world of the twenties and thirties through Mrs. Parker's short stories and soliloquies than through her verse, it is also more rewarding; to a startling degree, they have a substance, a solidity, that the poems do little to prepare us for. Not the least hint of the Round Table is detectable in the stories—no sassy showing off, no making a leg at the reader. The author keeps her distance, and sometimes it is a distance great enough to remind one of Flaubert. She has written her tales with grave care and given them a surface as hard and smooth as stone, and there is no need for her to flutter about in the foreground and call attention to her cleverness. We perceive from one sentence to the next that we are in the hands of a skilled and confident guide and that each story can be marched through from beginning to end without our stumbling into uncertain or gratuitous asides. One has only to sample the superlatively self-assured opening sentences of two or three of the stories:

> He was a very good-looking young man indeed, shaped to be annoyed.

> If the Bains had striven for years, they could have been no more successful in making their living-room into a small but admirably complete museum of objects suggesting strain, discomfort, or the tomb.

> The woman with the pink velvet poppies twined round the assisted gold of her hair . . .

The force of that "assisted," slipped so unobtrusively into the text, is like a hammer-blow. The opening paragraph of her late story, "The Lovely Leave," displays the Parker style at its simplest and best; not a word amiss:

> Her husband had telephoned her by long distance to tell her about the leave. She had not expected the call, and she had no words arranged. She threw away whole seconds explaining her surprise at hearing him, and reporting that it was raining hard in New York, and asking was it terribly hot where he was. He had stopped her to say, look, he didn't have time to talk long; and he had told her quickly that his squadron was to be moved to another field the next week and on the way he would have twenty-four hours' leave. It was difficult for her to hear. Behind his voice came a jagged chorus of young male voices, all crying the syllable "Hey!"

At the time she was writing them, Mrs. Parker's soliloquies caused a great stir among her readers and especially among her fellow writers. These soliloquies were like star turns by an acrobat working up at the top of the tent without a net, and part of the pleasure they gave lay in the reader's wondering how she could possibly bring off a feat so difficult. Like most feats of this order, they were made to look easy by the person performing them—what did they consist of, after all, but an unidentified woman nattering away to herself as a succession of thoughts tumbled helter-skelter across her consciousness?—but it soon turned out that, simple as the principle of the feats was, mastery of it was next to impossible; Mrs. Parker had few imitators. One of the more celebrated of her soliloquies was "The Telephone Call," which began:

> Please, God, let him telephone me now. Dear God, let him call me now. I won't ask anything else of You, truly I won't. It isn't very much to ask. It would be so little to You, God, such a little, little thing. Only let him telephone now. Please, God. Please, please, please.

Another was called "The Little Hours" and began:

> Now what's this? What's the object of all this darkness all over me? They haven't gone and buried me alive while my back was turned, have they? Ah, now would you think they'd do a thing like that! Oh, no, I know what it is. I'm awake. That's it. I've waked up in the middle of the night. Well, isn't that nice. Isn't that simply ideal.

In Wilson's review of the first edition of the Portable, he drew a contrast between the twenties and the forties that was notably unfavorable to the latter ⟨. . . .⟩ We are indeed in possession of a favorable climate for writing, and this may be one of the reasons that many of us are more powerfully drawn to the twenties than the usual processes of nostalgia would account for. A very deep and wide gulf separates us from those years, but we do not feel in the least estranged from them, as we do from the forties and fifties—sharper than ever to us are the lineaments of the writers we admire as we look back upon them over half a century. It is not surprising that we choose for good companions Fitzgerald, Lardner, Hemingway, and the other boys in the back room, nor is it surprising that there should pop up among them, glass in hand, hat askew, her well-bred voice full of soft apologies, the droll, tiny figure of Mrs. Parker.

—Brendan Gill, "Introduction" to *The Portable Dorothy Parker* (1973), excerpted in *Twentieth-Century American Literature*, ed. Harold Bloom (New York: Chelsea House Publishers, 1987), 3039–41

KATHY MACDERMOTT

In the 1920s the comic anti-realist position was characteristic of a group of writers of what has been called both literate humor and light humor, writers who found a reliable market for their work after the founding of the *New Yorker* in 1925—among them Dorothy Parker, Robert Benchley and S. J. Perelman. ⟨. . . They⟩ were prepared to regard realism as Literature; ⟨. . . they⟩ were prepared to displace the realist claim to be referential by emphasizing instead the transformative strategies of Art: style and the fictionalizing devices of plot, characterization and setting. Mainly they wrote essays—for the *New Yorker* at first, and formatively, but for other periodicals and even anthologies. They delivered reviews, observations "about town", pieces on the state of the arts—but these essays were always turning into vignettes and staying that way. That is to say, the expository function of the essay gets caught up in the forms of fiction and the text turns out to be ultimately about itself and its narrative strategies. This process is inscribed in the work of Dorothy Parker, who as "Constant Reader" reviewed for the *New Yorker* intermittently for six years, from 1927 to 1933. In Parker's reviews even direct literary judgments are suspended between connotation and denotation. That is, cultural and critical issues are posed in such a way as to refer back to their writer and their writing at least as much as outward to any external referent:

> Now *The Sun Also Rises* was as "starkly" written as Mr Hemingway's short stories; it dealt with subjects as "unpleasant." Why it should have been taken to the slightly damp bosom of the public while the (as it seems to me) superb *In Our Time* should have been disregarded will always be a puzzle to me. As I see it—I knew this conversation would get back to me sooner or later, preferably sooner—Mr Hemingway's style, this prose stripped to its firm young bones, is far more effective, far more moving, in the short story than in the novel. He is, to me, the greatest living writer of short stories; he is, also to me, not the greatest living novelist.

Constant Reader delights in raising the subject of herself—delights so clearly and so often that her self is transformed into a caricature, a convention in the process of defining itself. Even the Hemingway of this review is defined, repeatedly, by his effect on Constant Reader. Constant Reader's tendency to slip into broadly autobiographical gestures is symptomatic of literate humor's displacement of the satirist-reviewer by the raconteur-narrator. And that in turn is symptomatic of a shift, exhibited here in "The Short Story, Through a Couple of The Ages," away from referring to narrating and from reference to intertextuality:

> I read about bored and pampered wives who were right on the verge of eloping with slender-fingered, quizzical-eyed artists, but did not. I read of young suburban couples, caught up in the fast set about them, driven to separation by their false, nervous life, and restored to each other by the opportune illness of their baby. I read tales proving that Polak servant-girls have their feelings, too . . .
> And then I found that I was sluggish upon awakening in the morning, spots appeared before my eyes, and my friends shunned me. I also found that I was reading the same stories over and over, month

after month. So I stopped, like that. It is only an old wives' tale that you have to taper off.

Anti-realist comedy is characterized by a keen nose for clichés, which it recovers and exhibits to the reader with their formulaic ends foremost. In this way anti-realism directly asserts its distance from simple escapist or sensationalist writing while nevertheless drawing on the latter for materials and motifs. This means that the actual relationship between anti-realist comedy and the clichés it cites is not simply parodic or satiric. In the passage just quoted Constant Reader indeed satires clichés of plot in the first paragraph but then directly proceeds to anthologize clichés of style in the second—the style in this case being that of the advertisement in general and the radio advertisement in particular. The overall function of clichés here, then, is simply to textualize the subject under discussion, to remove it from referentiality, to turn it into Art. "Bored and pampered housewives" ceases, that is, to denote a group of people and suggests instead a literary prop, its new referent "bad stories I have read." Such anti-realist texts are ultimately bound to signify, more or less explicitly, "this is not-Life" ⟨. . . .⟩

—Kathy MacDermott, "Light Humor and the Dark Underside of Wish Fulfillment: Conservative Anti-realism," *Studies in Popular Culture* 10, no. 2 (1987): 39–41

ARTHUR F. KINNEY

Dorothy Rothschild Parker met Alexander Woollcott in 1919 when his love of desserts took him into the Algonquin Hotel for Frank Case's lunchtime delicacies, and her co-worker on *Vanity Fair*, Robert Benchley, introduced them. From the beginning, their friendship grew with a kind of instinctive, intimate solidarity: she found in his capacious energies, his love of parties, his incurable sociability and his verbal dexterity much that had come to be herself. "He has," she wrote in a *Vanity Fair* portrait she called "A Valentine for Mr. Woollcott," "between seven and eight hundred intimate friends, with all of whom he converses only in terms of atrocious insult. It is not, it is true, a mark of his affection if he insults you once or twice; but if he addresses you outrageously all the time, then you know you're in. . . . He is at the same time the busiest man I know and the most leisured. He even has time for the dear lost arts—letter-writing and conversation. . . . Alexander Woollcott's enthusiasm is his trademark; you know that never he has written a piece strained through boredom." He was, in fact, the only one who dared—and dared successfully—to call the half-Jewish Parker "Sheeny." She would not have tolerated this from anyone else.

Yet it is not difficult to see what brought these two together, however improbable the friendship might first appear between the pretty, popular woman and the ostentatious, idiosyncratic man. For they were both, despite their gregariousness, essentially lonely: highly sensitive, vulnerable, defensive. Effectively orphaned by their families, both had been fighting to establish themselves through their natural talents at writing in the hard, brash days of personal American journalism. They both had the knack for repartee, becoming two of the most publicized members of the Algonquin Round Table, the "vicious circle" of wits that F.P.A. (Franklin P. Adams) kept praising in his citations and quotations in the New York *World*. Fundamentally estranged from others and addicted to the theater, they both watched life as a spectacle others played; and both made their livings at the time as drama critics—Parker for *Vanity Fair* (succeeding P. G. Wodehouse) and later *The New Yorker* (substituting for the vacationing Robert Benchley), and Woollcott for *The New York Times*. Both developed a flashy, capsule kind of criticism, a sort of fashionable journalism notable for its personal prejudices and friendships, and both revealed streaks of sentimentality even when they tried hardest to hide it. They both became self-conscious about themselves and their careers, and self-styled in their performances of wit. They were both given to fits of depression as well as manic moments of joy; still, they thought of themselves as sophisticated, and this seemed confirmed when Harold Ross asked both of them to become advisory editors when he founded *The New Yorker* as the journal of urban culture in the summer of 1925. What these previously unpublished letters from Parker introduce, then, is not so much a flippant set of observations that seem resonant of F. Scott Fitzgerald's flappers but, more deeply, more tellingly, a language of shared insecurities only verbally buried in a vibrant slang.

Parker's first extant letter to Woollcott, written sometime in 1926, captures the buoyancy of the times and the artificiality of their apparently careless but actually carefully groomed style. Parker was then in the midst of her affair with Seward Collins, heir to a national chain of tobacco stores and editor of *The Bookman*, and had sailed to Europe with him (and with Ernest Hemingway and Donald Ogden Stewart and his wife). When her relationship with Collins became strained, she left him to stay with Gerald and Sara Murphy on the Riviera, although the Stewarts had just introduced her to them.

> *Villa America*
> *Cap d'Antibes*
> *A.M.*

> Dear Alec, so I thought you would like to know about the Murphy children's dog. It was a sort of joint dog, a present to all three of them. Naturally, there was a desparate [sic] time about finding a

name that was truly worthy of him, on account of the width of the field. They finally narrowed that by deciding that they would call him after the thing they liked best in all the world. Days passed, because new yearnings and old memories kept coming up and causing argument. But eventually they reached an agreement. The dog's name is Asparagus.

Young Baoth Murphy, who has gone in for poultry, did me the greatest honor of my life; he named a chicken Dorothy, after me. The christening was done, so to say, blind, and Dorothy has since turned out to be a rooster. But, as Baoth so well says, "What is that of difference?"

These opening sentences—both Parker and Woollcott are given to narrative as a form of communication—show how Parker could at once become a part of her day's jet set while standing deliberately outside, apart; the delicate balance is between an anxious involvement and a rueful sense of isolation.

It is entirely too lovely here now, and a person would be a fool to be any place else. All the younger sexual set has gone, and the weather is glorious—except the past few days, which have been given over to the equinox, making the water far too rough and full of currents for my purposes. Gerald Murphy, however, persists in his morning swim around the point of the Garoupe, so I think we can all look forward to a Smart Drowning any time now.

I am full of deferred health and twilit energy, and am working like a fool. Rotten it may be, and is, but it's an awful pile of work, just the same. And it's nothing, compared to what I tear up. Dear God, please make me stop writing like a woman. For Jesus Christ's sake, amen.

She had gone to the Antibes to write—a novel she said, for she wanted a career that was literary, not journalistic. But she found herself unable to start; the task was awesome, even threatening. Woollcott understood this, and her letter quickly becomes a series of avoidances.

—Arthur F. Kinney, "Dorothy Parker's Letters to Alexander Woollcott," *The Massachusetts Review* (Autumn 1989): 487–89

BIBLIOGRAPHY

Enough Rope. 1926.
Sunset Gun. 1928.
Close Harmony. 1929.
Laments for the Living. 1930.

Death and Taxes. 1931.
After Such Pleasures. 1933
Not So Deep as a Well. 1936.
Here Lies. 1939.
The Collected Stories of Dorothy Parker. 1942.
Collected Poetry of Dorothy Parker. 1944.
The Viking Portable Library: Dorothy Parker. 1944.
Smash-Up—The Story of a Woman. 1947.
The Fan. 1949.
The Coast of Illyria. 1949.
The Best of Dorothy Parker. 1952.
The Ladies of the Corridor (with Arnaud d'Usseau). 1953.
Short Story: A Thematic Anthology. 1965.
Constant Reader. 1970.
The Portable Dorothy Parker. 1973.
The Penguin Dorothy Parker. 1977.

ANN PETRY

B. 1908

ANN LANE was born on October 12, 1908, in Old Saybrook, Connecticut, a neighorhood with only one other black family. Ann and her older sister, Helen, were born above the family business, James Pharmacy & Soda Fountain, where her father was a pharmacist. Her mother was a hairdresser and chiropodist who also had a successful textile business. Storytelling was an important part of family gatherings: Ann's uncles and her father told stories of magical ancestors, adventures on the road, and aunts who had been "conjure women." Ann began writing stories and poems while at Old Saybrook High School, and when a teacher encouraged her to become a writer, she later said that it was "like being crowned."

After graduating, Ann attended the Connecticut College of Pharmacy in New Haven. During this time, she wrote short stories and submitted them to magazines, without success. She completed a Ph.D. and worked in the family pharmacies in Old Saybrook and Lyme for the next seven years.

Although she had vowed to wait until she was published, Ann married the mystery writer George D. Petry in 1938 and moved to Harlem. There she wrote advertising copy for the *Amsterdam News* from 1938 to 1941 and was a reporter for the *People's Voice* from 1941 to 1946, where she wrote a column called "The Lighter Side." Petry wrote short stories in her spare time. Her first published story, "Marie of the Cabin Club," appeared in the *Afro-American* of August 19, 1939, under the pseudonym Arnold Petri. In 1943, she enrolled in Mabel Louise Robinson's writing class at Columbia University, because, as she later told an interviewer, "I was still collecting rejection slips. I figured there were some secrets I was missing." Shortly thereafter she began publishing stories in *Crisis, Opportunity, Phylon,* and other journals. She also acted in a production of the American Negro Theater and became involved in her community. Working in an after-school program in Harlem, Petry was deeply affected by the circumstances of many children left on their own while parents—or an only parent—worked. In response, she formed a political group, called Negro Women, Inc.

"On a Saturday the Siren Sounds at Noon" (1943), one of Petry's most powerful short stories, about the violence of Harlem life and its impact on a family, attracted the interest of Houghton Mifflin, which invited her to apply for a stipend to finish a work that they would publish. The synopsis and first five chapters of what would become Petry's first novel, *The Street*, won her the Houghton Mifflin Literary Fellowship. The novel was published in 1946 and was critically acclaimed: Diana Trilling called the work "essential," and other critics praised Petry for her powerful depiction of a Harlem woman's life and the fate of her young son, who is lured into crime. The novel sold more than 1.5 million copies, and Petry, after a decade-long struggle, became a success.

Petry returned to Old Saybrook in 1947, gave birth to a daughter, Elizabeth, and published *Country Place*, a novel about small-town life in Connecticut. Although all the characters are white, Petry draws heavily upon her early life in Old Saybrook for many social and topographical details. Her story "Like a Winding Sheet" was included in *The Best American Short Stories: 1946*. In 1953, her third novel, *The Narrows*, appeared. Focusing upon an interracial affair between a black man and a white woman in Connecticut, it is perhaps Petry's most complex and ambitious work.

In 1949, Petry began writing children's literature, publishing *The Drugstore Cat* (1949), *Harriet Tubman, Conductor of the Underground Railroad* (1955), *Tituba of Salem Village* (1964), and *Legends of the Saints* (1970). Many of her short stories, previously published in magazines such as *Crisis*, *Redbook*, and *The New Yorker*, are collected in *Miss Muriel and Other Stories* (1971). Claiming that she would only repeat herself, Petry has not yet written another novel. She resides in Old Saybrook.

CRITICAL EXTRACTS

BUCKLIN MOON

The Street tells the story of Lutie Johnson, who tried unsuccessfully to make a normal life for herself and her young son Bub after she moved into a grubby little apartment on Harlem's 116th Street. Lutie, light-brown and luscious, had been a maid during the depression when Joe, her husband, had been without work; but taking a job in Connecticut while he remained in Harlem had meant that she lost him to another woman. Now, after a business course and a crack at the civil-service examinations, she has a precarious position as a white-collar worker while awaiting the security of a city job. After living with Pop, who had a succession of women after his wife died, and Granny, who was steeped in bitterness, this grimy little apartment seemed the key to a new and better life; yet at the same time the street outside seemed a menace. First there was Jones, the super, who wanted her, and the one bulwark against that ever present danger, Mrs. Hedges, the madam on the ground floor who ran a nice, quiet little house, and said the trouble with Jones was that he was "cellar-crazy." Then there was the neighborhood and its relationship to Bub, who was in school until three, but then on the street until she returned from her job at night. Later there was Boots Smith, an orchestra leader who heard her singing to herself in Mr. Junto's Bar and Grill and asked her to join his band, though she knew there were strings attached to his proposition. And finally there was Mr. Junto, the white man who controlled everything in the neighborhood and had a fixation about the color of a woman's skin.

With these elements Mrs. Petry has woven the rich tapestry of life on a Harlem street. She has done so with insight and courage, with the basic honesty toward Negro life that Richard Wright, and more recently Chester Himes, have projected into their novels, yet with something added to the sociological realism of a bitter pen. She can show the "cellar-crazed" super, Jones, who is sexually dangerous and a menace to society, not as a black brute who must be trampled to death by a mob, but as a product of what Roi Ottley calls "slum shock," the inevitable result of a wrong system, as a human being rather than a symbol. Or she can paint a picture of a Harlem madam, a great, gaunt amazon who has been badly burned in a fire and refuses to show her body to any man, badly as she wants one, because of a fierce inner pride. For Mrs. Petry knows what it is to live as a Negro in New York City and she also knows how to put it down on paper so that it is as scathing an indictment of our society as has ever appeared, notwithstanding the sugar-coating. Yet with all this—and to this reviewer Mrs. Petry is the most exciting new Negro writer of the last decade—still, there is a serious limitation in both the author and this book.

It is difficult to detract from something that seems so nearly perfect, and from a writer with such genuine talent, yet the truth of the matter is that there is a bad sag in the last third of the book which is almost fatal. In the midst of my real excitement (and an opening chapter which is as good writing as I have encountered almost anywhere), I was suddenly dumped into a bog of hopelessness that made me, as a reader, flounder rather badly. It seemed almost as though two people had collaborated on the book, one of them a sincere and honest writer, the other a slick-magazine technician with a completely mechanical heart and mind. The whole sequence of plot built around Lutie and her aspirations to sing in Boots Smith's band in order to get herself and Bub away from the street, and the relationship of them both toward Mr. Junto and its inevitable conclusion, are as banal and contrived as anything that ever appeared in the slicks. And even though Mrs. Petry has partially saved things by not going soft in the ending, one is left with a bad taste in the mouth that persists.

Normally, perhaps, one would not mention this, for certainly Mrs. Petry's batting average is high enough to stand one poop-out. Yet it seems to this reviewer that there is something basic here, something that not only concerns Mrs. Petry but all of us who are deeply interested in seeing the novel as an important factor in the fight against racial intolerance and for the logical integration of the Negro into the American life stream. Ann Petry has it within her power to be a vital force in that protest movement, or she can, almost as easily, become a popular writer who, within the taboos of marketability, will find success almost too easy. That she can be either is shown clearly in this book, but to be both, as also seems proved in these pages, makes her a writer whose work exhibits the flaws that may eventually alienate her from both audiences. That she is a real writer few, I think, will deny, but so long as she remains a paradox, the road before her may well be as menacing as 116th Street. Either fork will probably assure her a wide audience; which will bring her the greater inner satisfaction is for her to decide.

—Bucklin Moon, "Both Sides of the Street," *New Republic* (11 February 1946): 193–94

WRIGHT MORRIS

The heart of Miss Petry's story ⟨*The Narrows*⟩ is a love affair that various forces of evil bring to a tragic conclusion. The girl is Camilla Treadway, the beautiful daughter of a wealthy white family; the man is Link Williams, an educated Negro who has accepted the lowbrow life of The Narrows, a Negro community about two hours' drive from New York. Link is the adopted son of Abbie Crunch, who is a symbol of the old-fashioned virtues and discredited attitudes that Link has carefully examined and rejected. He chooses the more realistic world of Bill Hod and Creepy Williams at The Last Chance Saloon.

The girl meets Link Williams on the foggy night she drives into The Narrows to do a bit of slumming, and finds herself pursued by the Cat Jimmie, a human monster. Link rescues her—and, in the fog, she does not recognize him as a Negro until they enter a local night club.

Later they go for a drive in her red convertible. The high implausibility of this scene is symbolic of their subsequent love affair and the dilemma that Miss Petry is not able to resolve. The dramatic center of her story is never credible. The lovers meet many times, they have their troubles, quarrel. Finally, the girl, in a fit of temper, accuses Link of attacking her. This leads to his arrest, to scandal in the tabloids and to murder.

The other half of the story, the past, as it is revealed in a series of flashbacks, is always credible, and sometimes extremely good. But the reader is caught between an unreal present and a convincing past. Mamie Powther, a café-au-lait Molly Bloom, is real enough, whenever the author gets around to her, and so, at times, is her husband, the Treadway butler. The canvas has depth and complexity, but the surface drama central to the tragedy is like a tissue of tabloid daydreams, projected by the characters. The living past overwhelms the lifeless present, but the present is obliged to give the past its meaning.

It is hard to see why Miss Petry did not realize this herself. Her first novel, *The Street*, published several years ago, attracted well-deserved praise—and, though it dealt with the familiar elements of the Negro-problem novel, it seemed to point the way to a brilliant creative future. But *The Narrows* reads like the first draft of an ambitious conception that has not been labored into imaginative life. It indicates what the author might have done but did not do. The forces that have lowered the craft of fiction have made it more difficult, not less, to write the book that will cry havoc and be heard. Miss Petry can do it, but it will take more brooding labor—and less space.

—Wright Morris, "The Complexity of Evil," *The New York Times Book Review* (16 August 1953): 4

ROBERT BONE

One senses in Mrs. Petry's life and art a tension between metropolis and small town, between New York and Old Saybrook. In *The Street* she explores New York from an Old Saybrook point of view; in *Country Place* she reverses the process. Reminiscent of *Winesburg, Ohio* and *Spoon River*, the novel treats small-town life from the perspective of a refugee. Like the writers of the Chicago Renaissance who fled from Main Street to Fifty-Seventh Street, it was necessary for Mrs. Petry to renounce the village before she could realize its literary potential. A record of this experience, *Country Place* embodies both the struggle for emancipation and the desire, once liberated, to re-establish one's ties with the past through art.

Conceived in the spirit of revolt from the village, the novel probes beneath the quiet surface of a country town to the inquisitiveness, bigotry, and malice which are typical of its inner life. On the theory that village life revolves around the drugstore, Mrs. Petry introduces Doc, the druggist-narrator, who serves to "place" the action of the novel. To encompass the collective personality of the town, she employs a shifting point of view which rotates among the chief participants. The burden of conflict, however, is borne by Johnnie Roane, a returning veteran who has outgrown the town. His sole remaining tie is his young wife, Glory; when he discovers her infidelity with Ed, the town bull, he renounces his father's contracting business and embarks upon an apprenticeship as an artist in New York. ⟨. . .⟩

On its deepest level, the novel suggests that resistance to change is not a parochial trait but a universal human tendency. Seeking for certainty in a world of flux, man creates images or dreams which he tries to invest with timelessness. Each of the characters in *Country Place* pursues a "soapbubble dream"; each seeks to protect his heart's desire from the ravages of time. Glory and Lil defy time in the shallow fashion of the Hollywood glamor-merchant: Glory, by her restless search for romance and adventure; Lil, by her pathetic efforts to stave off middle age. Mrs. Gramby's defiance takes the form of a refusal to allow her son to grow up, to live his own life. Mearns Gramby tries to arrest time by making a middle-age marriage; Johnnie Roane expects time to have stood still during his absence overseas. All, in the end, are stripped of their illusions, but the positive characters are able to transform their loss into a source of growth.

It is from the theme of lost illusion that the narrative structure of the novel flows. *Country Place* develops a strong narrative drive, paced by a storm whose intensity is reminiscent of the New England hurricane of 1938. The action of the novel takes place in a single week (one cycle of weather), reaching a climax along with the storm. Through a kind of Lear motif the storm reduces each character to moral (or literal) nakedness. Faced with the death of their dreams, they are forced to reevaluate the past, balancing achievement with desire. The storm thus becomes considerably more than a narrative device; it suggests first of all the widespread uprootedness caused by the war. Ultimately it emerges as a symbol of time and flux, relentless killers of the dream.

Mrs. Petry's style, like her narrative strategy, supports her main intent. In the Wright School manner, she will describe a cat, mangled by an auto accident, without flinching. Her realism, however, expresses more than a conventional toughmindedness; it is well suited to a novel so largely concerned with deflating the romantic attitude. Beyond this, she achieves a metaphorical depth virtually unknown among Wright's disciples. Concrete, poetic, her style persistently seeks an "objective correlative" to human emotion. In the following passage she captures Glory's restless frustration through a vivid description of a marshy cove: "It was black, sullen, bordered by a ripple of white foam that gnawed restlessly at the edges of the marsh. The foam retreated and returned, retreated and then returned; and as she watched it she got the feeling that she could hear it snarl because it could not get free of the marsh that confined it."

From individual descriptive passages, image patterns and symbols emerge as part of a total design. The stifling atmosphere of small-town life is evoked, for example, by a recurrent image of confinement and restraint: "the grated window made the ticket-seller look as though he were in a cage." Each character, in fact, has his personal "cage," and through this symbol the essential village psychology is revealed. The townsfolk strive for an equal distribution of frustration; it is this that accounts for their vindictiveness. If the cage symbol is closed and static, the tree symbol is open and expansive. Initially the trees are used to dramatize the destructiveness of the storm, but later on they acquire another significance. Concern or indifference to their fate divides the positive from the negative characters. "Trees will grow," Mrs. Gramby insists, "people will live here." The town recovers from the storm, and life goes on. In a subtle movement which parallels the main direction of the novel, what has been a symbol of uprootedness becomes a symbol of growth.

Because of Mrs. Petry's technical proficiency it is especially difficult to account for the incredible lapse of taste which mars the closing pages of the novel. Somehow she can never manage (it is equally true of *The Street*) to remove her villains gracefully from the stage. Glory is handled throughout with unexceptionable irony, but in the final scene, during the reading of the will, Lil becomes an object of the author's unrestrained invective. The root of the trouble lies, one suspects, in Mrs. Petry's New England heritage. She understands evil, motivates her villains well, but fails to achieve distance in the end. Evil cannot go unpunished, even if the author has to administer the lash in person. This momentary loss of poise is unfortunate, but it cannot seriously detract from Mrs. Petry's distinguished achievement in *Country Place*.

—Robert Bone, "The Contemporary Negro Novel," *The Negro Novel in America* (1958), excerpted in *Twentieth-Century American Literature*, ed. Harold Bloom (New York: Chelsea House Publishers, 1987), 3085–87

ALFRED KAZIN

Ann Petry seems old-fashioned, so surprisingly "slow" in her narrative rhythm that you wonder if the title story in *Miss Muriel and Other Stories* took place in another century. Mrs. Petry's timing is as different from most contemporary black writing as is her locale, which in the best of these leisurely paced stories is a small upstate New York town where a pharmacist and his family are the only Negroes. Their life centers entirely around the drugstore itself. The longest and most successful of these stories, "Miss Muriel," tells of an eccentric elderly white shoemaker in the town, Mr. Bemish, who, to the astonishment and terror of the Negro family, falls in love with Aunt Sophronia. There is no "Muriel" in the story; the title is a sad joke about an old Negro who asked for "Muriel" cigars and was sternly told that *he* would have to ask for them as "Miss Muriel." But the feeling behind the "joke" is so strong in the small, isolated black family that poor Mr. Bemish not only doesn't get Aunt Sophronia, but is driven out of town for falling in love with a black lady.

This reversal of roles is typical of Mrs. Petry's quiet, always underplayed but deeply felt sense of situation. The other stories aren't as lovingly worked

out as "Miss Muriel"—which is an artful period piece that brings back a now legendary age of innocence in white-black relationships. Several stories are just tragic situations that are meant to touch you by that quality alone. A famous black drummer loses his adored wife to a pianist in his band, but the drumming must go on; a Harlem old-clothes man falls in love with the over-sized statue of a dark woman he calls "Mother Africa"; a Negro teacher is unable to stand up to a gang of young students and flees town, ashamed of not having played a more heroic part; a Negro woman at a convention is insulted by a white woman, and realizes in the morning, on learning that the other woman died of a heart attack during the night, that she might have saved her. These delicate points are characteristic of Mrs. Petry's quietly firm interest in fiction as moral dilemma. Clearly, her sense of the Negro situation is still "tragic." Her stories are very far from contemporary black nationalist writing, and by no means necessarily more interesting. But they are certainly different.
—Alfred Kazin, "Brothers Crying Out for More Access to Life," *Saturday Review* (2 October 1971): 34–35

ARTHUR P. DAVIS

Though it certainly holds the reader's interest, *The Narrows* has serious weaknesses as a novel. First, the author leans too heavily on flashbacks to tell her story. There are too many of them, and after the first few they begin to irritate. Second, Miss Petry puts a heavy strain on our "suspension of disbelief" when she asks us to believe that it would take an intelligent boy like Link Williams two or three months to find out who his girl friend actually was. And third, Ann Petry tries too often to create suspense by having her characters in moments of crisis think back, sometimes for as long as three pages, over past incidents in their lives. Although it may have its aesthetic value, this kind of interior monologue as used by Ann Petry somehow fails to impress.

The Narrows is an exciting work, and it does give us a fresh background, which is sorely needed in Afro-American fiction, but it is not a strong novel. Strangely enough, Miss Petry's delineation of white small-town New England life in *Country Place* is more convincing than her depiction of black life in *The Narrows*. *The Street* is Ann Petry's most impressive novel. ⟨. . .⟩

The short stories of Ann Petry show a great sensitivity. They tend to deal with those subtle aspects of racial hurt which are not always understood by nonblacks. For example, in "Like a Winding Sheet" she shows a Negro, confronted downtown by what he thinks is prejudice, coming home and beating his wife when she playfully calls him "nigger." "In Darkness and Confusion" depicts the action of two respectable, hard-working Harlemites who, thinking about the injustice meted out to their son in an army camp in Georgia, express their anger and frustrations in the Harlem Riot of 1943. Miss Petry's voice is low when she speaks of the tragedy of ghetto living in these stories—the broken homes, the deserted children, the faithless wives, the young girls going on the street—and it is more effective than shouting. These stories show a genuine concern for the unfortunate victims of American racism, and the sincerity of her feelings comes through in the stories. They also show an artist's concern for structure and effect.

Ann Petry's best story, however, differs slightly from the type described above. Entitled "The Bones of Louella Jones," it uses a rich blend of humor, satire, and superstition to poke fun at several things—the way the news is manipulated by journals, at racial science (the physician who was an authority on white and black physical differences), and at racial segregation. The story concerns the dilemma a certain town gets into when it wants to separate the bones (white) of Elizabeth Countess of Castro and the bones (black) of Louella Jones, her servant, after both have been long buried in the same cemetery. After the ghost of Louella has exerted a little pressure, an "either-or" slab has to be placed over the graves in Bedford Abbey.

The word *competent* best describes Ann Petry as a writer. She does several things well, but none superlatively. Her short stories will probably stand up best after the critical years have passed judgment.

—Arthur P. Davis, "Ann Petry," From the Dark Tower: Afro-American Writers 1900–1960 (1974), excerpted in Twentieth-Century American Literature, ed. Harold Bloom (New York: Chelsea House Publishers, 1987), 3088

MARGARET B. MCDOWELL

As in all her work, Petry excels in *The Narrows* in her use of concrete detail, her ability to dramatize a situation, and her ear for exact dialogue. She is a master at transcribing the details of a given milieu as she recreates, for example, the sound of the river lapping against the dock at night, the feeling that fog generates as it rolls up the street from the river, the smell of beer from the saloon across from Abbie's brick house, and the glare of sunlight on the River Wye. To help convey the sense of plenitude in the social scene that she recreates in her novel, she appeals to the auditory sense of her reader, as when Mamie Powther sings her plaintive blues throughout the novel.

Each place, object, and fragment of dialogue becomes important in creating the realistic milieu, but certain aspects of the Narrows generate abstract associations. The cemetery becomes segregated, as if the dead must not mingle across racial lines. A myriad of placards proclaiming rooms for rent and a growing number of drifters sleeping under Abbie's big tree suggest the increasingly transient nature of the population. The River Wye, though a beautiful stream, draws the desperate to suicide. In its growing pollution, the river symbolizes, to a degree, the economic exploitation of the area. The naming of the

Last Chance saloon promises fellowship as well as food and drink for the survival of the down-and-outer, but the name also implies an impending finality to those who need more than food and drink. It offers no further opportunities for the repressed of society to attain for themselves security, love or justice. Its neon sign is ugly and cheap, its owner's temper flares in murderous violence, and it is linked with lucrative prostitution and gambling enterprises which exploit the poor while providing them with specious pleasure. The Treadway estate—remote from the Narrows—is also symbolic. It is the site for an annual festival for the workers in a munitions plant, but the celebration is an impersonal gesture which expresses no true concern of the employers for their workers. The laborers, in turn, gossip viciously about Camilla Treadway's presence on the dock at Dumble Street at midnight when she was allegedly threatened with rape.

The motor cars of the Treadways—the Rolls-Royce and their fleet of Cadillacs—are symbolic of power. Camilla's automobiles make possible the anonymity which she and Link achieve by driving to Harlem. Camilla's impulsive, reckless driving suggests her instability. Treadway automobiles, in a more sinister context, facilitate the kidnaping of Link and the hauling away of his body. Bill Hod's secondhand Cadillacs represent the rewards of his shady dealings, many of which exploit his Black brothers and sisters, while F. K. Jackson's funeral limousine (with its whiskey bottle for the weary and its case of long black gloves and lace veil, available for any bereaved woman to wear for a half hour of proper mourning) reflects how superficial and conventional the rites of grief are to the capitalist entrepreneur.

—Margaret B. McDowell, "*The Narrows*: A Fuller View of Ann Petry," *Black American Literature Forum* 14, no. 4 (Winter 1980): 137

BERNARD W. BELL

Petry, like ⟨Chester⟩ Himes and ⟨Richard⟩ Wright, is adept at character delineation, but her protagonists are cut from a different cloth than those of her major contemporaries. Rather than sharing the pathology of a Bigger Thomas or Bob Jones or Lee Gordon, Lutie Johnson and Link Williams are intelligent, commonplace, middle-class aspiring blacks, who, despite the socialized ambivalence resulting from racism and economic exploitation, are not consumed by fear and hatred and rage. Petry's vision of black personality is not only different from that of Himes and Wright, but it is also more faithful to the complexities and varieties of black women, whether they are big-city characters like Mrs. Hedges in *The Street* or small-town characters like Abbie Crunch in *The Narrows*. Ann Petry thus moves beyond the naturalistic vision of

Himes and Wright to a demythologizing of American culture and Afro-American character.

—Bernard W. Bell, "Ann Petry's Demythologizing of American Culture and Afro-American Character," in *Conjuring: Black Women, Fiction, and Literary Tradition*, ed. Marjorie Pryse and Hortense J. Spillers (Bloomington: Indiana University Press, 1985), 114

NELLIE Y. MCKAY

In addition to its focus on a female protagonist, *The Street* is significantly different from its male counterparts in that while Petry lashes out uncompromisingly at racism, classism, and sexism, she undercuts the conventions of the naturalistic novel by refusing to make Lutie a mere victim of her social environment. Nor does this step on the part of the author lessen the impact of the oppression of that environment. Lutie may well have had greater success in achieving her goals had she been less innocent of the politics of race, class, and gender. Her uncritical acceptance of white middle-class values and the capitalist tenets of the American dream make her an easy prey for the greed and sexism of the black and white men who surround her. In addition, Lutie serves herself poorly by separating from any support she might have had from the black community and those values that have insured black survival in America since the first slaves arrived on its shores. Preoccupied with her ambitions for herself and her son to escape the poverty and disillusionment of black ghetto life and wholly uncritical of the white models to which she is exposed, she has no friends or relatives with whom she seeks association, attends no church, and in her attitudes, denies the possibilities of communal sources of strength. Consequently, she was vulnerable to the greed, anger, and sexism of those who were capable of destroying her.

—Nellie Y. McKay, "Ann Petry's *The Street* and *The Narrows*: A Study of the Influence of Class, Race, and Gender on Afro-American Women's Lives," in *Women and War: The Changing Status of American Women from the 1930s to the 1950s*, ed. Maria Diedrich and Dorothea Fischer-Hornung (New York: Berg, 1990), 134–35

KEITH CLARK

While something of an anachronism in the 1990s, the African-American protest novel of the 1940s and 1950s maintained a symbiotic relationship with the mythic American Dream: It decried a history of American racism which made achieving the Dream a chimera for blacks. While Richard Wright is considered the "father" of the genre, and *Native Son* (1940) its quintessential document, Ann Petry emerged as another strident voice—a progenitor or native daughter. While her novel *The Narrows* (1953) deviated somewhat, it nevertheless continued the Wrightian tradition. Link Williams, the protagonist, differs superficially from Bigger in that he has attained a Dartmouth education and enjoys relative freedom from economic hardships; it would *appear* that he has the means to acquire the bootstraps over which Bigger can only ruminate. However, Link's "success" cannot shield him in an America which insists upon his inhumanity. When he breaks the taboos of class and race by having an affair with a white New England heiress, his violent murder becomes ritual— an inexorable response to a black stepping out of his "place." While Petry's "New England" novel echoes *Native Son* thematically, more ostensibly it also foregrounds the black *male* as the victim of an America which denies African-Americans their very personhood. But in *The Street* (1946), Petry recasts the Herculean quest for the American Dream in an unequivocally female context. Indeed, the novel represents the "distaff" side of the African-American literary tradition, emerging as a groundbreaking work in its examination of the black woman's pursuit of happiness. Not only does Petry depict how women pursue the Dream in traditionally "American" terms, but, more deftly, she illustrates how black women subvert the quest for the American Dream and fulfill their own version of it. ⟨. . .⟩

Lutie Johnson, the protagonist in *The Street*, embodies the female version of the archetypal quest. Patterning her life after Benjamin Franklin's, Lutie embarks on an expedition she hopes will bestow the trappings of success upon herself and Bub, her eight-year-old son. However, Lutie's odyssey from Jamaica, New York, to Lyme, Connecticut, to Harlem bestows upon her little more than disillusionment. Ultimately, what Calvin Hernton calls the "three isms"—racism, capitalism and sexism—launch an implacable assault on Lutie, precipitating the novel's tragic conclusion.

While it would be tempting to view the novel as a treatise on how men, black and white, collude to destroy the All-American black girl, Petry's text discourages this sort of naturalistic preoccupation with character as subject and object. Instead, one might view this seminal examination of the black woman's search for the Dream as a mosaic—much like Alice Walker's tropological quilt—that includes other women, other stories, and other voices. In addition to presenting Lutie and her blind adherence to American values, Petry depicts two black female characters who circumvent the quest: Mrs. Hedges, who operates a bordello in the apartment building where Lutie lives and who also oversees the day-to-day events on "the street," and Min, the downtrodden and subservient companion of William Jones, the building superintendent.

Far from being minor characters, Mrs. Hedges and Min embody what I see as a history of black women *subverting* the vacuous Dream myth through an almost innate ability to secure their own space despite the twin scourges of racism and sexism. Existing in a milieu where the Dream's core assumptions belie their lived realities, these black women *undermine* the myth, altering it to ensure both economic survival and varying degrees of emotional stability. And because "traditional" principles have been the bane of black people since America's inception, questions involving "morality" of how these women survive become ancillary ones given their predatory, hostile environment.

Superficially, Mrs. Hedges and Min adhere to the ideals of "hard work" and "ingenuity" in a country where "anything is possible." However, these women more accurately replicate techniques used by such archetypal African-American trickster figures as Charles Chesnutt's Uncle Julius or black folklore's Peetie Wheatstraw in (re)inventing lives independent of the white American Dream. While denied opulent lifestyles and material objects, Petry's "minor" women attain life's basic necessities, and, given their tenuous existences, they (re)construct their own "dream" by tapping into a tradition of what Peter Wheatstraw in *Invisible Man* calls "'shit, grit and mother-wit.'" Thus, *The Street* transcends the boundaries of the *"roman-à-these,"* the thesis presumably being that white racism extinguishes all black hope. The denizens of Petry's Harlem face a world more Darwinian than Franklinian, and they act according to their individual circumstances.

—Keith Clark, "A Distaff Dream Deferred? Ann Petry and the Art of Subversion," *African American Review* 26, no. 3 (Fall 1992): 495–97

⌐ I ⌐ L I O ⌐ ⌐ A ⌐ ⌐ ⌐

The Street. 1946.
Country Place. 1947.
The Drugstore Cat. 1949.
The Narrows. 1953.
Harriet Tubman, Conductor on the Underground Railroad. 1955.
Tituba of Salem Village. 1964.
Legends of the Saints. 1970.
Miss Muriel and Other Stories. 1971.